Living & Working in New Zealand

Other related titles published by How To Books

Getting a Job in Australia
Secure well-paid work and a great new lifestyle

Getting into Australia
The complete immigration guide to gaining your visa

Getting a Job Abroad
The handbook for the international jobseeker: where the jobs are, how to get them

Retire Abroad
Your complete guide to a new life in the sun

howtobooks

Please send for a free copy of the latest catalogue:

How To Books
3 Newtec Place, Magdalen Road,
Oxford OX4 1RE, United Kingdom
email: info@howtobooks.co.uk
http://www.howtobooks.co.uk

Living & Working in New Zealand

*How to build a new life
in New Zealand*

JOY MUIRHEAD

6th edition

howtobooks

Cover images by kind permission of Tourism New Zealand.

Published by How To Books Ltd,
3 Newtec Place, Magdalen Road,
Oxford OX4 1RE. United Kingdom.
Tel: (01865) 793806. Fax: (01865) 248780.
e-mail: info@howtobooks.co.uk
http://www.howtobooks.co.uk

First published 1994
Second edition 1994
Third edition 1996
Fourth edition (revised) 1997
Fifth edition (revised) 2001
Reprinted 2002
Sixth edition 2004

British Library Cataloguing in Publication Data
A catalogue record for this book is available from
the British Library

Produced for How To Books by Deer Park Productions
Typeset by PDQ Typesetting, Newcastle-under-Lyme, Staffs.
Cover design by Baseline Arts Ltd., Oxford
Printed and bound by The Cromwell Press, Trowbridge,
Wiltshire

NOTE: The material contained in this book is set out in good
faith for general guidance and no liability can be accepted
for loss or expense incurred as a result of relying in particular
circumstances on statements made in the book. Laws and
regulations are complex and liable to change, and readers should
check the current position with the relevant authorities before
making personal arrangements.

Contents

List of Illustrations

Preface
to the sixth edition

Congratulations, you must have discovered that New Zealand is not just another part of Australia!

My husband and I brought our three children here in 1972. We had no friends or relations to come to: we just decided that it would be a good place in which to bring up our family. The only information we had received from New Zealand House in London was that we should buy a house in New Zealand before we arrived! We decided that was certainly not a good idea.

After poring over maps of New Zealand, we came to the conclusion that the North Island was going to be sub-tropical, and therefore we wouldn't need our warm English clothes, and told the children to take their last look at the pleasure of open fires, because we just would never see one again. This proved to be wrong; only north of Auckland in the Bay of Islands area does one find truly sub-tropical weather. As we settled in the Bay of Plenty, we found it very hot in summer, but when the temperature dropped to around 10 degrees Celsius after summer highs of 25–30 degrees Celsius, we certainly felt it cool enough to light a fire.

New Zealand lived up to the clean green image we had, the skies were certainly blue and the waters clear, and the sun was so bright we needed sunglasses to cut down the glare.

One day we were travelling from Hamilton in the North Island to Tauranga, a journey of perhaps one hour. After about 20 minutes I realised that there were no cars to be seen, and what's more, there were no people either! It felt as though a bomb had been dropped and we were the only people alive – a strange feeling. However, it now seems strange to meet many cars when on the open road; you only meet congestion and experience hold-ups when travelling through the cities.

The children got teased about their 'pommie accents' and it took a while for them to settle in at school and make friends, but that was in 1972 and there is a lot more tolerance these days towards new immigrants.

I hope that this book, based on more than 23 years' first-hand experience, will be of some help to you in planning your stay in New Zealand – and who knows? – perhaps making a whole new life here as so many have before. It is pleasing to see such great interest in New Zealand, making it necessary for a sixth edition of this book. This new edition has been revised and updated to reflect the latest information for visitors and new residents.

Finally, I would like to express my thanks to the following organisations for giving so much valuable help and advice during the preparation of this book:

NZ Immigration Service
NZ Police Department
KPMG Peat Marwick, Wellington office
Ministry of Education
Department of Statistics
New Zealand Medical Association
NZ Employment Service

Joy Muirhead

Fig. 1. Map of New Zealand.

Making the Big Decision

Aotearoa – The Land of the Long White Cloud
Kia-Ora – this is the traditional Maori welcome.

INTRODUCING THE COUNTRY

We have established that New Zealand is not just another part of Australia. It is also as far away from England as you can go without finding yourself on the way back again! It is 1,600 kilometres east of Australia and it consists of two major islands, the North Island and the South Island, plus a number of smaller islands, with a total land area of 270,500 square kilometres. It has a population of approximately 4 million people and 46 million sheep, that is about 12 sheep per head of population!

The islands of New Zealand have been ethnically and culturally connected to Polynesia for at least 1,000 years. Less than 200 years ago, its population and cultural heritage was wholly that of Polynesia, but now New Zealand is dominated by cultural traditions that are mainly European, emanating especially from Great Britain.

Some four-fifths of New Zealanders are of European origin, predominantly from the British Isles, but also including people from the Netherlands, former Yugoslavia, Germany and other nations. The indigenous Maori population make up the next largest group of the population, about 9.6%. The third main ethnic group is the Pacific Island Polynesians who make up about 6%.

New Zealand has a high standard of education and its qualifications are recognised internationally. Professor Marie Clay from Auckland University is well known for her remedial reading observations and recommendations.

The birds and the bees

One of the main factors in influencing me to make New Zealand my home was the fact that there are hardly any creepy crawlies here! There are no snakes or crocodiles. We do have one spider which is poisonous – the Katipo. I have never seen one although I do know that they can sometimes be found in decaying logs, so I just stay away from dead wood!

Twenty years ago there were no wasps here but there are now. We get mosquitoes, especially in the north of the North Island, and there are flies, but not in the horrendous numbers they have in Australia. Yes, we do have sharks in our waters and there have been a few attacks on swimmers.

First impressions

When you first arrive you will be enchanted by the gaily painted houses, which are mainly of wooden construction with tin roofs. You will be surprised at the spaciousness of everything, and even on a busy day on Queen Street, Auckland, you can still walk in reasonable comfort. You may notice the seemingly small selection of goods in the shops, and possibly be told, when enquiring for some-thing, that they are waiting for the next shipment!

Bare knees

New Zealand lifestyle is very casual. Shorts and shirts for the men and sundresses for the women are the norm during the summer. I found it strange to see butchers wearing shorts, knee socks and an apron! When I went to see the doctor, I had to try not to smile when he came around from his desk as he too was wearing shorts!

QUESTIONS AND ANSWERS

Does the water really go down the plughole in the opposite direction?
Yes, it does, all due to the earth's rotation and the fact that New Zealand is in the Antipodes.

Is sheep the only meat available in New Zealand?
No, even though sheep do outnumber people 12 to 1!

Is New Zealand sub-tropical?
In the north of the North Island it is.

Do the women wear grass skirts?
Definitely no! The women are very fashion conscious.

Has New Zealand ever been a penal colony?
No, but we have our fair share of criminals.

Do the trees grow twice as fast as anywhere else?
Yes, certain species do, because the growth doesn't stop during the winter.

THE ATTRACTIONS OF NEW ZEALAND

What are you looking for?

- A smaller population?
- A better climate?
- Long stretches of white sandy beaches?
- Clear blue skies?
- Freedom from terrorism?
- Nuclear free country?

Yes, you will find all these here, and there are still good opportunities for hard-working people who are adaptable to new lifestyles and traditions.

The beaches, especially from the Bay of Plenty in the North Island northwards, are spectacular with clean white sand and clear blue sea – you could be forgiven for thinking you were on a desert island. But the summers can be hot and dangerous. New Zealand now has the highest incidence of skin cancer in the world. We are constantly being reminded of the 'burntime' each day, and children in schools wear sunhats and everyone is urged to 'cover up' in the sun. Protective sun creams are essential. So think of these very real dangers if the climate is the main reason for your intended move.

John Burnett and his wife and family came to New Zealand from Surrey, England in the late 1960s. John and his wife were both schoolteachers. They bought their own home and soon acquired two cars and a boat for weekend pleasure trips. When the children left home John and his wife bought a new home with a view of the Pacific Ocean, and now they lead a much to be admired lifestyle.

Peter Spencer and his wife Joan and two boys arrived in New Zealand in 1989; Peter was an engineer. They were able to buy some land and start building their own home, but before it was finished they were so homesick for England they sold up and went back to Birmingham.

Jim and Sheila Murray-Hamilton came to New Zealand from England in 1990. They have set up a very successful fashion business in Wellington and say they love New Zealand because there is still a lot to offer here. Jim grew up in Scotland and Sheila grew up in Wolverhampton, England.

A non-nuclear region

In 1987 the New Zealand Government, at the time being the Labour Party led by David Lange, informed the American Government that we would no longer allow nuclear-powered ships in our waters, and this is still the case. New Zealand is proud to be a nuclear-free country, and after the Chernobyl type disasters this makes New Zealand appear a very attractive haven.

A pollution-free land?

Not quite: we do have water pollution. In the Hauraki Gulf, which is around the Auckland area, swimmers have been warned not to swim in certain areas because of pollution. Some parts of the Bay of Plenty, also in the North Island, have been declared unfit for swimmers, due to some degree of farm pollution pouring into the inner Tauranga Harbour.

Air pollution is also a problem in the Christchurch area, which is in the South Island. This is caused by open fires in the winter which create horrendous smogs which exceed the international safety standards.

In 1993 a natural phenomenon occurred which caused a type of pollution to our shellfish industry. An algae bloom caused a toxin infection to bivalves, which are shellfish with two shells i.e. scallops, oysters and mussels. When the toxin disappeared, and the shellfish had been washed clean by several clear tidal flows, they were inspected and declared fit for human consumption once more. However, some areas are still affected but they are expected to clear naturally, given time. Any shellfish for sale now are perfectly safe to eat, having first been cleared by the authorities.

CLIMATE

Weather varieties

The climate varies from sub-tropical in the far north to the almost continental in the mountainous areas of the South Island. However, because of the oceanic surroundings the climate is not extreme. There are, of course, always the exceptions. In 1991 there were three major floods and the worst affected regions were Westland and Otago in the South Island, and Wairarapa in the North Island.

The Westland flood was the worst in 30 years, and many people had to be evacuated from their homes. The total rainfall for January 1991 was the highest in 125 years. In the Wairarapa heavy rain caused severe flooding during 8–11 March when two rivers burst their banks. Stock losses were severe.

Greenhouse gases

New Zealand, with its large forested areas, low population and hydro-electric power generation, was believed to be a carbon dioxide sink, but testing has revealed that New Zealand is a net producer. This production has been associated with the high consumption of fossil fuels and gradual deforestation. New Zealand's emissions of carbon dioxide are twice the world average per capita.

We also have higher than average methane emissions: eight times the world average per capita. Most sources of methane have been identified, but there is still debate about how much can be attributed to each separate source. Amazingly enough, most is produced by micro-organisms working in the guts of such animals as sheep and cattle and with 46 million sheep alone, that is a lot of gas!

Earthquakes and volcanic eruptions

The level of seismic activity in New Zealand is moderate compared with other countries lying in the almost continuous belt of earthquake activity around the rim of the Pacific. A shock of Richter magnitude 6 or above happens on average about once a year, and a shock of magnitude 7 or above once in ten years, with a shock of magnitude 8 perhaps once a century.

There were two earthquakes of magnitude 6 or greater in 1990 and six exceeding 5.5. And in 1991 there were two earthquakes exceeding magnitude 6. The largest one in September was felt from the top of the North Island to the middle of the South Island.

In September 1995 Mount Ruapehu, in the centre of the North Island, erupted sending spectacular lava flows which ran like black streaks down the snow-clad mountain, disrupting the winter ski season. In June 1996 another spectacular fireworks display occurred, once again spoiling the ski season momentarily – the ash clouds disrupted air traffic across the centre of the North Island and carried inches of dust across the vineyards of Hawkes Bay.

Avalanches

We also get freak cold snaps, and in 1991 the Shotover River near Queenstown in the South Island froze over for the first time in a hundred years. Heavy snow also contributed to frequent avalanches on major ski fields and caused loss of life on Mount Ruapehu in the North Island. The Milford road in the South Island was closed for two weeks 6–20 August due to an avalanche risk.

Tornadoes

Occasionally we experience tornadoes, and sometimes there is building damage and people get injured. On 14 April 1991 a band of thunderstorms passed over Auckland in the North Island leaving behind a trail of damage, and a man was critically hurt. Tornadoes were also seen in the Bay of Plenty on 30 April 1991. I actually saw a garage roof lifted and blown across the road.

The seasons

Spring	September to November
Summer	December to February
Autumn	March to May
Winter	June to August

SOME BRIEF FACTS

Latitude	33° to 53° south
Longitude	162° to 173° west
Total area	26.9 million hectares
Farms	14.4 million hectares
Forest	8.1 million hectares
National parks	2.3 million hectares
Highest mountain	Mount Cook, South Island, 3,764m
Population	3.8 million (North Island, 2.8 million) (South Island 1 million) (approx)
Capital	Wellington, South Island

MULTICULTURALISM

Population
According to recent Department of Statistics figures, out of a total population of 4 million people, approximately 75% are New Zealand European, 10% New Zealand Maori, 6% Pacific Island Polynesian, 1.5% Chinese, 2% Asian, 1% Indian. (These groups do not total 100%. Some people are counted in two or more ethnic groups.)

Latest population growth figures
Statistics New Zealand stated recently that New Zealand's population grew by 70,000 (or 1.8%) during the June 2003 year compared with an increase of 58,000 (1.5%) in

the June 2002 year. Three-fifths of the growth was due to a net migration gain, and two-fifths due to natural increase. The average age was approximately 33.9 years compared with 33.6 in 1997.

Maori

The majority of Maori live in the north of the North Island, from Hamilton and the Bay of Plenty northwards. Today there is no true Maori, as intermarriage has diluted the race.

The modern Maori is well represented in the workforce, particularly in Government departments. The Maori people are represented by the Ministry of Maori Affairs which was formed on 1 July 1989. This Ministry provides a Maori perspective in policy making.

There are five Maori seats in Parliament, and as a result of the MMP (Multi Member Representation) voting system, Maori are now represented in a number of other electorates.

The language

The number of native speakers of Maori has been declining over the last hundred years in the face of strong competition from English, but in recent decades there has been a renewal of interest in the language on the part of the **Kohanga Reo** (Maori Language Pre-School Movement) and more recently the **Kura Kaupapa Maori** (Maori Language Immersion Primary Schools).

Many Maori radio programmes have now been established as well as Maori television programmes.

The Maori Queen
1991 marked the 25th anniversary of the coronation of Te Arikinui Dame Te Atairangikaahu as the Maori Queen and leader of the Kingitangi movement. She is the first woman to head the movement. Te Atairangikaahu belongs to the Waikato Confederation of Tribes and is a direct descendent of the famous Waikato leader Te Puea Herangi.

Maori legends
Maori legends abound, and one in particular tells of the formation of the North Island. Maui is said to have fished up the North Island of New Zealand – Te Ika a Maui – from his great canoe, the South Island. Maui and his brothers struggled with a large fish, beating and slashing it so that it writhed in agony creating the hills and valleys. When the fish died it became a great land where previously there had been nothing but the ocean.

The southern part of the North Island is said to be the head of the fish – Te upoko a te Ika. Wellington Harbour is the mouth of the fish – Te Waha o te Ika, and Lake Wairarapa the eye of the fish – Te Whatu o te Ika.

When the fish was hauled up, the mouth formed a lake separated from the sea by a barrier of land. This lake trapped two taniwha – sea monsters – named Ngake and Whaitaitai. Ngake didn't like being trapped so he smashed his way through to the open sea. The wreckage he left created the entrance to the harbour.

Whaitaitai decided he would go out to sea as well, but on the way he got stuck in the shallow water as the tide went

Fig. 2. The Welllngton area.

out. He remained there for two centuries, being revived by the tide washing in and out and preventing him from drying out.

In 1460 there was a great earthquake and Whaitaitai was uplifted and died, becoming the present day Miramar Peninsula. His soul, or wairua, left him in the form of a bird called Te keo and flew to a nearby hill and wept. The hill was thus called 'Tangi te keo', although the European name for it is Mount Victoria.

NEW ZEALAND'S MAIN CITIES

Wellington

Wellington is the capital of New Zealand, and it is nestled at the southern end of the North Island. It appears to be sprouting out from the creases of the many hills, like a plant searching for a hold. It has been the capital of New Zealand since 1865. It has a fine deep harbour which is said to be one of the most picturesque in the world. The population totals approximately 400,000.

Wellington is renowned as being the 'Windy City' with gusts of wind over 60 kilometres per hour. It has an average of 199 windy days per year. The climate fluctuates between 7 degrees Celsius and a high of approximately 23 degrees Celsius. The city is also reputed to have one restaurant for every day of the year!

Wellington is the world's most southern capital, and it is the only capital in the 'Roaring Forties' latitude. Nearly all Wellingtonians live within 3km of the sea, and Wellington Airport is the busiest in the South Pacific.

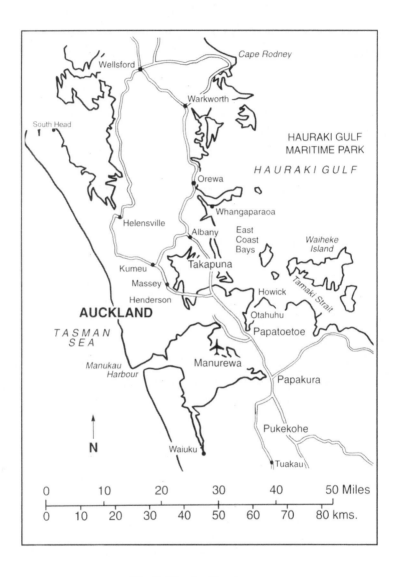

Fig. 3. The Auckland area.

Wellington is the National Headquarters for the National Museum, Art Gallery, National Archives, National Library, New Zealand School of Dance, Royal New Zealand Ballet Company, New Zealand Symphony Orchestra, New Zealand Drama School and government departments. A splendid new Museum of New Zealand opened in 1998, offering New Zealanders the very latest in technology and presentation.

Separated by Cook Strait, Wellington is the major connecting link with the South Island. You can catch the ferry at the Ferry Terminal, the cost being approximately $59 per adult and $35 per child one way in summer. Cars cost approximately $190 one way.

Auckland
Auckland is the second major city in the North Island, and it is New Zealand's largest urban centre with more than one-quarter of the national total population in a region of 5,580 square kilometres. The population totals 1.3 million. It is the largest Polynesian centre in the world.

Auckland is considered to be the commercial centre of New Zealand, and is also known as 'The City of Sails' because of the huge number of sailing craft moored in and around its waters. It has a superb coastline on each side of this narrow neck of land, with Waitemata Harbour on the east side and the Manukau Harbour on the west. The city's most scenic drive follows a coastal route, with views out to Rangitoto Island, the volcanic cone that is so much a part of Auckland.

The Waitemata Harbour and the Hauraki Gulf have a big influence on Auckland's leisure time. Auckland's Anniversary Day on 27 January brings out yachts for one of the largest one-day regattas in the world. Auckland will be the venue for the next America's Cup, which will be held on the Hauraki Gulf. The climate is close to sub-tropical but it is classified as a warm temperate which reaches an average of 23 degrees Celsius in the summer and around 15 degrees Celsius in the winter.

Hamilton

Hamilton is New Zealand's largest inland city and fifth largest urban area with a population of approximately 166,128. It is conveniently situated in the centre of the North Island, and is one of the richest pastoral farming regions of the world. Cambridge, which lies on the outskirts of Hamilton and is a 15-minute drive from the city, is world renowned for its horse breeding. Hamilton is a drive of approximately 90 minutes from Auckland. The Waikato River runs through the centre of Hamilton – this is the longest river in New Zealand.

Within a radius of 150 kilometres of Hamilton there are more than 2.3 million people, that is over 60% of New Zealand's total population. It is located on four State Highways and has the biggest railway junction in New Zealand.

There are enormous recreational opportunities within Hamilton and the immediate surroundings. Trout fishing, sailing, wind surfing and water skiing are available on the region's rivers and lakes. World-class rowing facilities are available at Lake Karapiro, a 20-minute drive from Hamilton.

Winters can be cold, with an average temperature of 13 degrees Celsius during the day and an occasional low of 0 degrees Celsius during the night. Summer days can be long, warm and sunny, with temperatures around 20 to 25 degrees Celsius. There is abundant rainfall, between 800 and 1,500mm per year. Rain falls throughout the year, with more falling in the winter.

New Plymouth

Around a thousand years ago, a giant flightless bird moved through virgin indigenous forests and browsed at the edge of vast flax swamps of a still active volcanic cone. This was the scene discovered in about the 11th century by the first settlers to the Taranaki areas who stalked the large bird for food, called it the **Moa**, and harvested the flax to make clothing.

The Moa is now extinct, but its cousin the **Kiwi**, a much smaller flightless bird, still frequents remaining forest areas. Much of the forest was cleared for farming by European settlers who began arriving in the 1840s. Small townships sprang up, the first being New Plymouth, which became a city in 1948 and is the main servicing centre for the province of Taranaki.

New Plymouth is situated on the west coast of the North Island, and is dominated by the majestic Mount Egmont/ Taranaki, which stands 2,518m high and is only 32 kilometres south of the city. The life and climate of New

Fig. 4. The Christchurch area.

Plymouth seems to be dominated by this fabulous mountain, which some days can remain hidden from view by strange large clouds gathered around its peak, and yet the rest of the skies can be clear.

New Plymouth was made affluent by the exploitation of oil and gas reserves. The local oil industry is said to be one of the oldest established in the world. There are lots of attractions for its 68,000 residents in the form of seven golf courses, rivers, lakes and beaches. The summer temperature averages 17–20 degrees Celsius, and in the winter 10 degrees Celsius.

Christchurch
Cathedral City, Garden City of the Plains, English City – the most English city outside England. These are all phrases to describe the capital of Canterbury in the South Island. The Botanic Gardens bordered by the gentle flowing Avon River are said to be among the best in the world.

When English settlers arrived in 1850 on the 'First Four Ships' they began building their city, and the English influence is still seen today. It was designed as a model Anglican settlement, a clean geometric grid of a city laid over wild swamp and scrubby plainsland. By the late 1890s the English immigrants had already turned it into a tree studded, neo-gothic re-creation of 'home'.

Christchurch is at the centre of New Zealand's third most populous area after Auckland and Wellington, with a population of 334,107. The metropolitan areas sprawl over the Canterbury Plains and lower Northern Plains. It is linked to its seaport at Lyttleton Harbour, 11 kilometres south of the city centre by rail and tunnel. It also has an International Airport, as Christchurch is the gateway to the Southern Alps and Queenstown, which is a very busy tourist attraction. It is also the base for Antarctic expeditions, and it is here that you can get a real taste of the Antarctic by visiting the International Antarctic Centre.

Christchurch is very flat and a very popular form of transport is by bicycle. There are eight skifields to choose from within two hours' drive of the city, including the internationally renowned slopes of Mount Hutt.

Located 43 degrees south of the Equator, Christchurch has an unpredictable climate, with a summer temperature of around 25 degrees and a winter temperature of approximately 9 degrees Celsius, but these temperatures can fluctuate at any time of the year, and it is not unknown for Christchurch to experience a temperature of 20 degrees Celsius in the winter!

Dunedin

Dunedin, capital of the province of Otago, is located at the head of Otago Harbour on the lower east coast of the South Island. It was founded in 1848 by Scottish migrants and is a four-hour drive to Christchurch and a comfortable four-hour drive to the Alpine resort of Queenstown. It is the second largest urban area in the South Island, after Christchurch, and has a population of around 107,088.

Dunedin is the coldest of the main centres. The summer temperature is around 19 degrees Celsius, and a minimum of 2.5 degrees Celsius in the winter. Its rainfall is spread throughout the year.

Culture mingles side by side with recreation in Dunedin. Amongst the city's parks and playing areas should be mentioned Carisbrook Park, scene of many important cricket and rugby games. The nearby beaches of St Clair and St Kilda attract thousands of bathers in the summer. The southern Lakes District is just three hours' drive away, and from there the inspiring grandeur of Fiordland and South Westland a mere stone's throw away.

Invercargill

Invercargill is the southernmost city in the British Commonwealth. It was founded on the shores of the Waihopai River estuary in 1856. Legendary whaler and farmer Johnny Jones is said to have bought a huge block of land which included Invercargill from the Maori and the price he is said to have paid was 12 muskets and a whaleboat!

The first inhabitant is said to have been John Kelly, an Irishman who saw a business possibility as a boatman ferrying new settlers ashore from the vessels that brought them to New Zealand. Invercargill attracted a large number of Scottish immigrants, and the Scottish street names bear witness to this.

Invercargill is very flat and symmetrically laid out, and has a population of approximately 52,000. It is the capital of the province of Southland. The giant aluminium smelter at Bluff plays a very important part in the economic life of Invercargill. The province also produces wool, wheat, barley, beef and the deer farmed in the area produce velvet. The temperature is approximately 18 degrees Celsius in the summer, with a winter temperature of approximately 7 degrees Celsius.

Minnie Dean

The most infamous character in the history of Invercargill was Minnie Dean. She was Minnie McCulloch and a widow when she arrived in Invercargill in 1868. She was only 21 years of age and she had two daughters from her first marriage. It was said that she was the niece of the first European woman to live in the town.

Within four years she had married Charles Dean. After 14 years they were still childless and her two other daughters had grown up and presumably moved away. They adopted Mary Cameron and bought a house on 20 acres.

Minnie set herself up as a 'baby farmer'. Victorian attitudes meant that unmarried mothers were sinful and babies were hastily given for adoption. Minnie adopted children outright, or kept them until foster homes could be found. At times there were as many as ten children including babies a few months old in the small three-roomed house.

Mary Cameron, her adopted daughter, found work as a dressmaker and was out of the house during the day; her husband also worked during the day. She would tell them that adoptive parents had been found for several of the children, as they left and were replaced by 'new' ones. The truth was, Minnie disposed of some of the children to make room for more. It is said that she killed some of them with laudanum, and buried them in her garden.

The trial was closely followed throughout New Zealand, and particularly in Invercargill. Minnie said that dozens of 'her' children were in foster homes, but she couldn't say where as she had never kept records. Minnie was sentenced to death. She was hanged at 8a.m. on 12 August 1895 protesting her innocence. She was 47 years old.

Minnie Dean was the only woman ever to be hanged in New Zealand.

(2)

Immigration

MORE MIGRANTS NEEDED

New Zealand welcomes applications from people wishing to come here, whether it is to visit, study, work or live. New Zealand needs people who are 'keen to make a go of it', people with qualifications and experience, who would not be a drain on our resources.

It will cost you money to process your application for residency, and unfortunately if you find that you have not been successful, you will not receive a rebate of the fees you have paid. So it is a good idea to assess your chances before having to 'pay up', by filling in the specimen self assessment form in this chapter. If after having assessed your points you wish to proceed further, go to your nearest immigration office and apply for a residency permit. Remember, you then have to go through *their* assessment. Do *not* make any serious plans to move *until you have received your residency permit.*

There are many New Zealand Immigration Offices around the world where expert help and information can be received, and the necessary application forms applied for. See addresses at the back of this book.

Policy in the temporary field has been aimed at facilitating the entry of tourists and business visitors, and New Zealand has arrangements for visa-free entry for citizens of over 25 countries. See the section on Visitors for a list of these countries.

If, on the other hand, you are not from a visa-waiver country, or if:

- you want to study
- you want to work at a job you have already arranged
- you are sponsored for a visit by a relative or friend in New Zealand
- you want to get medical treatment

then you will need to apply for a visa. Three months is the standard period for a visit to New Zealand for visitors from both visa-waiver and visa-required countries.

If you wish to extend your visit, you must demonstrate viable means of support or other good reasons, before a further three month permit will be granted. British citizens only can receive a six months' permit on arrival. You may also apply for a further visitor's permit if there are good reasons why you cannot leave New Zealand, or if you are a genuine tourist.

If you know you want to visit New Zealand for more than three months before you arrive, then you should apply for a visa to stay the length of time you require (up to 12 months) *before* travelling to New Zealand, whether you are from a visa-required or visa-waiver country.

Visitors who do not apply in advance for a longer stay are usually only permitted to be in New Zealand for a stay of up to six months in any 12-month period. You must then leave this country, and stay away for the same period you were here, e.g. if you were here for six months, then you must stay away for six months before returning to New Zealand as a visitor.

Applications for work permits are considered in the light of the local labour market. Policy allows entry on student visas of people wishing to undertake long-term courses at universities and other tertiary institutions, although some courses of less than three months' duration can be attended without a student permit. Provision is also made for people to enter New Zealand for medical treatment in certain circumstances.

In March 2002 the Government introduced a Residence from Work Category which encompasses the following:

(a) Talent (Accredited Employers) Residence Policy
(b) Talent (Arts, Culture and Sports) Residence Policy
(c) Priority Occupations List Residence Policy.

The categories
Now we come to the 'hard bit' – delving through numerous pages of information on immigration requirements. So that you can pick out the part that is relevant to you we have divided the sections as follows:

◆ Visitor's permit
◆ Study permit

- Work permit
- Residency.

Advance Passenger Screening

A new system called Advance Passenger Screening now affects all travellers entering New Zealand. Traditionally, visas, passports and other travel documents have been checked when you arrive in New Zealand. Under Advance Passenger Screening, your documents will also be checked before you board the flight that is bringing you to New Zealand.

Therefore, in order to board your flight, it is critical that you have the correct documentation, and that it is valid and current. Incorrect travel documents may result in your experiencing delays at check-in, or even not being allowed to board your flight to New Zealand.

OBTAINING A VISITOR'S VISA/PERMIT

Visitors may come to New Zealand:

- as tourists
- for business talks
- to see friends or relatives
- to play sport or perform in cultural events (without pay)
- for medical treatment or medical consultation.

You will definitely need a visitor's visa *before* you travel here unless you are:

- an Australian citizen travelling on an Australian passport (you *do not* need a visa and are exempt from the requirement to hold a permit to be in New Zealand)

♦ an Australian resident with a current Australian resident return visa (you *do not* need a visa and are granted a residence permit when you arrive)

♦ a citizen of any of the following countries, which have visa-waiver agreements with New Zealand.

Note: you *must* apply for a visa if you plan to visit for more than the time stated below:

For visits up to 30 days
Citizens of France living in Tahiti or New Caledonia.

For visits up to three months
Citizens of Austria, Belgium, Brunei, Canada, Denmark, Finland, France[1], Germany, Greece, Iceland, Indonesia, Ireland, Italy, Japan, Korea (South), Kiribati, Liechtenstein, Luxembourg, Malaysia, Malta, Monaco, Nauru, Netherlands, Norway, Portugal[2], Singapore, Spain, Sweden, Switzerland, Thailand, Tuvalu, United States of America.

Notes: [1]French citizens living in France only. [2]Portuguese passport holders must have the right to live permanently in Portugal.

For visits up to six months
British citizens and other British passport holders who have evidence of the right to live permanently in the United Kingdom.

If you are a citizen of one of the above stated countries,

you can apply for a visitor's permit (see page 31) by completing an arrival card when you arrive in New Zealand.

Visitor's visas

A visitor's visa is an endorsement in your passport *before* you come to New Zealand. You should apply for your visitor's permit when you complete an arrival card upon entering New Zealand. The period of time you are allowed to stay will be written inside your visa and permit, and you are *not* entitled to work in New Zealand. Visas are to enable you to:

♦ study or train for a single course of not more than three months

♦ undergo medical treatment

♦ take a holiday.

You will need to supply a completed **Application for Visitor's Visa**, fee, passport, and a recent passport-size photo. You may also be required to show that you have enough money to support yourself during your stay here, i.e. NZ $1,000 for each person per month or NZ $400 each person per month if your accommodation is already paid, and evidence of this – prepaid hotel vouchers – must be available. Details of your travel arrangements to leave New Zealand must also be shown.

If you wish to make more than one journey to New Zealand, you should apply for a multiple visa.

Medical treatment

If you are coming to New Zealand for medical treatment you may have to give details of treatment by completing a **Details of Intended Medical Treatment** form. You will also need a letter from a New Zealand hospital (Crown Health Enterprise) or Regional Health Authority to your doctor confirming your acceptance for treatment. For private sector treatment, you will need a letter from a New Zealand doctor or hospital confirming that you have been accepted for treatment. Evidence that you will be able to pay for treatment is also required.

Yacht and private aircraft

You will require a visa if you are travelling by private aircraft or yacht, unless you are a citizen of one of the visa-waiver countries listed in this chapter, also if you are only visiting for no longer than the time stated in that section. Application for a visitor's permit is made by completing an arrival card when you land in New Zealand.

What is a visitor's permit?

A visitor's permit is endorsed in your passport. It shows that you have permission to be in New Zealand. The period of time you are allowed to stay here is written on the permit.

You *may not* work here if you have a visitor's permit. It is also illegal for you to study for longer than three months if you have a visitor's permit. If you have a visitor's permit and want to work in New Zealand or to study for longer than three months you must make an application to either change to a work or student permit or change the conditions of your visitor's permit.

You will only be granted permission to work if there are no suitable New Zealand job seekers who could do the job you have been offered. Also, you will only be able to work for the remaining time you are entitled to stay as a visitor.

How do I apply for a visitor's permit?

When you arrive in New Zealand you apply for a visitor's permit by completing an arrival card. You will need to show your passport which must be valid until at least three months past the date you plan to leave New Zealand, and your visitor's visa (if you had to obtain one before you travelled to New Zealand). If you are already in New Zealand you should apply to an office of the New Zealand Immigration Service (see the addresses at the back of this book).

Documents

To make an application you will need to supply:

1. a completed *Application for Visitor's Permit* form
2. the application fee (see this chapter)
3. your passport (which must be valid until at least three months past the date you plan to leave New Zealand)
4. a recent passport-sized photo.

Money

You will also be asked to show that you have enough money to support yourself whilst in New Zealand, see this chapter for details, plus evidence of funds which can be in the form of traveller's cheques, bank draft, letters of credit or a New Zealand bank account in your name.

Cash or credit cards may be accepted as evidence of funds.

Guarantees

If you do not have enough money you will need a guarantee of accommodation and maintenance from a friend or relative who lives in New Zealand. In this case you must use the form **Sponsoring a Visitor**. In addition, you will need to show details of travel arrangements for your departure from New Zealand, such as valid tickets to a country to which you have the right of entry.

How long can I stay?

The length of stay shown in the permit granted on your arrival will depend on whether you entered under a visa-waiver agreement and were able to meet the requirements for a visit of the time specified in the agreement, or you obtained a visitor's visa before you departed for New Zealand.

All visitors to New Zealand are allowed a stay of up to nine months, provided they apply for further permits (if required) and meet normal visitor requirements. You *must* apply for a further permit if you want to extend your stay. A further visitor's permit allowing a stay of more than nine months many only be granted to people who are genuine tourists, or who have lodged a residence application for the first time, and this is being considered, or if you cannot leave New Zealand because of circumstances beyond your control. This permit will be for a period of not more than three months, to a maximum stay of twelve months, from the date of your arrival.

You might also be granted a further visitor's permit if you are undergoing medical treatment or your private yacht or aircraft needs repair. Owners of private craft may be granted further permits beyond the standard maximum stay when their craft needs to undergo refitting or major repairs. You will need to show evidence of this.

Finding a sponsor

If you are applying for a visitor's visa or visitor's permit, but do not have enough money for your living expenses or onward travel, you may be sponsored by a friend or relative in New Zealand.

Such sponsors must be resident in New Zealand and be a New Zealand citizen or have a residence permit *without requirements*, or be exempt from the requirements to hold a permit.

They must be prepared to cover the cost of your maintenance (or living expenses), accommodation and tickets for you to leave New Zealand. Any dependants must also be listed on this form. Your sponsor should complete the form **Sponsoring a Visitor** and take it to an office of the New Zealand Immigration Service in New Zealand for approval. After approval, your sponsor should send it to you so that you can attach it to your application for a visitor's visa.

It must be noted that if sponsors fail to carry out their undertaking, the New Zealand Government may recover from them any costs incurred in respect of that failure (this could include the cost of accommodation and tickets for departure if the person has to be removed from New Zealand).

Could I be refused a visa or permit?

Yes, you could if you did not meet the standard requirements for getting a visitor's visa or permit, or if you are not eligible for a permit under Section Seven of the **Immigration Act 1987**. You could be refused entry if:

♦ you have been convicted and sentenced to prison for five years or more†

♦ in the past ten years you have been convicted and sentenced to prison for twelve months or more†

♦ you have been deported from any country

♦ you are subject to a current New Zealand removal warrant or removal order

♦ the authorities suspect you of being a terrorist or likely to commit a crime.

† This applies even if your offences have been later taken off the record.

OBTAINING A STUDY VISA/PERMIT

Visas

A visa is an endorsement placed in your passport *before* you depart for New Zealand. Visas allow you to travel to New Zealand until the specified date; they do not give you permission to be in New Zealand, but do indicate that the holder has permission to travel to New Zealand, and that the issuing officer knows of no reason why a permit should not be issued upon arrival. You must apply for a visa *unless* the course of study or training is for three months or less. A visa shows the length of your stay, e.g. up to four years. This will also be shown on your permit.

If you wish to enquire about technical institutions, universities and schools, you can contact either the Ministry of Education, International Division, Private Bag, Wellington, New Zealand. Tel: 64 4 473 5544 or Fax 64 4 499 1327, or the institution of your choice. The addresses can be found at the back of this book, together with the Immigration Service Offices (NZ addresses) and the New Zealand Ministry of Education offices (see Chapter 4 on education).

Before you apply

There are two courses of action to take *before* applying for a visa:

1. You must have a letter of acceptance for the course of your choice, from the New Zealand institution of your choice. A specimen application form is shown on page 175.

2. You must show that the fees have been paid, by presenting your receipt.

You must then have the following information which must be attached to your application for a visa:

(a) Your passport or certificate of identity. Your passport must be valid for the period of time you are applying to study for.

(b) A completed and signed **Application for Student Visa** form, with a passport-size photograph. You will be required to pay a non-refundable student visa application fee of approximately NZ$188.00.

(c) A written offer of a place, which notifies you that you have been accepted by an educational institution in New Zealand to undertake a course of study.

(d) Either a receipt for payment of course fees (you are not required to produce the receipt before your application has been approved in principle), or evidence that you are exempt from course fees, e.g. by a New Zealand Government Scholarship. To find out more about this please contact your nearest New Zealand Embassy office.

(e) A guarantee of accommodation – a written assurance from an educational institution or other person, that suitable residential accommodation is available to you in New Zealand.

(f) Evidence that funds are available for your maintenance throughout your stay. The following is acceptable:

- A completed **Sponsoring a Student** form, in which your sponsor gives a financial undertaking that he or she can transfer to New Zealand approximately NZ$7,000 per year.

- A letter from your educational institution confirming that your living costs have already been paid.

- A bank document showing the funds of the amount required will be available to you in New Zealand e.g. approximately NZ$1,000 for each month of your stay for short-term study, or approximately NZ$7,000 per year for long-term study.

◆ An award of a full New Zealand scholarship.

(g) Evidence of arrangements for onward travel from New Zealand. If you are undertaking a long-term course, a completed **Sponsoring a Student** form will usually satisfy this requirement. If you intend taking a short-term course, you will need to provide a return ticket to show that you have the funds to do so.

If you intend studying in New Zealand for more than two years you will need to show New Zealand Immigration Service medical and chest X-ray certificates, plus character clearances, which must be:

◆ two original character references if under 17 years of age or

◆ a local police clearance if you are 17 years of age and over. You will be advised of the procedure for obtaining these by the New Zealand Government office of your country.

All of the above are essential before a student visa is issued. When the New Zealand Government office overseas is satisfied that your application is complete and in order you will be issued a student visa.

If your course of study is less than three months, a student visa is not required.

If you are in New Zealand, or entering New Zealand on a visitor's visa, or under a visa-waiver agreement, or as the dependant of a visitor for a short time, you may be admitted to a primary or secondary school without charge for a period of up to 28 consecutive days, at the discretion of the principal, and beyond 28 days with the approval of the Secretary of Education.

Permits

When you arrive in New Zealand your passport will be endorsed with a permit which will allow you to be here for study or training whilst it is current. If you need an extension of your permit, you must apply before the original permit expires. Failure to do so will mean that you are here unlawfully, and may be removed. If you leave New Zealand before your permit expires, it will automatically cancel.

Further information for students

New Zealand Immigration Service will issue a visa or permit to a school student for one year, on the basis of one term's fees. However, if an instalment of fees is for less than one term, a visa or permit will be issued for only the period covered by the instalment. A permit renewal fee is payable.

If you wish to transfer to another course or institution, you must obtain a variation to your student permit, specifying the course and institution and, if appropriate, the extended validity of the permit.

Health benefits for students

As a full-fee foreign student you are eligible for health

KEY FEATURES

1. Last date by which holder must arrive in New Zealand
2. Issued for multiple/single journeys
3. Usually children travelling on the same passport may be included here
4. Limiting factors such as occupation or place of study may be inserted here

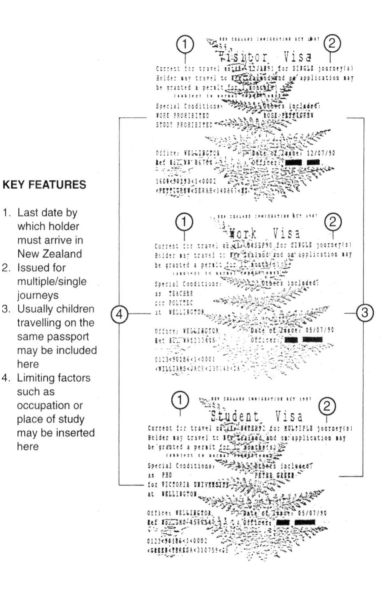

Fig. 5. Examples of New Zealand visas.

KEY FEATURES

1. Date on which
   permit comes
   into force
2. Date permit
   expires
3. Usually children
   travelling on the
   same passport
   may be included
   here
4. Limiting factors
   such as
   occupation or
   place of study
   may be inserted
   here

Fig. 6. Examples of New Zealand permits.

benefits if your course of study is of two or more years' duration. It is strongly recommended that all foreign students obtain medical insurance cover, especially students on shorter courses of up to two years' duration. Information on medical insurance will be available from New Zealand Government offices overseas.

Full-fee students from the United Kingdom and Australia are eligible for health benefits during courses of study lasting less than two years if they meet the requirements of the reciprocal health agreements New Zealand has with these countries.

Income support
You will not be eligible for income support assistance. A condition of your student visa is that you will be able to meet the full costs of education, accommodation and other living costs.

Accident compensation
You will be eligible for accident compensation on the same basis as resident New Zealand citizens. This will include earnings-related compensation if you are working.

Student allowances
Foreign students will not be entitled to student loans or to allowances under the Student Allowances Regulations 1991. Australian citizens or those who have been granted the right to reside permanently in Australia will be entitled to student loans. They may also apply for student allowances, provided they make a statutory declaration of their intention to reside permanently in New Zealand.

Restrictions on student employment

Holiday employment
You need to apply for special permission from the nearest office of the New Zealand Immigration Service before you commence holiday employment. You may work only during the long summer holidays and only if you are taking a full-time course of more than 12 months' duration.

Course-related employment
The New Zealand Immigration Service will grant approval for you to work during the year if it is work experience related to course requirements. They may also give you permission to remain in New Zealand and work for up to two years in employment related to your course if it has not been possible to gain work experience during your studies and if this work experience is a condition of being awarded a certificate.

Application for spouses of students to work
If your spouse wishes to work while you are in New Zealand, an application must be made through an office of the New Zealand Immigration Service. (See the addresses at the back of this book.)

Decisions on applications will depend on whether there are any unemployed New Zealand residents who can do the job which has been offered. For this reason, no definite assurance can be given whether an application would be successful.

Postgraduate study
If you have already completed an undergraduate course at

a New Zealand university, you can apply for a further permit to do postgraduate study.

OBTAINING A WORK PERMIT

Anyone who arranges a job before arriving in New Zealand, or who intends to come to New Zealand to work, must apply in their own country for a work visa. Do not make arrangements to travel here until you have written approval of your application.

How to apply

If you have a current work, visitor's or student permit and you now want a work permit to stay longer, you must apply before your current permit expires. Your work permit application will be considered according to the local job market. A permit will normally be issued only if a suitable New Zealand citizen or resident is not available locally for the job.

You will need to supply:

- a completed **Application for Work Permit**
- your passport or certificate of identity, which must be valid for one month beyond the proposed date of leaving New Zealand, or three months if your passport has to be sent outside New Zealand for renewal
- a recent passport-size photo
- the application fee.

The person or firm offering you the job must provide you with the following information in writing to give to the

New Zealand Immigration Service:

◆ the name, address, telephone and/or fax number of company or employer

◆ a job description including –
Job title
Type of work or duties
Pay and conditions
Qualifications or training or experience required
Duration of the job
Details of attempts to recruit New Zealanders and reasons why none was suitable.

You must supply evidence that you are suitably qualified by training and experience to do the job, and if the salary or pay from your prospective employer is not considered enough to cover your maintenance and/or outward travel, you may also be asked to produce evidence of money or means of support and an outward ticket or other evidence of the travel arrangements you have made to leave at the end of your stay. It is very important that you make a careful note of the expiry date of your permit, because if you stay in New Zealand after that date you will be here unlawfully and will be liable for removal.

Other conditions of a work permit
You may not study without obtaining:

◆ a student permit, or

◆ a change to the conditions of your work permit to let you study for a short time, unless the course is one single course of not more than three months' duration.

United Kingdom Working Holiday Scheme

British residents aged between 18 and 30, and unaccompanied by children, are allowed to have one-year working holidays in New Zealand, under the **Temporary Work Permit Scheme**.

New Zealand allows 500 people per year, on a first come first served basis. All applicants have to satisfy the New Zealand Immigration officers in London that their primary intention is to holiday in New Zealand. They are then only allowed to perform 'incidental or temporary work' whilst in New Zealand.

PERMANENT MIGRANTS

There are four main categories permanent migrants will be considered under:

- Skilled Migrant Category
- Business Investment Category
- Family Category
- Humanitarian Category.

Skilled Migrant Category (SMC)

In August 2003 the New Zealand Government announced sweeping changes to the immigration policy, the greatest in a decade. SMC is to replace the old General Skills Category, and will place more emphasis on job offers. It has been designed to ensure the best possible outcome for both skilled migrants, and New Zealand as a whole.

I am unable to give you the final details regarding this new category, as the New Zealand Government will not be releasing this information until late 2003/early 2004. I urge you to contact your nearest NZIS or *www.immigration.govt.nz* to avail yourself of these changes.

Briefly, SMC will allow would-be migrants to register an 'expression of interest', on the appropriate forms, and then be admitted to a pool for which there will be a pass mark. The highest ranking applicants will then be asked to apply for residence, and required to pay a fee, which has yet to be decided. The NZIS will release information on a regular basis giving the number of applicants selected from the pool, and their points total. This will give some indication of the quality of migrants being selected.

When an applicant is selected from the pool, he/she will be asked to pay an application fee. After this you will either gain permanent residence, or go through a two year work-to-residence scheme. This scheme will facilitate the entry of people whose skills or talents are in demand, and provide them with a pathway to residence.

The SMC is expected to shift the emphasis on scoring enough points to gain residence, to ensuring skills and talents are properly utilised. In order to help the skill-starved provinces, bonus points will be available to those who choose not to settle in Auckland.

The self assessment chart on page 52 will become obsolete, but until a new chart is available it will give you some idea of how points can be scored, bearing in mind that the 'Work Experience' section is to be changed, and possibly 'Settlement Factors' could change. However, English language requirements will still stay the same and character, health and police checks will all still be obligatory.

The main areas tested will be –

◆ *Employability*
This is the major element and will relate to qualifications and work experience. You will need to supply *original* or *certified* true copies of your qualifications, and evidence that you were employed in your stated occupation for the given length of time.

◆ *Qualifications*
The following rules apply:
  – You can only obtain points for one qualification.
  – Partially completed qualifications will not be accepted.
  – Your qualifications must be of a comparable standard to a New Zealand qualification.

Note: in New Zealand there are certain occupations for which you must have membership of and/or registration with a professional or industrial organisation. Some examples of such occupations are:

Dental technicians	Optometrists	Radio/TV servicing
Electricians	Pharmacists	personnel
Town planners	Plumbers and	Veterinarians
Medical personnel	gas fitters	

If you wish to apply for residence in New Zealand you do not have to be registered. If you are registered, however, this will assist the New Zealand Immigration Service in making a correct assessment of your qualification (see Chapter 3).

Work experience
You can score points for work experience that is:

◆ sound, continuous and relevant to your qualification (which you obtained after the completion of your schooling) for which you by obtain points.

Your work experience must have been obtained after you completed your qualification, or be:

◆ sound, continuous and in an approved occupation.

An approved occupation is one which is considered skilled in New Zealand and appears on the New Zealand Immigration Service's Register of Approved Occupations. To score points in this area you must have had at least five years' experience in your approved occupation. You may wish to contact your local New Zealand Immigration Service office for advice on whether you are working in an approved occupation.

Note: if you have a post-schooling qualification and work experience which is not directly related to that qualification, you cannot claim points for both the work experience and the qualification, even if the work experience is in an approved occupation. You can, however, claim points for both twelve years' schooling and work experience in an approved occupation.

Age

You will be allocated points for the age that you are at the time you lodge your application. If you are over the maximum age limit of 55 years, you are not eligible to be approved under the General Category.

Settlement factors

If you claim points for settlement funds, your investment funds must be additional to your settlement funds.

Settlement funds

To score points, your settlement funds (i.e. the value of your house, cash, shares, stocks find any other assets, minus all your debts) *must* be worth at least NZ$100,000.

Investment funds

To score points you must have between NZ$100,000 and NZ$300,000 and must be willing and able to have it transferred to, and invested in, New Zealand for at least two years. This investment must, in normal circumstances, provide a commercial return on the funds invested. Applicants will not be permitted to invest the funds in the purchase of possessions that could be for personal use, such as a house or car.

Note: you should note that settlement funds of $100,000 will attract two points, while the same amount of investment funds attract one point.

Sponsorship

To score points for a sponsor, you must have a family sponsor who is your adult brother or sister, or parent, or adult child, who is a New Zealand resident, who has been lawfully permanently living in New Zealand for at least three years immediately prior to the application, and is prepared to accept family sponsorship obligations.

Your community sponsor must be prepared to accept community sponsorship obligations, and be approved by the New Zealand Immigration Service.

Offer of skilled employment

To score points for an offer of skilled employment, you must have a firm and genuine job offer which will be kept open for six months. (For further details contact your nearest Immigration Office.)

Business and investment migrant category

The Government recognises that business migrants can significantly add to the wealth of New Zealand, and as a result, consideration will be given to applicants with substantial capital and business skills who can create jobs and enhance development.

Applicants in this category will be required to bring into New Zealand a minimum of NZ$750,000.

Though in general business migrants will be allowed to place their money in investments of their choice, a residence visa will *not* be granted until funds have been lodged in a New Zealand investment, and if those funds are not kept there for at least two years, the residence permit may be revoked.

Applicants must be able to show that the business investment funds are the direct result of their own business or professional record over a period of at least three years, and that their business or professional record extends over a minimum period of ten years. This category will be open to business people of all ages, and will require a minimum level of English language ability on the part of the principal applicant or their spouse or an adult child over 17.

Self assessment

Having got this far you must be anxious to see if you will qualify. This you can do by using the Self Assessment Form on page 52.

Business investor category

The aim of the business investor category is to ensure that high quality migrants with excellent, proven business skills and experience gain entry to New Zealand. Generally, they are also expected to invest business funds in New Zealand. You will be granted residence under the business investor category if you score enough points to meet the pass mark and you meet the compulsory requirements. Contact the New Zealand Immigration Service for the current pass mark.

Family migrant category

This category covers three situations – marriage to a New Zealand citizen or resident; de facto/homosexual relationship with a citizen or resident; parents, dependent children and single adult brothers and sisters and

Self assessment

POINTS FACTOR	POINTS		YOUR SCORE	
	You	Spouse	You	Spouse
EMPLOYABILITY FACTORS Points may be scored for both Qualifications and Work Experience				
1. Qualifications: Any equivalent to a base degree, trade or 3 yr diploma/certificate Any advanced trade or professional qualification Any equivalent of a Masters or better	10 11 12	1 – 2		
2. Work Experience: (Must be relevant to Post Secondary Qualifications or in an Approved Occupation) 2 complete years 4 complete years 6 complete years 8 complete years 10 complete years 12 complete years 14 complete years 16 complete years 18 complete years 20 complete years	 1 2 3 4 5 6 7 8 9 10			
Maximum points for Employability factor: 25				
3. Age: 18-24 years 25-29 years 30-34 years 35-39 years 40-44 years 45-49 years Maximum age limit: 55 years	 8 10 8 6 4 2			
Maximum points for Age factor: 10				
4. Settlement Factors: NZ$100,000 settlement funds (max 2 points) Family sponsor 1 point for each additional NZ$100,000 investments funds, up to a max of $300,000 Offer of Skilled employment (full time)	 1 3 3 5			
MAXIMUM POINTS: 40 **TOTAL:**				

Fig. 7. General category – points system.

children. A legally married spouse of a New Zealand resident or citizen may qualify for residence. De facto or homosexual partners of New Zealand citizens or residents may be considered for residence. Once again, approval is not automatic, and an interview with both partners may be held. The couple will need to show they are living together in a stable, lasting relationship. The relationship must be of at least two years' duration in the case of a de facto couple, and four years if the relationship is homosexual.

If you are a parent, you are eligible to be reunited with your adult children in New Zealand (provided all your adult children are living permanently outside your home country, or you have an equal or greater number of adult children lawfully permanently resident in New Zealand than anywhere else).

Limited provisions exist for parents with dependent children. Single adult brothers, sisters and children of New Zealand citizens or residents (including persons who are divorced or widowed) are eligible for residence provided they have no children and have no immediate family in their home country.

If you are applying under family reunification you will need a sponsor or support from the New Zealand based relative.

Unmarried dependent children under 17 are eligible for residence if they:

- are joining their parent(s) in New Zealand
- have no children of their own
- were declared in their parents' application for residence, and provided their parents are lawfully and permanently living in New Zealand.

APPEALS

There are two appeal authorities which can review declined applications.

The **Residence Appeal Authority** will provide unsuccessful residence applicants with an opportunity to have the decision independently reviewed. The Authority may approve cases where it is satisfied they fall within policy.

The **Removal Review Authority** will have the power to quash a removal order where there are exceptional humanitarian grounds for allowing the person to remain in New Zealand, or where a person has been determined not to be an overstayer.

There is provision for appeals on questions of law to be taken to the High Court.

Provision is also made in the Immigration Act for the reconsideration of any refusal by an immigration officer to grant a temporary permit.

IMMIGRATION FEES

New fees were introduced in July 2003. Your application will not be considered unless your fee is paid. Fees must be paid by bank cheque, building society cheque, money order or acceptable credit/debit card. Cheques must be made payable to 'The New Zealand Immigration Service'. Cash payments are acceptable if paying in person. Do not send cash payments by mail. *All fees must be paid in pounds sterling, no other currency is accepted.* Acceptable debit/credit cards are: Visa, Delta, Switch, Eurocard/Mastercard. Irrespective of outcome, visa fees are *non-refundable.*

For further information on possible changes check *www.immigration.govt.nz.* Please ensure you have the correct information and current forms when you submit your application to the office.

Type of Visa	UK £
Visitor's Visa	45.00
Work Visa (temporary)	75.00
Work visa (talent)	105.00
Working Holiday Visa	45.00
Work – Long-Term Business Visa	830.00
Student Visa (temporary)	75.00
Residence (general and family migrants)	435.00
Residence (business investor/entrepreneur)	795.00
Residence (family quota)	410.00
Migrant Levy (general and business categories – to be paid when residence application approved in principle)	85.00pp
Migrant Levy (family category – to be paid when residence application approved in principle)	45.00pp
Returning Resident's Visa (RRV)	60.00
Transit Visa	60.00
Transfer of Label	40.00

Business immigration category application fees do not include Goods & Services Tax (GST) as they are assessed outside New Zealand. GST (12.5%) is payable when the service is provided in New Zealand.

It is possible to lodge an appeal asking for reconsideration of decisions made. The appropriate fees for this can be obtained from *www.immigration.govt.nz*.

Family applications

Your spouse to de facto partner (either heterosexual or same sex) and any unmarried dependent children 24 years of age or younger do not need to make a separate application or pay a separate fee if they are included in your application for a residence visa or permit.

Children who are 25 years of age or younger who are not dependant and children who are 25 years of age or older must make their own application for a residence visa or permit and pay a separate fee.

OBTAINING A POLICE CERTIFICATE

All applicants applying for residence in New Zealand must provide a Police Certificate at the same time as a residence application is lodged. This Certificate must be less than two months old at the time the application is lodged.

You must apply for this from your country of residence, but contact the nearest New Zealand Immigration office. If you have lived for periods of 12 months or more in other countries during the last ten years, you must obtain certificates from these countries also. The certificates must be in English, or on an official letterhead as a certified translation, with a stamp or signature of the translator.

HUMANITARIAN CATEGORY

This covers people whose circumstances are exceptionally difficult. The applicant must have at least one close relative who is a New Zealand citizen or resident, and who supports the application. Applicants will be assessed under the following criteria:

+ their circumstances must be such that they, or a New Zealand party, is suffering serious physical or emotional harm, and

+ their application is supported by a close family member who is a New Zealand citizen or resident, and

+ they produce evidence to show why their situation can only be resolved by their being granted residence in New Zealand, and

+ it would not be contrary to the public interest to allow the applicants to reside in New Zealand.

A close family member is defined for the purposes of the Humanitarian Category as a parent, sibling or child, aunt, uncle, nephew, niece, grandparent or a person who has lived with, and been part of, the applicant's family for many years.

QUESTIONS AND ANSWERS ON IMMIGRATION

How long does it take to process residence applicants?

It can take up to six months. However, if you ensure that your application is complete and all the necessary material is enclosed with your application, i.e. original documents or certified copies, then you stand a much better chance of getting an early reply.

How can I find out about work prospects?

By obtaining New Zealand newspapers or by contacting your nearest Immigration Office. You could also contact an Employment Bureau in New Zealand (see end of book for addresses). If funds allow, you could always come here first on a visitor's visa to check the situation out for yourself before applying for New Zealand residency and selling up in your homeland.

Is it possible that a visitor wouldn't be allowed a permit upon arrival in New Zealand?

Yes, but only if something unusual had happened in between your getting your visa and your arrival in New Zealand.

INWARDS AND OUTWARDS MIGRATION

The flow of people isn't just inwards into New Zealand. Several New Zealanders have had to abandon, temporarily or otherwise, their country of birth to earn a living overseas.

Rachael Hunter, who was a photographers' model, made her name as a very highly paid model in America. She met Rod Stewart, famous English pop singer, they got married, and now she lives permanently in the USA. She would have had to live 'outside' New Zealand even if she hadn't met Rocker Rod.

Sam Neill, the sexy superstar, started off small time acting in New Zealand, but he didn't achieve world fame and fortune until he went overseas. Now he just comes home for a visit to 'wind down'.

Kiri Te Kanawa, the world-acclaimed opera singer, went overseas for furtherance of her career, and now lives outside London. She, too, is just an occasional visitor to these shores.

Bob Charles, well-known golf champion, now travels overseas to play the golf circuits as a veteran golfer. He earns his income overseas, and very rarely competes in New Zealand. He does come back to his New Zealand home occasionally.

Application *for* Visiting New Zealand

(to travel to New Zealand or to be in New Zealand to visit)

Application No. | For NZIS Use Only

This form may be used by a single applicant or a family (which may include a principal applicant, partner, and dependent children under 20), and may be used to apply for a Visitor's Visa or Permit or a Limited Purpose Visa or Permit.

Please note: If you decide to apply directly for a Limited Purpose Visa and you are subsequently granted a Limited Purpose Permit, your immigration rights in New Zealand are restricted to fulfilling the express purpose for which you came.

☐ Number of persons included on this form

☐ Number of visitor visas applied for on this form

☐ Number of visitor permits applied for on this form

☐ Number of limited purpose visas/permits (delete one) applied for on this form.

Please note: if you are in New Zealand and applying for a further permit, you need to allow sufficient time for a decision to be made on your application before your current permit expires. If your permit does expire, your application for a further permit does not make your stay in New Zealand lawful or give you the right to remain in New Zealand while your application is being considered.

Section A   Personal Details

Principal applicant   Client number: ☐

A1 Name as shown in passport
    Family: _____ Given: _____

A2 Preferred title   Mr ☐ Mrs ☐ Ms ☐ Miss ☐ Dr ☐ Other _____
    (please specify)

Attach one recent passport size photograph of yourself here. Write your name on the back.

A3 Other names you are known by _____

A4 Your name in ethnic script _____

A5 Gender   Male ☐ Female ☐   **A6** Date of birth ☐ day ☐ month ☐ year

A7 Place and country of birth   Place: _____ Country: _____

A8 Passport details   Number: _____ Country: _____
    Expiry Date: ☐ day ☐ month ☐ year

A9 Your citizenship _____

A10 Other citizenships currently held _____

A11 Partnership status   ☐ Married   ☐ Never married   ☐ De Facto   ☐ Separated
    ☐ Engaged   ☐ Widowed   ☐ Divorced

③

Fig. 8. Application for a visitor's pass or permit.

60

A12 If you are applying for a visa/permit on the basis of a partnership:
- are you living in a genuine and stable partnership? ☐ Yes ☐ No

If no please explain

- will your partner be in New Zealand for the same period of time? ☐ Yes ☐ No
- do you meet the minimum requirements for the recognition of a partnership? ☐ Yes ☐ No
- do you intend to apply for residence under Partnership policy? ☐ Yes ☐ No
- If yes, will your New Zealand citizen or resident partner be eligible to sponsor your application? ☐ Yes ☐ No

Additional information

Principal applicant, please complete for yourself and on behalf of any accompanying family members.

A13 I may be contacted at this New Zealand residential address and telephone number:

	Telephone

A14 Name and address of any friends, relatives or contacts I have in New Zealand are:

Name	Relationship
Address	

Name	Relationship
Address	

Name	Relationship
Address	

A15 My postal address and contact phone number for this application are:

Address:	Telephone
	Email

A16 My residential address in my home country is:

A17 I am employed by, and my regular occupation is:
(Please give name and address of employer. If not employed, please state this.)

Employer details:
Your occupation:

A18 My stay in New Zealand will be financially supported in the following way:

A19 The arrangement I have made for outward travel from New Zealand is:

4 If requested, please attach a copy of your travel itinerary or air ticket out of New Zealand.

Fig. 8. Continued.

Principal Applicant: Application Details – Visitor's Visa or Permit

DO NOT complete this section if you are applying for a **Limited Purpose Visa** or **Permit** (see questions A24 to A27)

A20
☐ I am applying for a Visitor's Visa to travel to New Zealand, or
☐ I am applying for a Visitor's Permit to be in New Zealand, or
☐ I am applying for a Visitor's Permit and a Visitor's Visa as I am already in New Zealand

A21 If applying for a Visitor's Visa:
This is the date I will enter or re-enter New Zealand:

| day | month | year |

This is the date I will finally depart New Zealand:

| day | month | year |

☐ I would like a **single** journey Visitor's Visa, or
☐ I would like a **multiple** journey Visitor's Visa

A22 The purpose of this application is to **visit** New Zealand for:
☐ General (tourist, or visit friends or family) ☐ Business ☐ Medical
Other | Please specify

If you wish to apply to study or work in New Zealand please use a study or work application form.

A23 If applying for a **Visitor's Permit**:
This is the date I arrived in New Zealand:

| day | month | year |

This is the date I request my **Visitor's Permit** be valid to:

| day | month | year |

This is the date I will finally depart New Zealand:

| day | month | year |

Limited Purpose Visa or Permit Complete questions A24 to A27.

DO NOT complete questions A24 to A27 if you are applying for a Visitor's Visa or Permit.
Only complete this section if:
• you are travelling to New Zealand for an "express purpose" and you wish to have a Limited Purpose Permit in New Zealand,
or
• your existing Limited Purpose Permit will not last long enough for you to achieve your "express purpose" and you therefore require a further one.

Such permits mean that you are **not** able to apply for any other type of permit in New Zealand or seek to stay longer or indefinitely in New Zealand. For general information and a list of "express purposes" see the **Information Leaflet on Limited Purpose Visas and Permits** (NZIS 1070).

Principal Applicant: Application Details – Limited Purpose

A24
☐ I am applying for a **Limited Purpose Visa** to travel to New Zealand, or
☐ I am applying for a further **Limited Purpose Permit** to be in New Zealand

(you may only apply for a further Limited Purpose Permit if you already have a Limited Purpose Permit and you need further time to achieve the "express purpose").

5

Fig. 8. Continued.

A25 The limited purpose application is for the **"express purpose"** of:
- Attendance at an event such as a wedding, funeral, conference, seminar, graduation, sports tournament or match, religious event, or other significant ceremony; or
- Medical treatment in New Zealand; or
- Family emergencies such as illness or accident affecting a family member or relative of the applicant in New Zealand; or
- "Milestone" events such as reunions or anniversaries; or
- Any other specific purpose other than employment, where the circumstances warrant the issue of a Limited Purpose Visa.

Please specify the "express purpose", the date the "express purpose" begins and the date the "express purpose" will be completed below.

"Express purpose" details:

If your **"express purpose"** is to study in New Zealand please use the **Application to Study in New Zealand** (NZIS 1012) form.

A26 If applying for a **Limited Purpose Visa:**
This is the date I will enter New Zealand:

| day | month | year |

This is the date I will finally depart New Zealand:

| day | month | year |

A27 If applying for a **Limited Purpose Permit:**
This is the date I arrived in New Zealand on a **Limited Purpose Visa:**

| day | month | year |

This is the date I will finally depart New Zealand:

| day | month | year |

Please list the reasons why you require a further **Limited Purpose Permit:**

Section B — Application for the purpose of a culturally arranged marriage

Complete this section ONLY if you are applying for a visa/permit for the purpose of culturally arranged marriage.

B1 Are you coming to New Zealand for the purpose of entering a marriage in accordance with an identified cultural tradition where the arrangements for the marriage, including the initial selection of the persons to be married, are made by persons who are not parties to the marriage? Yes ☐ No ☐

B2 Do you intend to marry within 3 months of your arrival in New Zealand? Yes ☐ No ☐

B3 Please mark the box to confirm you have supplied the following items:

☐ Evidence that the person you intend to marry is a New Zealand citizen or resident; and

☐ Evidence that the New Zealand citizen or resident you intend to marry:

   ☐ supports your application in writing; and

   ☐ is eligible to sponsor your application

☐ Evidence that there is no legal impediment to the intended marriage; and

☐ Evidence that the marriage follows an identified cultural tradition; and

☐ Evidence that you and the New Zealand citizen or resident you intend to marry comply with the minimum requirements for the recognition of partnership.

6

Fig. 8. Continued.

Section C Family Details

Partner

C1 Name as shown in passport

Family: [_____] Given: [_____]

C2 Preferred title Mr ☐ Mrs ☐ Ms ☐ Miss ☐ Dr ☐ other [____]
(please specify)

Attach one recent passport size photograph. Write name on back.

C3 Other names they are known by [_____]

C4 Name in ethnic script [_____]

C5 Gender Male ☐ Female ☐ **C6** Date of birth [_____]
day month year

C7 Place and country of birth Place: [_____] Country: [_____]

C8 Your citizenship [_____]

C9 Passport details Number: [_____] Country: [_____]

C10 Other citizenships currently held [_____]

C11 Is your partner included in this application? Yes ☐ No ☐

Dependent Children

C12 Supply the following details for each dependent child included in this application:

Child's name as shown in passport

Family: [_____] Given: [_____]

Dependent Child 1

Attach one recent passport size photograph. Write name on back.

C13 Male ☐ Female ☐ **C14** Date of birth [_____] day month year

C15 Country of birth [_____]

C16 Passport number [_____]

C17 Country of citizenship [_____]

C18 Other citizenships currently held [_____]

C19 Child's name as shown in passport

Family: [_____] Given: [_____]

Dependent Child 2

Attach one recent passport size photograph. Write name on back.

C20 Male ☐ Female ☐ **C21** Date of birth [_____] day month year

C22 Country of birth [_____]

C23 Passport number [_____]

C24 Country of citizenship [_____]

C25 Other citizenships currently held [_____]

7

Fig. 8. Continued.

Dependent Child 3

| C26 | Child's name as shown in passport |
| Family: | Given: |

| C27 | Male ☐ Female ☐ | C28 | Date of birth | day month year |

Attach one recent passport size photograph. Write name on back.

C29	Country of birth	
C30	Passport number	
C31	Country of citizenship	
C32	Other citizenships currently held	

Dependent Child 4

| C33 | Child's name as shown in passport |
| Family: | Given: |

| C34 | Male ☐ Female ☐ | C35 | Date of birth | day month year |

Attach one recent passport size photograph. Write name on back.

B36	Country of birth	
C37	Passport number	
C38	Country of citizenship	
C39	Other citizenships currently held	

Character Details

Have you or any person included in this application been:

- convicted   Yes ☐   No ☐
- charged   Yes ☐   No ☐
- under investigation   Yes ☐   No ☐

for any offence(s) against the law in any country; or

- deported   Yes ☐   No ☐
- excluded (refused entry) Yes ☐   No ☐
- removed   Yes ☐   No ☐

from any country.

If you have marked **Yes** to any of the above. Please provide details below:

8

Fig. 8. Continued.

Health Details

Are you, or any person included in the application, currently receiving, or likely to require during your time in New Zealand:

- dialysis treatment, or a consultant physician has indicated that such treatment will be required in the future; or — Yes ☐ No ☐
- treatment for active tuberculosis; or — Yes ☐ No ☐
- treatment for a mental disorder or intellectual disability that has needed care in a hospital or supervised residence for more than 90 days in the last 2 years; or — Yes ☐ No ☐
- treatment for a physical incapacity that requires full-time care — Yes ☐ No ☐

If you have answered **Yes** to any of the above questions, please provide details below:

Please Note: All immigration visa and permit holders who access health services in New Zealand should carry a current passport to enable health providers to document eligibility status. We strongly recommend that you have comprehensive health insurance for the duration of your visit. For more information visit the Ministry of Health website at www.moh.govt.nz.

Declaration

I understand the questions and contents of this form, and the information I have provided is true and correct.

I understand that if, between the time that I make this application and the time it is decided, or between the time I am issued with a visa and the time I travel to New Zealand, any relevant matter relating to the application changes, I am obliged to inform the NZIS.

I understand I am responsible for making sure I leave New Zealand before my permit expires and that if I do not I may face removal action.

Residents and people holding work permits for a stay of two years or more (and their dependent children) are eligible for publicly funded health and disability services. Other work permit holders, students, and visitor permit holders generally are not eligible. People covered by New Zealand's Reciprocal Health Agreements with Australia and the UK are entitled to publicly funded health care for immediately necessary medical treatment only. I understand that if not entitled to free treatment, I will pay for any health care or medical assistance I or any person included in my application may require in New Zealand.

I authorise NZIS to provide information about my state of health and my immigration status to any health service agency. I authorise any health service agency to provide information about my state of health to the NZIS.

I authorise NZIS to make any enquiries it considers necessary in respect of information provided on this form in order to make a decision on this application and enquiries about my subsequent immigration status. I authorise any agency which holds information (including personal information) relevant to those matters to disclose that information to NZIS.

If granted a Limited Purpose Permit I understand that I am subject to immediate removal from New Zealand without appeal if I fail to leave New Zealand on or before the expiry date of that Permit.

Signature of principal applicant	day month year
Signature of partner	day month year
Signature of dependent child	day month year
Signature of dependent child	day month year
Signature of dependent child	day month year

Note: a parent or guardian may sign on behalf of any children aged under 17 years.

Important Note

If you are an applicant who is using this form to apply for a Limited Purpose Visa you should have specifically chosen to take the Limited Purpose Visa option rather than apply for a Visitor's Visa. You will also have specified an "express purpose" in coming to New Zealand and will understand the limitations of a Limited Purpose Permit compared to a Visitor's Permit.

9

Fig. 8. Continued.

Declaration for Person Assisting the Applicant to Complete This Form

To be completed and signed by any person who has assisted the applicant to complete this form by explaining, translating or filling in the form for the applicant.

Full name of person assisting:

Address of person assisting:

I understand that after the applicant has signed this form it is an offence to alter or enter further information on it, alter any material attached to it, or attach any further material to it, unless the person making the alteration or addition states on the form what information or material has been altered or attached, why and by whom. I understand that the maximum penalty for this offence is a fine of up to NZ$100,000 and/or a term of imprisonment of up to 7 years.

I certify that I have assisted in the completion of this form and any additional forms at the request of the applicant **and** that the applicant understood the content of the form(s) and agreed that the information provided is correct before signing the declaration. I have assisted the applicant as a:

lawyer ☐   agent, consultant ☐   translator ☐   friend or ☐   other advisor ☐
                or representative   family member   Please specify:

Signature of person assisting:

day   month   year

Payment Details

Amount enclosed

☐ I am paying by cash   ☐ I am paying by electronic direct debit (eg EFTPOS).

☐ I am paying by cheque   ☐ Please charge to my Visa/Mastercard: details as follows:

Note: For credit card or personal cheque payments outside New Zealand please check with your nearest diplomatic or consular office.
Card type   Expiry date   Card number   Name of card holder

Signature   day   month   year

Collection Details

☐ I wish to collect my documents when ready.

☐ Please return all documents to me by "secure" post at the address given.

Fig. 8. Continued.

Application to Study in New Zealand

(to travel to New Zealand or to be in New Zealand to study)

Please note: If you decide to apply directly for a Limited Purpose Visa and you are subsequently granted a Limited Purpose Permit, your immigration rights in New Zealand are restricted to fulfilling the "express purpose" to study for which you came.

This form may be used to apply for a Student Visa or Permit, or Limited Purpose Visa or Permit to study.

- [ ] I am applying for a Student Visa to travel to New Zealand, or
- [ ] I am applying for a Student Permit to be in New Zealand, or
- [ ] I am applying for a Student Permit and Visa as I am already in New Zealand, or
- [ ] I am applying for a Limited Purpose Visa/Permit (delete one) to study

Please note: if you are in New Zealand and applying for a further Permit, you need to allow sufficient time for a decision to be made on your application before your current Permit expires. If your Permit does expire, your application for a further Permit does not make your stay in New Zealand lawful or give you the right to remain in New Zealand while your application is being considered.

Section A   Personal Details

Principal applicant

Client number:

A1 Name as shown in passport

Family: Given:

A2 Preferred title   Mr [ ]   Mrs [ ]   Ms [ ]   Miss [ ]   Dr [ ]   other [   ]
(please specify)

Attach one recent passport size photograph of yourself here. Write your name on the back.

A3 Other names you are known by

A4 Your name in ethnic script

A5 Gender   Male [ ]   Female [ ]   **A6** Date of birth [   ]
day   month   year

A7 Place and country of birth   Place: Country:

A8 Passport details   Number: Country:

Expiry Date: [   ]
day   month   year

A9 Your citizenship

A10 Other citizenships currently held

A11 Partnership status   [ ] Married   [ ] Never married   [ ] De Facto   [ ] Separated
[ ] Engaged   [ ] Widowed   [ ] Divorced

3

Fig. 9. Application for a student visa.

Additional information

A12 I may be contacted at this New Zealand residential address and telephone number:

	Telephone

A13 Name and address of any friends, relatives or contacts I have in New Zealand are:

Name	Relationship
Address	
Name	Relationship
Address	
Name	Relationship
Address	

A14 Name and address for correspondence about this application:

	Telephone - day
	Telephone - night
	Fax
	Email

A15 If you have given the name and address of an agent in A14, do you authorise that agent to act on your behalf?   Yes ☐   No ☐

A16 My residential address in my home country is:

A17 I am employed by, and my regular occupation is:
(Please give name and address of employer. If not employed, please state this.)

Employer details:

Occupation:

A18 My stay in New Zealand will be financially supported in the following way:

A19 The arrangement I have made for outward travel from New Zealand is:

4

Fig. 9. Continued.

Application Details – Student Visa or Permit

Complete questions A20 to A25.

DO NOT complete this section if you are applying for a **Limited Purpose Visa** or **Limited Purpose Permit** to study (see questions A25 to A29).

A20 If applying for a Student Visa:
This is the date I will enter or re-enter New Zealand:

day	month	year

A21 If applying for a Student Permit:
This is the date I will enter or re-enter New Zealand:

day	month	year

A22 This is the date my course starts

day	month	year

A23 This is the date my course finishes:

day	month	year

A24 Date to which fees have been paid or length of scholarship (if applicable)

day	month	year

A25 My course(s) details in New Zealand are:

Name of institution where I will be studying	Qualification I will be studying	Location in New Zealand where I will be studying

---

Limited Purpose Visa or Permit

Complete questions A26 to A30.

DO NOT complete questions A26 to A30 if you are applying for a Student Visa or Permit.

Only complete this section if:
- you are travelling to New Zealand for the "express purpose" of studying and you wish to have a Limited Purpose Permit to study in New Zealand,
or
- if your existing Limited Purpose Permit to study will not last long enough for you to achieve your "express purpose" to study and you therefore require a further one.

Such permits mean that you are **not** able to apply for any other type of permit in new Zealand or seek to stay longer or indefinitely in New Zealand. For general information and a list of **"express purposes"** see the *Information Leaflet on Limited Purpose Visas and Permits* (NZIS 1070).

Principal Applicant: Application Details – Limited Purpose

A26 ☐ I am applying for a **Limited Purpose Visa** to travel to New Zealand to study, or

☐ I am applying for a further **Limited Purpose Permit** to be in New Zealand to study

(you may only apply for a further Limited Purpose Permit if you already have a Limited Purpose Permit to study and you need further time to complete the "express purpose" to study).

A27 If applying for a **Limited Purpose Visa to study:**
This is the date I will enter New Zealand:

day	month	year

A28 If applying for a further **Limited Purpose Permit to study:**
This is the date I arrived in New Zealand on a **Limited Purpose Visa:**

day	month	year

Please list the reasons why you require a further **Limited Purpose Permit:**

⑤

Fig. 9. Continued.

A29 This is the date my course starts:

day	month	year

This is the date my course finishes:

day	month	year

Date to which fees have been paid:

day	month	year

A30 The limited purpose application is for the **"express purpose"** of study:

My course(s) details in New Zealand are:

Name of institution where I will be studying	Qualification I will be studying	Location in New Zealand where I will be studying

If your **"express purpose"** is other than to study in New Zealand please use the *Application for Visiting New Zealand* (NZIS 1017) form.

Section B   Character Details

B1 Have you been:

• convicted		Yes ☐	No ☐
• charged		Yes ☐	No ☐
• under investigation		Yes ☐	No ☐

for any offence(s) against the law in any country; or

• deported		Yes ☐	No ☐
• excluded (refused entry)		Yes ☐	No ☐
• removed		Yes ☐	No ☐

from any country.

If you have marked **Yes** to any of the above, please provide details below:

B2 Are you intending to study in New Zealand for 2 years or longer?   Yes ☐ No ☐

If no, or you are 16 years or younger, please go to Section C.

B3 If yes, and your are aged 17 or over, have you attached police certificates from:

• all countries in which you have lived for 5 years or more since attaining the age of 17 years?   Yes ☐ No ☐

• your country(ies) of citizenship?   Yes ☐ No ☐

• If no, please state any country(ies) of which you are a citizen but for which you have not provided police certificates because you have never lived there.

6

Fig. 9. Continued.

Section C   Health Details

Are you currently receiving, or likely to require during your time in New Zealand:

- dialysis treatment, or a consultant physician has indicated that such
  treatment will be required in the immediate future; or   Yes ☐   No ☐
- treatment for active tuberculosis; or   Yes ☐   No ☐
- treatment for a mental disorder or intellectual disability that has
  needed care in a hospital or supervised residence for more than 90
  days in the last 2 years; or   Yes ☐   No ☐
- treatment for a physical incapacity that requires full-time care.   Yes ☐   No ☐

If you have answered **Yes** to any of the above questions, please provide details below:

Please Note: All immigration visa and permit holders who access health services in New Zealand should carry a current passport to enable health providers to document eligibility status. We strongly recommend that you have comprehensive health insurance for the duration of your visit. For more information visit the Ministry of Health website at www.moh.govt.nz.

Declaration

I understand the questions and contents of this form, and the information I have provided is true and correct.

I understand that if, between the time that I make this application and the time it is decided, or between the time I am issued with a visa and the time I travel to New Zealand, any relevant matter relating to the application changes, I am obliged to inform the NZIS.

I understand I am responsible for making sure I leave New Zealand before my permit expires and that if I do not I may face removal action.

Residents and people holding work permits for a stay of two years or more (and their dependent children) are eligible for publicly funded health and disability services. Other work permit holders, students, and visitor permit holders generally are not eligible. People covered by New Zealand's Reciprocal Health Agreements with Australia and the United Kingdom are entitled to publicly funded health care for immediately necessary medical treatment only. I understand that if not entitled to free treatment, I will pay for any health care or medical assistance I or any person included in my application may require in New Zealand.

I authorise NZIS to provide information about my state of health and my immigration status to any health service agency. I authorise any health service agency to provide information about my state of health to the NZIS.

I authorise NZIS to make any enquiries it considers necessary in respect of information provided on this form in order to make a decision on this application and enquiries about my subsequent immigration status. I authorise any agency which holds information (including personal information) relevant to those matters to disclose that information to NZIS.

If granted a Limited Purpose Permit I understand that I am subject to immediate removal from New Zealand without appeal if I fail to leave New Zealand on or before the expiry date of that Permit.

Signature of principal applicant   day   month   year

Important Note: Limited Purpose Visas

If you are an applicant who is using this form to apply for a Limited Purpose Visa you should have specifically chosen to take the Limited Purpose Visa option rather than apply for a Student Visa. You will also have specified an "express purpose" in coming to New Zealand and will understand the limitations of a Limited Purpose Permit compared to a Student Permit.

Fig. 9. Continued.

Declaration for Person Assisting the Applicant to Complete This Form

To be completed and signed by any person who has assisted the applicant to complete this form by explaining, translating or filling in the form for the applicant.

Full name of person assisting:

Address of person assisting:

I understand that after the applicant has signed this form it is an offence to alter or enter further information on it, alter any material attached to it, or attach any further material to it, unless the person making the alteration or addition states on the form what information or material has been altered or attached, why, and by whom. I understand that the maximum penalty for this offence is a fine of up to $NZ100,000 and/or a term of imprisonment of up to 7 years.

I certify that I have assisted in the completion of this form and any additional forms at the request of the applicant **and** that the applicant understood the content of the form(s) and agreed that the information provided is correct before signing the declaration. I have assisted the applicant as a:

lawyer ☐   agent, consultant ☐   translator ☐   friend or ☐   other advisor ☐
or representative   family member   Please specify:

Signature of person assisting:

day   month   year

Payment Details

☐ I enclose cash for the required amount.
☐ I enclose a cheque for the required amount.
☐ I am paying by electronic direct debit (eg, EFTPOS).
☐ Please charge to my Visa/Mastercard; details as follows:

Note: For credit card or personal cheque payments outside New Zealand please check with your nearest diplomatic or consular office.

Card type	Expiry date	Card number	Name of card holder

Signature

day   month   year

Collection Details

☐ I wish to collect my documents when ready.
☐ Please return all documents to me by "secure" post at the address given.

Privacy Act

The information about you on this form is collected to determine your eligibility for a Student Visa or Permit or a Limited Purpose Visa or Permit to study.

The main recipient of the information is the New Zealand Immigration Service of the Department of Labour but it may also be shared with other Government agencies which are entitled to this information under applicable legislation, or with other agencies in accordance with an authority in the form.

The address of the New Zealand Immigration Service is PO Box 3705, Wellington, New Zealand. **This is not where your application should be sent.**

The collection of the information is authorised by the Immigration Act 1987 and the Immigration Regulations made under that Act. The supply of the information is voluntary, but if you do not supply it then your application is likely to be declined.

You will, if you come to New Zealand, have a right to see the information about you held by the New Zealand Immigration Service and to ask for any of it to be corrected if you think that is necessary.

Your application should be sent to your nearest New Zealand Immigration Service Branch or New Zealand Embassy or High Commission.

8   This form has been approved under s132(1) Immigration Act 1987   NZIS 1012
September 2003

Fig. 9. Continued.

Application *to* Work in New Zealand
(to travel to New Zealand or to be in New Zealand temporarily to work)

Application No.　　　*For NZIS Use Only*

This form may be used to apply for a visa or permit, or both.

☐ I am applying for a **work visa.** Mark this box if you want to travel to New Zealand to work **or** if you already have a work permit and want to leave New Zealand and return to continue working.

☐ I am applying for a **work permit.** Mark this box if you are in New Zealand and want to work here temporarily **or** if you already have a work permit and want a further work permit.

☐ I am applying for a **work permit** and a **work visa.** Mark this box if you are in New Zealand and want to work here temporarily **and** you also want to be able to leave New Zealand while your work permit is current and return to continue working.

What Work Visa and Permit policy are you applying under?

Work to Residence ☐　　General Work ☐　　Family ☐　　Other (please specify) ☐

Please note: if you are in New Zealand and applying for a further permit, you need to allow sufficient time for a decision to be made on your application before your current permit expires.

If your permit does expire, your application for a further permit does not make your stay in New Zealand lawful or give you the right to remain in New Zealand while your application is being considered.

Section A　　Personal Details

Principal applicant
Client number: ☐

A1 Name as shown in passport
Family: ☐　　Given: ☐

Attach one recent passport size photograph of yourself here. Write your name on the back.

A2 Preferred title　Mr ☐　Mrs ☐　Ms ☐　Miss ☐　Dr ☐　other ☐
(please specify)

A3 Other names you are known by ☐

A4 Your name in ethnic script ☐

A5 Gender　Male ☐　Female ☐　　**A6** Date of birth ☐
　　　　　　　　　　　　　　　　　　　　day　month　year

A7 Place and country of birth　Place: ☐　　Country: ☐

A8 Passport details　Number: ☐　　Country: ☐
　　　　　　Expiry Date: ☐
　　　　　　　　　　day　month　year

A9 Your citizenship ☐

A10 Other citizenships currently held ☐

A11 Partnership status　☐ Married　☐ Never married　☐ De Facto　☐ Separated
　　　　　　　　　　　☐ Engaged　☐ Widowed　☐ Divorced

A12 If you are applying for a visa/permit on the basis of a partnership:
- are you living in a genuine and stable partnership?　　Yes ☐　No ☐
If no please explain
☐

- will your partner be in New Zealand for the same period of time?　　Yes ☐　No ☐
- do you meet the minimum requirements for the recognition of a partnership?　　Yes ☐　No ☐
- do you intend to apply for residence under Partnership policy?　　Yes ☐　No ☐
- if yes, will your New Zealand citizen or resident partner be eligible to sponsor this application and any application for residence under Partnership policy within 12 months?　　Yes ☐　No ☐
- How long have you been living together in this partnership?　Years ☐　Months ☐

Note: You may be required to meet health and character requirements, however you will not need to provide this documentation unless the NZIS requests you to do so.

1

Fig. 10. Application for a work visa.

Additional information

A13 I may be contacted at this New Zealand residential address and telephone number:

	Telephone

A14 Name and address of any friends, relatives or contacts I have in New Zealand are:

Name	Relationship
Address	
Name	Relationship
Address	
Name	Relationship
Address	

A15 Name and address for correspondence about this application:

	Phone - day:
	Phone - night:
	Fax:
	Email:

A16 If you have given the name and address of an agent in A15, do you authorise that agent to act on you behalf?   Yes ☐   No ☐

A17 My residential address in my home country is:

A18 I am currently employed by and my main occupation is:
(Please give name and address of employer. If not employed, please state this.)

Employer name:	Telephone:	Fax:
Employer address:	Email:	
Main Occupation:		

Your main occupation is the job you spent most hours doing in the last 12 months. If you have not worked in the last 12 months, please state your previous occupation. If you have not worked in the last 5 years or more, please state "Not applicable".

A19 I have the following qualifications:
(Please give details of all qualification(s) below. If you have no qualifications please state this.)

Name of qualification	Date obtained	Institution where gained
	/ /	
	/ /	
	/ /	

A20 My stay in New Zealand will be financially supported in the following way:

2

Fig. 10. Continued.

A21 The arrangement I have made for my outward travel from New Zealand is:

Application Details

A22 If applying for a **work visa**:
This is the date I will enter or re-enter New Zealand:

day month year

This is the date I will finally depart New Zealand

day month year

☐ I would like a **single** journey work visa

☐ I would like a **multiple** journey work visa

A23 If applying for a **work permit**:
This is the date I will be leaving New Zealand:

day month year

This is the date I request my **work permit** to be current to:

day month year

A24 Do you have a job offer in New Zealand? Yes ☐ No ☐

If **Yes**, please provide the information requested below.

Employer name:	Telephone:	Fax:
Employer address:	Email:	
Name of position offered:		

- Do you have qualifications relevant to your job offer? Yes ☐ No ☐
  If **Yes**, please attach evidence.
- Do you have work experience relevant to your job offer? Yes ☐ No ☐
  If **Yes**, please attach evidence.

Note: If registration with a professional body is required for this job, please provide this also.

Health and Character Requirements

(If you are 17 years of age or over you must include evidence of your health and character if you intend to stay in New Zealand for more than 24 months or a specific Work Permit or Work Visa Policy requires you to. For details see our **Guide for Working in New Zealand** *(NZIS 1016))*

Note: If you intend to stay in New Zealand for less than 24 months you may be required to meet health and character requirements, however you will not need to provide this documentation unless the NZIS requests you to do so.

A25 Is a NZIS **Medical and X-Ray Certificate** form (NZIS 1007) included? Yes ☐ No ☐

A26 Have you attached police certificates from:
* all countries in which you have lived for 5 years or more since attaining the age of 17 years? Yes ☐ No ☐

* your country(ies) of citizenship? Yes ☐ No ☐

If no, please state any country(ies) of which you are a citizen but for which you have not provided police certificates because you have never lived there.

If you are applying under **Work to Residence** policy go to **Section B**.
If you are applying under **General Work** policy go to **Section C**.
If you are applying under **Family** policy go to **Section D**.
You must provide **all** information requested for the *relevant* policy you are applying under.

If you are **not** applying under one of these three policies go to **Section E**.

3

Fig. 10. Continued.

Section B   Work to Residence Policy Requirements

B1   **Talent (Accredited Employers) Work Policy**

Please mark the box to confirm you have supplied the following items:
- Offer of full time employment in New Zealand for a period of at least 24 months from an Accredited Employer for a position with a salary of NZ$45,000 or more *(salary amount may be waived if you provide evidence to show you have exceptional talent in a field of art, culture or sport)* ☐
- Evidence you are aged 55 years or under
- Evidence you have met or are able to meet any New Zealand registration requirements necessary to take up your offer of employment. *(If you do not have to meet any registration requirements state "N/A".)* ☐

OR

B2   **Talent (Arts, Culture and Sports) Work Policy**

a) Please briefly describe the particular field of art, culture or sport you consider you have exceptional talent in *(this will be treated as your 'declared field' for the purposes of this policy).*

b) Please mark the box to confirm you have supplied the following items:

A fully completed and signed *Talent (Arts, Culture and Sports) Sponsorship Form* (NZIS 1091) ☐

Evidence that you have exceptional talent in the field of art, culture or sport you have described in B2 a) above. This must include:
- Evidence of your international reputation and record of excellence in your declared field, and
- Evidence that you are still prominent in your declared field, and
- Any additional evidence to show that your presence in New Zealand will enhance the quality of New Zealand's accomplishments and participation in your declared field. ☐

Evidence you are aged 55 years or under. ☐

OR

B3   **Priority Occupations List Work Policy**

Please mark the box to confirm you have supplied the following items:
- Offer of full time employment in New Zealand for a period of at least 24 months in an occupation currently included on the Priority Occupations List (POL) that meets the specifications for that occupation. ☐
- Evidence you have met or are able to meet any New Zealand registration requirements necessary to take up your offer of employment. *(If you do not have to meet any registration requirements state "N/A".)* ☐

Note: All applicants under the three Work to Residence policies above **must** include evidence of their health and character (see questions A24 and A25 in this form).

If you have completed the questions relevant to your application in **Section B** or have been invited to apply under the **Job Search Policy for General Skills Category Residence Applicants** please go to **Section E**.

B4   How many people do you intend to include on your residence application? ☐

Section C   General Work Policy Requirements

C1   Please mark the box to confirm you have supplied the following items:
- An offer of employment in New Zealand in an occupation currently included on the Occupational Shortages List (OSL). ☐

OR
- An offer of employment in New Zealand from an employer who has a current approval in principle from the NZIS to recruit non-New Zealand citizen or resident workers. *(Please include a copy of your employer's approval in principle from NZIS if you have it.)* ☐

OR
- An offer of employment in New Zealand **and** evidence from your potential employer that shows:
  - genuine attempts have been made to attract and recruit suitable staff from within New Zealand, and
  - the reasons why suitable New Zealand citizen or resident workers were not suitable, or refused to perform the work, and
  - why New Zealand citizen or resident workers may not be readily trained to do the work. ☐

C2   **General Work Policy - Other Categories**

You need to supply evidence to show you meet the specific requirements for the policy relevant to your application. For details on specific requirements see our *Guide for Working in New Zealand* (NZIS 1016).

4

Fig. 10. Continued.

Section D Family Work Policy Requirements

D1 **Partners of a New Zealand citizen/resident**
Please mark the box to confirm you have supplied the following items:
- evidence that you and your partner are living together in a genuine and stable relationship ☐
- evidence of your partner's New Zealand citizenship or residence status in New Zealand ☐
- a letter from your partner supporting this application ☐
- evidence you and your partner (meet the minimum requirements for the recognition of a partnership) ☐
  * are both aged 18 years or older (or evidence of parental/guardian/other support if aged between 16 years and 19 years)
  * have met prior to this application being made
  * are not close relatives
- evidence that your partner is eligible to sponsor this application to work in New Zealand and a residence application ☐
- evidence of the duration of your partnership ☐

D2 **Partners of persons holding a work permit current for more than six months**
Please mark the box to confirm you have supplied the following items:
- evidence that you and your partner are living together in a genuine and stable relationship. ☐
- evidence you and your partner are intending to live in New Zealand for the same period of time e.g. evidence of intended travel to New Zealand if you are both overseas. ☐
- evidence of your partner's work visa or work permit or eligibility to obtain a work visa or work permit e.g. a letter from NZIS giving approval in principle to the issue of a work visa or grant of a work permit. ☐

Section E Character Details

Have you been:

• convicted	Yes ☐	No ☐
• charged	Yes ☐	No ☐
• under investigation	Yes ☐	No ☐

for any offence(s) against the law in any country; or

• deported	Yes ☐	No ☐
• excluded (refused entry)	Yes ☐	No ☐
• removed	Yes ☐	No ☐

from any country.
If you have marked **Yes** to any of the above. Please provide details below:

5

Fig. 10. Continued.

Section F   Health Details

Are you currently receiving, or likely to require during your time in New Zealand:

- dialysis treatment, or a consultant physician has indicated that such treatment will be required in the future; or   Yes ☐   No ☐
- treatment for active tuberculosis; or   Yes ☐   No ☐
- treatment for a mental disorder or intellectual disability that has needed care in a hospital or supervised residence for more than 90 days in the last 2 years; or   Yes ☐   No ☐
- treatment for a physical incapacity that requires full-time care.   Yes ☐   No ☐

If you have answered **Yes** to any of the above questions, please provide details below:

Please Note: All immigration visa and permit holders who access health services in New Zealand should carry a current passport to enable health providers to document eligibility status. We strongly recommend that you have comprehensive health insurance for the duration of your visit. For more information visit the Ministry of Health website at www.moh.govt.nz.

Section G   Declaration

I understand the questions and contents of this form, and the information I have provided is true and correct.

I understand that if, between the time that I make this application and the time it is decided, or between the time I am issued with a visa and the time I travel to New Zealand, any relevant matter relating to the application changes, I am obliged to inform the NZIS.

I understand I am responsible for making sure I leave New Zealand before my permit expires and that if I do not I may face removal action.

Residents and people holding work permits for a stay of two years or more (and their dependent children) are eligible for publicly funded health and disability services. Other work permit holders, students, and visitor permit holders generally are not eligible. People covered by New Zealand's Reciprocal Health Agreements with Australia and the United Kingdom are entitled to publicly funded health care for immediately necessary medical treatment only. I understand that if not entitled to free treatment, I will pay for any health care or medical assistance I or any person included in my application may require in New Zealand.

I authorise NZIS to provide information about my state of health and my immigration status to any health service agency. I authorise any health service agency to provide information about my state of health to the NZIS.

I authorise NZIS to make any enquiries it considers necessary in respect of information provided on this form in order to make a decision on this application and enquiries about my subsequent immigration status. I authorise any agency which holds information (including personal information) relevant to those matters to disclose that information to NZIS.

If granted a Limited Purpose Permit I understand that I am subject to immediate removal from New Zealand without appeal if I remain in New Zealand after the expiry date of that Permit.

Signature of principal applicant   day   month   year

Important Note: It is in your own interest to submit with your application the information and documents requested in this form, plus any other item you think will show you meet the Work Visa and Permit policy you are applying under. The NZIS does not have to seek any additional information from you and may make a decision based on the information contained in your application alone if that is all you provide. Failure to supply the information required at the time you make application could also delay the processing of your application.

6

Fig. 10. Continued.

Section H — Declaration for Person Assisting the Applicant to Complete This Form

To be completed and signed by any person who has assisted the applicant to complete this form by explaining, translating or filling in the form for the applicant.

Full name of person assisting:

Address of person assisting:

I understand that after the applicant has signed this form it is an offence to alter or enter further information on it, alter any material attached to it, or attach any further material to it, unless the person making the alteration or addition states on the form what information or material has been altered or attached, why, and by whom. I understand that the maximum penalty for this offence is a fine of up to $NZ100,000 and/or a term of imprisonment of up to 7 years.

I certify that I have assisted in the completion of this form and any additional forms at the request of the applicant **and** that the applicant understood the content of the form(s) and agreed that the information provided is correct before signing the declaration. I have assisted the applicant as a:

lawyer ☐   agent, consultant ☐   translator ☐   friend or ☐   other advisor ☐
              or representative   family member   Please specify:

Signature of person assisting:

day   month   year

Section I — Payment Details

☐   I enclose cash for the required amount.

☐   I enclose a cheque for the required amount.

☐   I am paying by electronic direct debit (eg, EFTPOS).

☐   Please charge to my Visa/Mastercard; details as follows:

Note: For credit card or personal cheque payments outside New Zealand please check with your nearest diplomatic or consular office.

Card type	Expiry date	Card number	Name of card holder

Signature   day   month   year

Collection Details

☐   I wish to collect my documents when ready.

☐   Please return all documents to me by "secure" post at the address given.

7

Fig. 10. Continued.

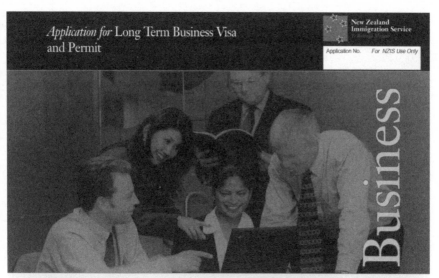

Application for Long Term Business Visa and Permit

New Zealand Immigration Service

Application No.   *For NZIS Use Only*

For help completing this form, refer to the *"Guide to Applying for Long Term Business Visa and Permit"* (NZIS 1059).

Note: If there is not enough room on this application form to answer a question fully, please answer on a separate sheet of paper and state on the form that you have done so. **Please sign each additional sheet of paper.**

Section A   Personal Details

Client number:

Principal applicant

A1 Name as shown in passport

Family: Given:

Pin or staple two recent passport size photographs of yourself here. Write your name on the back of each photograph.

A2 Preferred title   Mr ☐   Mrs ☐   Ms ☐   Miss ☐   Dr ☐   other
(please specify)

A3 Other names you are known by

A4 Your name in ethnic script

A5 Gender   Male ☐   Female ☐   **A6**   Date of birth
day   month   year

A7 Place and country of birth   Place: Country:

A8 Passport details   Number: Country:

A9 Other citizenships currently held

A10 Name and address for correspondence (or agent details). Use both English and own language where required.

Phone/ day:
Phone/ night:
Fax:
Email:

1

Fig. 11. Application for long-term business visa and permit.

A11 Your current home address and telephone number.
Are we able to contact you directly regarding your application?   Yes ☐   No ☐

	Phone/ day:
	Phone/ night:
	Fax:
	Email:

Address in your home country

A12 Partnership status   ☐ Married   ☐ Never married   ☐ De Facto   ☐ Separated
☐ Engaged   ☐ Widowed   ☐ Divorced

A13 Give details of ALL your family, whether migrating with you or not.
It is not necessary to list deceased family members.

Full name	Gender M/F	Date of birth	Partnership status	Country of residence
Parents (birth and adoptive)				

Brothers and sisters (including full, half and adopted brothers and sisters)

Does the person intend to accompany you to NZ?
Yes   No

Children (including from previous partnerships)

					Yes	No
					☐	☐
					☐	☐
					☐	☐
					☐	☐
					☐	☐
					☐	☐
					☐	☐
					☐	☐

2

Fig. 11. Continued.

Partner

A14 Name as shown in passport

Family: [_____] Given: [_____]

A15 Preferred title Mr ☐ Mrs ☐ Ms ☐ Miss ☐ Dr ☐ other [_____]
(please specify)

Attach two recent passport size photographs. Write name on back.

A16 Other names they are known by [_____]

A17 Name in ethnic script [_____]

A18 Gender Male ☐ Female ☐   **A19** Date of birth [__|__|__]
day month year

A20 Place and country of birth   Place: [_____]   Country: [_____]

A21 Passport details   Number: [_____]   Country: [_____]

A22 Other citizenships currently held [_____]

A23 Please indicate whether your partner is applying for a work or visitor visa or permit.   Work ☐   Visitor ☐

A24 How long have you been living together in this partnership?   Years [____]   Months [____]

A25 Do you meet the minimum requirements for recognition of partnership?   Yes ☐   No ☐

A26 Are you living together in a genuine and stable partnership?   Yes ☐   No ☐
If you are not living together please explain.

[_____]
[_____]
[_____]

A27 Give details of ALL your partner's family, whether migrating with you or not.
It is not necessary to list deceased family members.

Full name	Gender M/F	Date of birth	Partnership status	Country of residence
Parents (birth and adoptive)				
Brothers and sisters (including full, half and adopted brothers and sisters)				

Does the person intend to accompany you to NZ?

Children (including from previous partnerships)	Gender M/F	Date of birth	Partnership status	Country of residence	Yes	No
					☐	☐
					☐	☐
					☐	☐
					☐	☐
					☐	☐

3

Fig. 11. Continued.

Supply the following details for each dependent child included in this application

Dependent Child 1

A28   Child's name as shown in passport

Family: [ ]   Given: [ ]

Attach two recent passport size photographs. Write name on back.

A29   Male [ ]   Female [ ]   A30   Date of birth [ ]   day month year

A31   Country of birth [ ]

A32   Passport number [ ]

A33   Country of citizenship [ ]

A34   Other citizenships currently held [ ]

A35   Please indicate whether your child is applying for a student or visitor visa or permit.   Student [ ]   Visitor [ ]

Dependent Child 2

A36   Child's name as shown in passport

Family: [ ]   Given: [ ]

Attach two recent passport size photographs. Write name on back.

A37   Male [ ]   Female [ ]   A38   Date of birth [ ]   day month year

A39   Country of birth [ ]

A40   Passport number [ ]

A41   Country of citizenship [ ]

A42   Other citizenships currently held [ ]

A43   Please indicate whether your child is applying for a student or visitor visa or permit.   Student [ ]   Visitor [ ]

Dependent Child 3

A44   Child's name as shown in passport

Family: [ ]   Given: [ ]

Attach two recent passport size photographs. Write name on back.

A45   Male [ ]   Female [ ]   A46   Date of birth [ ]   day month year

A47   Country of birth [ ]

A48   Passport number [ ]

A49   Country of citizenship [ ]

A50   Other citizenships currently held [ ]

A51   Please indicate whether your child is applying for a student or visitor visa or permit.   Student [ ]   Visitor [ ]

Dependent Child 4

A52   Child's name as shown in passport

Family: [ ]   Given: [ ]

Attach two recent passport size photographs. Write name on back.

A53   Male [ ]   Female [ ]   A54   Date of birth [ ]   day month year

A55   Country of birth [ ]

A56   Passport number [ ]

A57   Country of citizenship [ ]

A58   Other citizenships currently held [ ]

A59   Please indicate whether your child is applying for a student or visitor visa or permit.   Student [ ]   Visitor [ ]

A60   Does any person not included in this application have custody or visitation rights over any of the above children?

No [ ]   Yes [ ]   If yes, supply evidence that you have been granted the right to bring this child permanently to New Zealand.

4

Fig. 11. Continued.

Character requirements

Please answer A61 and A62 in respect of every person in your application over 17 years of age if:
- **this is your first application under LTBV policy; or**
- **you have held a Work Visa or Permit under LTBV policy for 3 years and are applying for a further Work Visa or Permit.**

A61 List the countries, including all countries of citizenship, you and/or your family (if applicable) have lived in for more than 5 years since attaining the age of 17 and attach police certificates from each of these countries.

Name	Name of country	Date of arrival	Date of departure

A62 Are you and/or any of your accompanying family members currently under investigation, or wanted, by any law enforcement agency in any country?   Yes ☐   No ☐

Have you and/or any of your accompanying family members ever been:

- Convicted or found guilty of any offence(s) against the law in any country?   Yes ☐   No ☐
- Sentenced to serve a period of time in prison or other form of detention?   Yes ☐   No ☐
- Placed on probation?   Yes ☐   No ☐
- Charged with any offences against the law in any country?   Yes ☐   No ☐
- Deported, excluded or removed from any country, including New Zealand?   Yes ☐   No ☐
- Asked to leave any country, including New Zealand?   Yes ☐   No ☐
- Refused entry to any country, including New Zealand?   Yes ☐   No ☐
- Refused a visa/permit to visit, work, study or reside in any country, including New Zealand?   Yes ☐   No ☐
- Involved in any terrorist activities or advocated similar violent activities?   Yes ☐   No ☐
- A member of, or adhered to, any terrorist organisation?   Yes ☐   No ☐
- Involved in the illicit drug trade?   Yes ☐   No ☐
- A member of, or adhered to, any organisation or group with criminal objectives or which has engaged in criminal activities or advocated such activities?   Yes ☐   No ☐
- A member of, or adhered to, any group of persons or organisation which, at the time of membership or adherence, had objectives which were based on hostility against persons or groups of persons on the basis of their colour, race, or ethnic or national origin, or were based on a representation that persons of a particular race or colour are inherently inferior or superior to other races or colours?   Yes ☐   No ☐
- Convicted of an offence (including a traffic offence), committed within the last five years, involving dangerous driving, driving having consumed excessive alcohol (including drunk driving and driving with a blood or breath alcohol content in excess of a specified limit) or driving having consumed drugs?   Yes ☐   No ☐

If you answered "Yes" to any of the above questions, give full details and the name of the family member(s).

_____
_____
_____
_____
_____
_____

5

Fig. 11. Continued.

Medical requirement

Please answer A63 if:
- **this is your first application under LTBV policy; or**
- **you have held a Work Visa or Permit under LTBV policy for 3 years and are applying for a further Work Visa or Permit.**

A63 Have you attached a **Medical and X-ray Certificate Form** (NZIS 1007) for you and each of your accompanying family members?   Yes ☐   No ☐

English language requirements

Minimum English language requirements apply to first time applicants or applicants seeking a further 3 year Long Term Business Visa and Permit who have not previously met English language requirements. For details see the **Guide to Applying for Long Term Business Visa and Permit** (NZIS 1059).

A64 Do you meet the minimum level of English language   Yes ☐   No ☐

If yes, please provide evidence of your English language ability.

Section B   Business Plan Information

Note: If you have held a Work Visa or Permit under LTBV policy for less than 3 years, you are applying for a further work visa or permit, and the business proposal consented to by the NZIS has not changed, you do not need to answer the questions in Sections B-F.

Questions **B1** and **B2** are for statistical purposes only. All details of a business proposal should be covered in the Business Plan.

B1 Your intended business (tick one box only)

Administration/customer service	☐	Finance	☐	Retail	☐
Advertising/media/public relations	☐	Healthcare	☐	Sales/Marketing	☐
Agriculture/forestry/fishing	☐	Hospitality/restaurant	☐	Sports	☐
Arts/culture/entertainment	☐	Human resources	☐	Telecommunication	☐
Central government	☐	Information technology	☐	Tourism/accommodation	☐
Education/training	☐	Legal	☐	Water/gas/electricity	☐
Engineering/science	☐	Local government	☐	Other (specify)	
Film/video	☐	Manufacturing	☐		

B2 In which town or city do you intend to locate your business?

B3 Please state the amount of funds available for the maintenance and accommodation costs of all family members included in the application. This must be sufficient for three years and must be additional to the investment capital required for your business.

Please attach evidence.

B4 What is the status of your proposed business?   ☐ new   ☐ established

B5 Please state the amount of funds in $NZ that you have available to start up your proposed business.

6

Fig. 11. Continued.

Section C Business Outline

C1 Please give details of your proposed business venture, including type of business, industry, position in the market, targeted customers, suppliers and distributors, required assets etc.

C2 What do you expect the business to achieve in its first three years?

C3 What is the proposed ownership structure of the business?

☐ Sole trader ☐ Partnership ☐ Limited liability company
☐ Subsidiary of overseas company ☐ Other

C4 Will the business have any links with other overseas businesses?

☐ Yes ☐ No

If yes, please give details of overseas company, activities, location, and nature of proposed relationship.

C5 How will your proposed business benefit New Zealand?

7

Fig. 11. Continued.

C6 What is your intended involvement/role in the operation of the proposed business?

C7 How many full-time employees will the business require?

C8 What type of skills will these employees require, and are these skills readily available in New Zealand?

C9 Provide details of the proposed marketing strategy of the business, including details on market size, estimated market share, market positioning, competitor analysis, distribution and pricing strategy.

C10 Prepare a brief SWOT analysis of the proposed business
— strengths, weaknesses, opportunities, threats.

Strengths	Weaknesses
Opportunities	Threats

C11 Provide details of the operational plan and timeline for establishing the business in New Zealand, including an estimation of the time required for establishing the company, obtaining approvals (if required), finding premises, purchasing equipment, recruiting staff and establishing a distribution network etc.

8

Fig. 11. Continued.

Section D Financial Information

Financial forecasts

D1
Please provide details of the start-up costs for the business, research and development, recruitment, asset purchase, including legal and professional fees etc.

_____
_____
_____
_____
_____

D2
Please provide details of the forecast profit and loss statements for the business in the format detailed below. Please complete form or attach forecasts separately.

Forecast Profit and Loss Statement

NZ$000	Year 1	Year 2	Year 3
Revenue (A)			
Cost of sales (B):			
Labour			
Overheads			
Raw materials			
....			
Gross Margin (C=A-B)			
Expenses (D):			
Salaries			
Rent			
Depreciation			
Administration			
Audit fees			
Legal fees			
....			
....			
Earnings before interest (E=C-D)			
Interest (F)			
Net Profit (G=E-F)			
Tax (H =G x 33%)			
Net Profit after Tax, available to shareholders (I=G-H)			
Ratios			
Gross Margin % (= C/A x100)			
Net profit after Tax/ Revenue % (=I/A x100)			
Interest Cover — times (=E/F)			

9

Fig. 11. Continued.

D3 Please provide a three-year cash flow forecast for the proposed business, in the format detailed below. Please complete the form below or attach forecasts separately.

Cash-flow forecasts

NZ$000	Year 1	Year 2	Year 3
Net profit after tax			
Add: Depreciation			
Gross cash-flow			
Working capital required			
Debtors			
Inventory			
Creditors			
Other assets			
Creditors			
Other liabilities			
Cash flow from operations (A)			
Financing activities			
Increase/(decrease) in bank debt			
Increase/(decrease) in overdraft			
Increase/(decrease) in capital			
Dividend payments			
Cash provided from financing (B)			
Investment activities			
Sale/(purchase) of fixed assets (before depreciation)			
Increase/(decrease) in shareholder loans			
Increase/(decrease of inter-company loans			
Cash provided from investing (C)			
Net cash flow (D=A+B+C)			
Opening cash balance (E)			
Plus/(minus) net cash flow (F=D)			
Closing cash balance profits (G=E+F)			

Financing options

D4 What level of capital investment will the business require? *(please attach third party evidence that you have these funds available)*

D5 What level of capital will you bring into the business?

D6 Will the business require additional financing?

D7 How are you intending to arrange financing for your business? Include with your answer details of potential financiers or equity partners.

(10)

Fig. 11. Continued.

Section E   Business Experience

E1 Please describe your past and present business management experience. Include details of how you started out, and the type and nature of businesses you have been involved in. Give specific details of your responsibilities and duties within the company(ies).

E2 Provide details of your existing businesses, including business type, background, turnover, profitability, and number of employees. Please provide contact details for the businesses.

E3 What is your share of ownership in each of your existing businesses?

E4 Have you ever been involved in a business failure or bankruptcy?

☐ Yes ☐ No

If yes, please provide details.

E5 Have you ever been convicted of fraud or financial impropriety?

☐ Yes ☐ No

If yes, please provide details

11

Fig. 11. Continued.

E6   Provide details of any business or trade qualifications and university degrees, including institution, date and qualification type, and attach certified copies of these.

E7   Does your proposed business require you to utilise any professional qualifications?

☐ Yes   ☐ No

If yes, please provide proof that you have obtained full registration of these qualifications in New Zealand.

Section F   Knowledge of New Zealand Market

F1   Describe the extent of your knowledge regarding the New Zealand business environment.

F2   Have you had any previous involvement with/in any business in New Zealand?

☐ Yes   ☐ No

If yes, please provide details of the involvement.

F3   Have you made contact or sought advice from any relevant trade associations in New Zealand?

☐ Yes   ☐ No

If yes, please provide details of the contact.

F4   Have you commissioned any independent research regarding the potential regarding the viability of your proposed business in New Zealand?

☐ Yes   ☐ No

If yes, please provide details of the research.

12

Fig. 11. Continued.

F5 Have you received any professional advice regarding the establishment of the business?

☐ Yes ☐ No

If yes, please provide details of the advice and the outcome.

F6 Will your business require any consents under the Resource Management Act or the Overseas Investment Act?

☐ Yes ☐ No

If yes, please provide details.

F7 Do you have any family members or associates who are currently operating similar businesses in NZ?

☐ Yes ☐ No

If yes, please provide details of this business.

Section G   Contact Details

G1 Name as shown in passport

Family: [   ]   Given: [   ]

Preferred title   Mrs ☐   Mr ☐   Ms ☐   Miss ☐   Dr ☐   Other [   ]
(please specify)

G2 Name and address for correspondence (or agent details).

	Phone/ day:	
	Phone/ night:	
	Fax:	
	Email:	

13

Fig. 11. Continued.

This part must be signed by the principal applicant, partner and dependent children aged 17 years and over. Make sure you understand the declarations below before you sign them.

Important

I understand that if I make any false statements, or provide any false or misleading information, or have changed or altered this form in any way, my application may be declined, or my visa or permit may later be revoked, and that I may also be committing an offence and liable to prosecution.

I understand that I am required to inform NZIS about any relevant changes to my circumstances that occur after I lodge this application.

I understand the notes and questions in this form and I declare the information given about myself, partner and any children is true and complete.

I declare that there are no matters or warrants outstanding, or investigations of any kind, which could have any current or future effect on the assessment of my good character or the good character of any other persons included in this application.

I authorise the NZIS to make any enquiries it deems necessary in respect of the information provided on this form and to share information about me with other government agencies (including overseas agencies) to the extent necessary to make decisions about my immigration status. I also consent to any organisation providing relevant information to the NZIS about me.

I authorise the NZIS to provide information about my state of health and my immigration status to any health service agency.

I authorise any health service agency to provide information about my state of health to the NZIS.

I accept that any advice given to me by the NZIS before lodging this application was intended to assist me and acting on that does not mean that my application for a long term business visa and permit will be approved.

I understand that in order to work in certain occupations in New Zealand registration is required by law. I accept that the grant of a permit does not guarantee that registration will be granted.

I agree that information about my personal resources and the contents of this form may be provided to the New Zealand Department of Work and Income (DWI) if I apply for an emergency benefit. I understand that I will need to give a copy of this declaration to DWI if I apply for an emergency benefit.

Should my application be approved I agree to participate in an evaluation of the Long Term Business Visa/Permit category for a period of up to 5 years after the approval of my application. I agree to inform NZIS of any changes to my postal/contact address within 5 years from the date of approval for the purpose of participating in the aforementioned evaluation.

Signature of principal applicant

| |
| |

day   month   year

Signature of partner (if applicable)

| |
| |

day   month   year

Signature of parent or guardian if principal applicant is under 17 years of age

| |
| |

day   month   year

Signature of accompanying dependent children over 17 years of age (if applicable)

| | |
| | |

day   month   year

Fig. 11. Continued.

Declaration for Person Assisting the Applicant to Complete this Form

To be completed and signed by any person who has assisted the applicant to complete this form by explaining, translating or filling in the form for the applicant.

Full name of person assisting:

Address of person assisting:

I understand that after the applicant has signed this form it is an offence to alter or enter further information on it, alter any material attached to it, or attach any further material to it, unless the person making the alteration or addition states on the form what information or material has been altered or attached, why, and by whom. I understand that the maximum penalty for this offence is a fine of up to NZ$100,000 and/or a term of imprisonment of up to 7 years.

I certify that I have assisted in the completion of this form and any additional forms at the request of the applicant **and** that the applicant understood the content of the form(s), **including the business plan**, and agreed that the information provided is correct before signing the declaration. I have assisted the applicant as a:

lawyer ☐   agent, consultant ☐   translator ☐   friend or ☐   other advisor ☐
           or representative   family member   Please specify:

Signature of person assisting:

day   month   year

Payment Details

I enclose (amount)

Cash ☐   Cheque ☐   Electronic credit card or SWITCH ☐

SWITCH card issue number (in UK only):

Credit card (specify type):   Mastercard ☐   Visa ☐

Name of card holder   Card number   Expiry date

Signature   day   month   year

How do you want your documents returned to you?

By mail ☐   Collected by you or a nominated person ☐

15

Fig. 11. Continued.

Earning a Dollar

JOB HUNTING

Unlike Australia, New Zealand does not maintain an occupations list, i.e. a list of preferred professionals and likely job vacancies.

The New Zealand Immigration Department does not feel it would be helpful to issue such a list, as it would be continually out of date. The preferred system is for a person to qualify with the points system. If for instance they issued a list saying that the country was in need of electronic engineers, by the time the list was circulated, it would probably be out of date and New Zealand would then be overrun with electronic engineers insisting that they were needed!

The labour force

The very best way to get a good idea of salaries and conditions in New Zealand is to access The Kiwi Careers' website. It has comprehensive lists of job outlines grouped either in industry, alphabetical order, or by interests areas. Details of salary ranges, current market demand, training requirements and typical work conditions are provided for each job category.

Visit: *www.careers.co.nz*
Select: Job outlines

Job by alphabetical listing
Specific job category
Sidebar: employment conditions

LABOUR RELATIONS

On 15 May 1991 the new Government repealed the Labour Relations Act 1987 and enacted the **Employment Contracts Act**.

This Act provided a fundamentally different framework for the conduct of industrial relations. Rather than being based on a conflict model of industrial relations, it is based on two quite different assumptions:

- Employers and their employees have a mutual interest in maintaining the wealth and profitability of their enterprises.

- Employers and their employees are in the best position to make decisions on what arrangements should govern their employment relationship.

To achieve these ends, the Act removes union monopolies over coverage and bargaining; it gives employees the right to decide whether or not they wish to belong to an employee organisation such as a union and the right to choose who, if anybody, they want to represent them. It aims to encourage bargaining outcomes that are relevant to the workplace and enables employers and employees to negotiate either individual or collective employment contracts directly.

Employees are now required to sign an **employment contract**. Bargaining can be done by the person involved, or they may elect to have someone bargain for them. A bargaining agent must not have been convicted of an offence punishable by five years or more in prison, within the last ten years.

No smoking

It is not unusual to see groups of people standing outside office blocks smoking. This is because many offices now have a ban on smoking, so the people who smoke have to go outside when they want a quick 'drag'. When applying for a job you will quite possibly be asked if you smoke, and you will probably find that a condition of the job is that you do not smoke.

FINDING A JOB

There are three conventional ways in which to track down the 'right' job:

◆ the newspapers
◆ New Zealand Employment Bureau
◆ private employment bureaux.

The newspapers

Write to a New Zealand newspaper office, enquiring as to the cost of sending you the latest editions, or view the latest news online.

> *The New Zealand Herald*, Box 32, Auckland. Website: *www.nzherald.co.nz*
> *The Dominion*, Box 1297, Wellington
> *The Otago Times*, Box 517 Dunedin
> *The Christchurch Star*, Box 1467, Christchurch.

It would be a good idea to mention that you are interested in 'situations vacant' and would therefore like the issue with the largest selection – Saturday for some papers and Wednesday/Thursday for others.

New Zealand Employment Service

These offices are run by the Labour Department, and their main purpose is to help people find work. Unlike the private employment bureaux, the New Zealand Employment Bureau does not make a charge. The offices are as follows:

New Zealand Employment Service:

PO Box 23 358, Auckland. Tel: 64 9 278 0905.
PO Box 5065, Whangarei. Tel: 64 09 438 8875.
PO Box 9446, Wellington. Tel: 64 4 81 5277.
PO Box 4441,Christchurch. Tel: 64 3 377 0530.
PO Box 859, Dunedin. Tel: 64 3 477 5395.
PO Box 545, Napier. Tel: 64 6 835 8569.

Private employment bureaux

There are many employment bureaux, and some of them specialise in different areas, so here are a few of the larger and better known:

Hospitality industry
Kelly Services (NZ) Ltd. Box 10151, Wellington. Tel: 64 4 499 2825. Fax: 64 4 499 2821.
Hotel & Hospitality Employment Service, Box 90198, Auckland. Tel: 64 9 379 7532 Website: *www.hhes.co.nz*

Two major hotel chains you could try:

Quality Hotels, 280 Queen St, Auckland.
   Email: *sales.marketing@cdlhms.co.nz*
Scenic Circle Hotels, Christchurch. Tel: 64 3 357 1900.
   Website: *www.scenic-circle.co.nz*

Some ski resort hotels
Holiday Inn, Queenstown. Tel: 64 3 442 6600.
Southern Cross Ski Hotel, Canterbury. Tel: 64 3 302 8464.
Mount Hutt Country Club, Canterbury. Tel: 64 3 302
   8721.
Pembroke Inn, Wanaka, Central Otago. Tel: 64 3 433 7296.
Edgewater Resort, Wanaka, Central Otago. Tel: 64 3 433
   8311.
Shotover Resort Hotel, Queenstown. Tel: 64 3 442 7850.
Quality Hotel, Queenstown. Tel: 64 3 442 8123.
The Queenstown Parkroyal, Queenstown. Tel: 64 3 442
   7750.

Info-technology
IT@Work Recruitment Ltd, PO Box 47-881, Ponsonby,
   Auckland. Tel: 64 9 360 6151.
   Website: *www.itworks.co.nz*
New Zealand IT Limited, Auckland. Tel: 64 9 620 0633.
   Website: *www.NewZealandIT.co.nz*

Engineering/technical/chemical/scientific
A-Trade NZ, 78 Worcester St, Christchurch. Tel: 64 3 365
   557.
Engineering Design Consultants Ltd, 227 Main Road,
   Albany, Auckland. Tel: 64 9 419 6662. Website:
   www.edc.co.nz
Holmes Consulting Group, Box 99-450, Newmarket
   Auckland. Tel: 64 9 522 4596.

Finance & accounting specialists

Doyle Consulting Ltd, Auckland. Tel: 64 9 529 9369.
Email: *jan@doyle.consulting.co.nz*

Banking Personnel Ltd, West Plaza Building, Albert St,
Auckland. Tel: 64 9 358 0888.
Website: *www.debbiegraham.co.nz*

General

Drake International, Box 10063, Wellington. Tel: 64 4 472
6972.

Drake International, Box 13275, Tauranga. Tel: 64 7 571
0283.

Drake International, Tower Centre, Queen St, Auckland.
Tel: 64 9 379 5610. Website: *www.drakeintl.com*

Advanced Personnel Services, 611 Great South Rd,
Manukau Central, Auckland 1701. Tel: 64 9 263 4322.

Alpha Personnel Recruitment, Box 99256, Newmarket,
Auckland. Tel: 64 0 524 2336.
Website: *www.alphajobs.co.nz*

Job leads

Did you know, however, that 70 per cent of jobs are not
advertised? These are usually the jobs that are found by
people who do their own job seeking. There is more to
finding a job than just looking in the local newspaper. The
following are vital sources of job openings:

- professional publications
- professional associations
- the head office of the organisation you would like to
  work in
- advertising in the paper yourself for the job you are
  seeking

Fig. 12. Some typical New Zealand job advertisements.

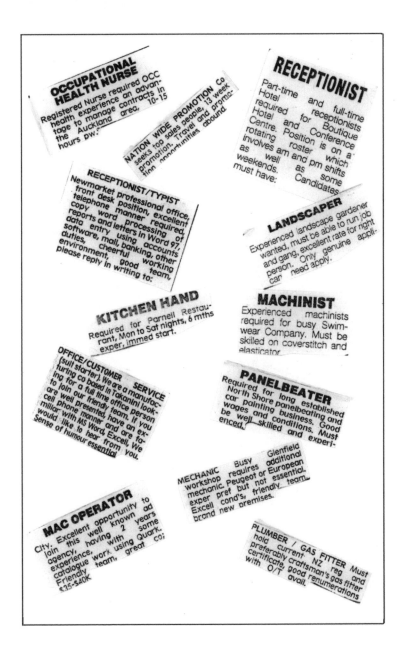

Fig. 12. Continued.

◆ circulating your details to professional organisations and consultants.

GETTING STARTED

Finding the right job may not be easy, so the better prepared you are the more chances you have of finding one. Here are a few ideas to get you started.

Make sure you have an up-to-date Curriculum Vitae (CV) prepared. Curriculum Vitae is Latin for 'Course of Life'. It should contain two or three pages of information. A CV is your personal sales document. It details all the skills and experiences that you've gained, your interests and hobbies and your work history. Most employers ask for a CV or résumé. Its main purpose is to get you an interview. Résumé is French for 'Summary'. A résumé is usually one page of information about yourself, but not in as much detail as a CV. If an employer asks for a résumé instead of a CV this usually means they would like just the information most relevant to the job.

The main types of CVs are:

◆ functional
◆ chronological.

Creating a functional CV

This highlights the particular skills you have that match a specific job you are applying for. A functional CV will have:

◆ a clearly stated job objective (relevant to the job you are applying for)

* your skills directly related to the job objective
* a brief list of your work history, and
* details of your education and training.

If you are applying for different jobs, prepare a different CV for each job application. Each CV should highlight the skills you have that best fit the job you are applying for. (See Figure 13.)

Creating a chronological CV
This is a record of all your jobs and education in the order you did them. A chronological CV is a very structured CV and can be used for a variety of job applications. (See Figure 14.)

What about references?
References, either written or verbal, are very important. They tell an employer what you are like as a worker or how well you have worked.

You need to ask the permission of the person whose name you want to use as a verbal reference on your CV.

If you don't have written references, you could ask for one from someone you have done some voluntary work for. You could also ask for a reference from someone, other than family, who has known you a while.

TACKLING TYPICAL INTERVIEW QUESTIONS
The following are some typical questions used by employers when interviewing for job vacancies. What would your answers be?

* Why do you want to work here?

Personal Details

Name	Aroha Hylton
Address	1/80 Pine Crescent
	Blockhouse Bay
	Auckland
Telephone	0 9 882 0956

Objective

To further develop my supervisory skills

Highlights of Experience

- Three years' experience as assistant Check-Out Supervisor
- Trained new staff in supermarket procedures

Relevant Experience

Numeracy Skills

Dealing with numbers/figures has always been my specialty. My background includes:
- treasurer for local sports club and association (hockey)
- balancing my own and friend's cheque books
- helping friends budget their finances

Organisation skills

I pay attention to detail and can delegate effectively. My organisation skills have developed well and this is shown in my involvement with:
- social functions for work
- fundraising for local sports club
- written correspondence for cricket club

Communication skills

My communication skills are excellent. I pride myself in being able to put my view across in an assertive manner. I have:
- captained a local hockey team – guiding and directing team members
- experience as assistant check-out supervisor for three years
- attended courses on effective communication skills

Employment History

1999–2003 General Food Supermarket – Assistant Check-out Supervisor
1997–1998 Foodtown Supermarket – Shop Assistant

Education/Training

1996–1997 Regional Polytechnic
 Effective Communication Skills
1992–1995 Four years secondary education

Referees

Ms Kay Arland (Check-out Supervisor)
General Food Supermarket, Henderson
Telephone: 0 9 345 9876

Mr W Whetu (Sports Co-ordinator)
Sports Foundation
Telephone: 0 9 234 8765

Fig. 13. Sample functional CV.

Personal Details
Name   Matthew Reid
Address   57 Kowhai Street
                                 Brighton
                                 Christchurch
Telephone   0 3 234 5678

Personal Statement   Throughout my school and working career I have
                                       prided myself on being a self motivated, reliable and
                                       hardworking person. More than anything, these are
                                       the qualities I wish to recommend to you.

Education and Training
            2003   **Carrington Polytechnic**
                           Training Opportunity Programme (TOPs course)
                           Building and Landscaping Skills
      1994–1997   **Mt Albert Grammar School**
                           Subjects taken at sixth form level:
                           Horticulture and Art

Work History
      1998–2003   **Harvey's Brick & Blocklayers**
                           Labourer
                           Duties included: heavy lifting, spreading sand and
                           gravel, laying bricks into patterns and driving.
                           Position made redundant when the firm was sold.
      1997–1998   **Robinson & Walker Construction**
                           Builder's Labourer (temporary)
                           Duties included: Cleaning tools, measuring to
                           instructions, assisting tradesmen with general
                           duties.
            1997   **Beechcroft's Orchards – Henderson**
                           Vineyard Labourer (seasonal)
                           Duties included: General duties, packing, cleaning
                           sheds

Additional Information   Clean driver's licence (A, B, F)
                                        Own reliable transport

Interests/Hobbies   Running, squash, landscape gardening

Referees   **Keith Harvey** (former manager Harvey's Brick &
                                  Blocklayers)
                                  37 Oakland Avenue
                                  Glen Eden
                                  Auckland
                                  Telephone: 0 9 345 6789

                                  Susan Anderson (owner of Beechcroft's Orchards)
                                  88 Rimu Drive
                                  Henderson
                                  Auckland
                                  Telephone: 0 9 876 5432

Fig. 14. Sample chronological CV.

- ◆ What interests you most about this job?
- ◆ Have you done this type of work before?
- ◆ Why should we hire you and not someone else?
- ◆ What skills can you bring to this job?
- ◆ Tell me about yourself, your hobbies and other interests.
- ◆ What are your strengths and weaknesses?
- ◆ How well do you work with other people?
- ◆ What did you most enjoy about your last job?
- ◆ Why did you leave your last job?
- ◆ What are your plans for the future?
- ◆ What level of wage or salary do you want?
- ◆ Who can we contact for a reference?

The following are some questions you might like to ask at an interview:

- ◆ Could you tell me more about the job?
- ◆ Where and with whom would I be working?
- ◆ What are the dress standards?
- ◆ Are there other conditions or requirements?
- ◆ When will you decide who gets the job?

CHOOSING YOUR OCCUPATION

Below are described some of the opportunities available in a wide range of careers and professions. Useful addresses are listed to help you follow up particular areas of interest and obtain more detailed information. At the end of the chapter there is a comprehensive list of personnel consultants who may also be able to advise and assist you.

Advertising

I was told by Saatchi & Saatchi Advertising in Wellington that they are always on the look out for new exceptional talent. There are several people from England and Australia already working in their office. The best advice I can give is for you to contact any of the advertising agencies listed below, and they will be able to give you up-to-date information on their needs.

Useful addresses

Saatchi & Saatchi Advertising, 101–103 Courtney Pl, Wellington. Tel: 64 4 385 6524. Fax: 64 4 385 9678.

Now known as: Clemenger BBDO Ltd Advertising Agency, Clemenger BBDO House, 8 Kent Terrace, PO Box 9440, Wellington. Tel: 04 802 3333.

Donnithorne Fordyce Vintiner Birss & Young, 128–132 The Terrace, Wellington. Tel: 64 4 473 1129.

McCann Erickson Ltd, 382 Manukau Rd, Epsom, Auckland. Tel: 09 6388 075.

Aviation

The aviation industry in New Zealand comprises the commercial airlines, e.g. Air New Zealand and Ansett. There are numerous small airlines, e.g. Air Chathams which operates from the Chatham Islands; Gt Barrier Airlines which operates from Gt Barrier Island; Mt Cook Airlines; Rex Aviation, specialist in corporate jets, turbo props, freight operations and aircraft charters; Soundsair, which operates an amphibian service to the Marlborough Sounds and three scheduled flights daily from Wellington to Picton plus charter flights anywhere in New Zealand.

There are aviation opportunities available in New Zealand and it would be a good start to contact the following:

Useful addresses

The Civil Aviation Authority of New Zealand, Aviation House, 1 Market Grove, PO Box 31-441, Lower Hutt, Wellington. Tel: 64 4 560 9400. Fax: 64 4 569 2024. Website: *www.caa.govt.nz*

Aviation Industry Association, Agriculture House, 12 Johnstone Street, Wellington. Tel: 64 4 472 2707. Website: *www.caa.govt.nz*

Massey School of Aviation, Private Bag 11222, Palmerston North. Tel: 64 6 356 9099. (Training and general aviation enquiries.)
Website: *www.aviation.massey.ac.nz/*

Accountancy

McLay & So (NZ) Ltd of Wellington recently informed me that the market is fairly buoyant for accountants with banking backgrounds and manufacturing backgrounds.

Firstly check out if your qualifications enable you do work in New Zealand by contacting the New Zealand Society of Accountants, PO Box 11-342, Wellington. Tel: 64 4 473 8544. Fax: 64 4 472 6282.

Useful address

Chartered Institute of Management Accountants, PO Box 11269, Wellington. Tel: 64 4 384 7393. Fax: 64 4 385 4279.

Agriculture

Even though there is unemployment in New Zealand there is still a demand for *skilled* agricultural labour. The Government has allowed Marvin Farm Services to bring a limited number of overseas young farmers into New Zealand to participate in their Agricultural Work Study Tour. Well over 500 young farmers have undertaken this programme in the last ten years. The requirements to apply for entry to this scheme are for young farmers to have sound practical dairy farming experience.

The North Island of New Zealand is mainly rolling contour with dairy farming on the lowlands and sheep and cattle on the hills. The South Island is very mountainous, with mainly sheep, arable and beef farming.

The summer season commences in November and ends about the middle of March. Winter conditions vary between mild and wet in the North Island and cold and snowy in the South Island.

As New Zealand is an agricultural country, most of its earnings come from producing and exporting butter, milk products, meat and wool. Marvin Farm Services provide a service to farmers, supplying them with labour when they are short-handed because of sickness, holidays or extra work.

Barry Hazlehurst of Marvin Farm Services advises me that successful applicants *must* arrive between mid July and early August. This is when dairy farmers require staff to assist them over the calving period. Overseas young farmers can almost be assured of a full work programme from this time until mid February or possibly a full 12 months. At times Marvin Farm Services send labour to Western Australia during the wheat-planting season in April through to the end of June.

Some important points to remember:

- Marvin Farm Services only employ young farmers from the United Kingdom and Ireland.
- They arrange temporary work permits for *successful* applicants.
- The scheme starts in July or very early August each year.
- *Compulsory* seven months' work although up to 12 months' work available.
- Successful applicants must have had a fair amount of practical dairy farming experience.
- Preferred age is 20–30 and you *must* be single.

For further details about this Work Study Tour please contact: Barry Hazlehurst, Marvin Farm Services, 95 Arawa St, PO Box 248, Matamata. Tel: 64 7 888 6025. Fax: 64 7 888 5014.

Lance Orr of Central Employment informs me that he employs backpackers for farm work during the July/ August period. If you travel to New Zealand as a visitor on a visitor's permit you are *not* allowed to work until you have applied for and received a work permit from the Immigration Department. For further information please contact: Lance Orr, Central Employment, R.D.2,

Tuakau, South Auckland. Tel: 64 9 232 8005. Fax: 64 9 233 4889. Email: *Lance@ps.gen.nz*

Useful addresses

Ministry of Agriculture and Forestry, Wellington.
    Website: *www.maf.gov.nz*
Federated Farmers of New Zealand Inc, Box 715, Wellington. Tel: 64 4 473 7269. Fax: 64 4 473 1081.
    Website: *www.fedfarm.org.nz*
    Email: *Wellingtonoffice@fedfarm.org.nz*
New Zealand Dairy Board, Box 417, Wellington. Tel: 64 4 463 2000. Fax: 64 4 463 2073.
    Website: *www.nzmilk.com*
Meat New Zealand, PO Box 121, Wellington. Tel: 64 4 473 9150. Fax: 64 4 474 0800.
    Website: *www.meatnz.co.nz*
New Zealand Wool Board, Wool House, 10 Brandon St, Box 3225, Wellington. Tel: 64 4 472 6888. Fax: 64 4 473 7872. Website: *www.nzwool.co.nz*

Automotive mechanical engineers
The Motor Trade Association Inc indicated that there is a shortage of automotive mechanical engineers in New Zealand because of a shortage of apprentices. If you:

- have City & Guilds qualifications
- are versatile with all makes and models
- are willing to live anywhere in New Zealand
- have your own tools

then you can start tomorrow!

To find vacancies you should arrange to receive copies of New Zealand newspapers:

The New Zealand Herald, Box 32, Auckland (whole of NZ). Website: *www.netclassifieds.co.nz* and *www.nz. herald.co.nz/*

The Dominion, Press House, 40 Boulcott St, Box 3740, Wellington (North Island).

The Otago Daily Times, Box 517, 52–66 Lower Stuart St, Dunedin (South Island). Tel: 64 3 477 4760. Website: *www.odt.co.nz*

The Christchurch Star, Box 1467, Christchurch (South Island). Tel: 64 3 379 7100. Fax: 64 3 364 7480. Website: *www.wilsonandhorton.co.nz/ wh_companies/newspapers/christchurch_star.html*

Write to the paper of your choice enclosing NZ$8 per copy. You can pay by cheque, credit card or bank draft.

Useful address

Motor Trade Association Inc, Level 2, 79 Taranaki St, Box 9244, Courtenay Place, Wellington. Tel: 64 4 385 8859. Fax: 64 4 385 9517. Website: *www.mta.org.nz* Email: *mta@motor-trade.co.nz*

Building trades

Qualification requirements are the same as in the UK. There are limited job opportunities available. Vacancies are usually advertised in the newspapers. Direct all enquiries to the Building Industry Authority.

Useful address

Building Industry Authority, Greenock House, 39 The Terrace, PO Box 11846, Wellington. Tel: 64 4 471 0794. Fax: 64 4 471 0798.
Website: *www.bia.govt.nz/* Email: *bia@bia.co.nz*

The New Zealand telephone directory is now on the web. Website: *www.whitepages.co.nz* and *www.yellowpages. co.nz*

Beauty therapy

More and more women are taking advantage of the wide range of services, such as aromatherapy, waxing, manicure, pedicure, acne treatment, therapeutic massage, electrolysis, facials, red vein treatment, etc., now available from beauty therapy clinics. Jobs in this area can be found in the newspapers. For further information contact Association of Beauty Therapists, Box 28026, Remuera, Auckland 5. Tel: 64 9 303 3238. Website: *www.beautynz.org.nz/*

Hairdressing

It would be advisable to look in the newspaper in the area of your choice for hairdressing positions. (For details of newspapers, see above under Automotive mechanical engineers.)

Chiropractors

Chiropractic clinics can be found in most centres. They are widely used for sporting injuries and general consultation. For further details contact the New Zealand Chiropractic Association.

Useful address

New Zealand Chiropractic Association, Box 46127, Herne Bay, Auckland. Tel: 64 9 360 2089. Fax: 64 9 360 2091. Website: *www.chiropractic.org.nz/*

Computing

John Jennings of IDPE Holdings Limited, Wellington,

informed me that the skills which are especially short in New Zealand at the moment include relational database, open systems, client server and networking. Although relatively newer skills such as Oracle, C++, Windows, object-oriented programming, business process re-engineering and SAP are in demand, there has been a resurgence of interest in mainframe skills such as Cobol/CICS and DB2. Good mid-range experience is also sought on a regular basis.

A Ministry of Commerce survey revealed a dramatic increase in the number of people employed in the IT industry since 1989. The report also revealed that salaries for people with highly specialised skills increased by 15–20%.

Employers looking for contract staff focus primarily on the technical skills of an applicant, but for permanent roles a real commitment to remain in New Zealand is as important as anything else. Britain is a logical market from which to recruit staff for New Zealand because of cultural similarities, language and past experience.

Dentistry and dental technicians
Private dental practitioners and government agencies collaborate to provide oral health care in New Zealand. The school dental service, staffed by operating auxiliaries, is a distinctive feature of the system.

A recent survey showed there were approximately 1,500 dentists in the active workforce. The New Zealand Dental Association is recognised as the organised voice of dental

practitioners and approximately 95% of registered dentists belong. The Dental Association Council is the Association's governing body. More information can be had by using the website.
Website: *www.dentalcouncil.org.nz*

Clinical dental technicians are able to supply and fit dentures directly to the public. They are represented by the Institute of Dental Technologists. Contact the Dental Technicians Board for more information.

There are many overseas-trained doctors and dentists registered as unemployed. In many cases this is because their qualifications are not sufficient to allow them to practise in New Zealand. They are required to sit an expensive three-part Medical Council registration exam, which I am told many fail at the first attempt.

Useful addresses
Dental Technicians Board, PO Box 11053, Ellerslie, Auckland. Tel: 64 9 579 7096. Fax: 64 9 525 1169.
    Website: *www.dentaltec.org.nz*
Dental Council of New Zealand.
    Website: *www.dentalcouncil.org.nz*

Economists, finance and banking
The most likely sources of employment are through the banks.

Useful addresses
ANZ Banking Group (NZ) Ltd, Box 1492, Wellington.
    Tel: 64 4 496 7000. Fax: 64 4 473 6919.
    Website: *www.anz.com/nz/*

ASB Bank (Auckland Savings Bank), Corner of Jervois Quay and Hunter Street, Wellington. Tel: 64 4 499 4422. Fax: 64 4 499 7766.

Bank of New Zealand, State Insurance Tower, 1 Willis Street, Wellington. Tel: 64 4 474 6351. Fax: 64 4 474 6531.

National Bank of NZ Limited, 170-186 Featherston Street, Wellington Tel: 64 4 494 4000. Fax: 64 4 498 6092. Website: *www.nationalbank.co.nz*

Reserve Bank of New Zealand, 2 The Terrace, Wellington. Tel: 64 4 472 2029. Fax: 64 4 473 8554.
Website: *www.rbnz.govt.nz*

Westpac Banking Corporation, 318-324 Lambton Quay, Wellington. Tel: (from New Zealand) 0800 400 600, (from abroad) 64 9 912 8000.
Website: *www.westpactrust.co.nz*

Industry

In a recent survey published by the Northern Employers and Manufacturers Association, Wellington, the word is that manufacturing is 'humming'. Export sales are up 21% on October 1998. Domestic sales are up 9% and staffing up 10%.

When the Asian economy crashed, it badly affected the Tourism industry. Tourism is now seen as a new and exciting growth industry, which is expected to chalk up nearly 2 million visitors for the current year with greater predictions for the future. It accounts for 1 in 12 jobs and is one of New Zealand's largest foreign exchange earners at NZ$3.7 billion, slightly below the Diary Board at NZ$4.8 billion.

Law

There are always places for good keen applicants, but good qualifications are a necessity. To ascertain that your qualifications reach New Zealand standards you must apply to the Council of Legal Education, 26 Waring Taylor Street, Wellington. Tel: 64 4 472 7837. Fax: 64 4 473 7909. Website: *www.nz-lawsoc.org.nz* Legal vacancies are generally advertised in the newspapers (see above under Automotive mechanical engineers details of New Zealand newspapers) and positions are also advertised by personnel consultants.

Useful addresses
Wellington District Law Society, 26 Waring Taylor Street,
    Wellington. Tel: 64 4 472 8978. Fax: 64 4 471 0375.
    Email: *wellaw@wellaw.co.nz*
    Website: *www.wellaw.co.nz*
Auckland District Law Society, PO Box 58, Auckland.
    Tel: 64 9 303 5270. Fax: 64 9 309 3726.
    Website: *www.adls.org.nz*

Working in the office environment

The following information was made available to me by the Lampen Group. It was compiled from a summary of findings from the 1999 Lampen Salary Survey.

Wellington

Secretarial/word processing
Skill shortages exist as candidates require more variety and challenge than roles limited to a high WP content. There has been an increase in multi-skilling in this area. Finding people interested in straight WP work has become increasingly difficult.

Reception
There is a shortage of suitable candidates with appropriate personality, grooming and oral/written communication skills.

Information Technology
As this industry develops so rapidly, skill-based training is needed to allow staff to match their skill level to the pace of industry development.

Accounts
There is a market perception that accounts roles are 'backroom', yet employers' expectations are that customer services and frontline people skills are required in such roles. There is a shortage of people with CHRIS payroll experience. There is a greater emphasis on people skills for accounting graduates. Accountants have experienced marked salary increases.

Clerical
There has been an increase in intermediate to advanced administration roles which include multiple responsibilities, i.e. there is a higher expectation that a PA will complete advanced administration tasks as well as word processing work which requires high computer literacy.

Marketing and customer service
These roles are currently very popular. Telemarketing and Telesales are growing rapidly with the increase in customer focus and technology, i.e. the increase in use of 0800 lines (free phones). These roles are replacing sales representatives in some cases.

Sales

Many applicants lack an understanding of the sales process, i.e. specialist product knowledge and negotiation skills. Sales salary packages frequently include faxes and mobile phones.

Graduates

Are being most frequently employed in legal, policy or human resource roles.

Legal

There has been a chronic and consistent shortage of legal secretaries, and many firms are training up secretarial staff into these roles. Skilled legal executives are commanding high salaries. An increase in speech recognition software usage attempts to deal with the increase in OSS/RSI and the emphasis on typing speed as a prerequisite for many roles.

> *Note*: there is a massive skills shortage in the New Zealand employment market. In Wellington it is concentrated in legal, secretarial, technical and payroll CHRIS areas.

Auckland

Auckland businesses are currently facing a skill shortage. The skill areas most affected are sales and marketing, secretarial (especially secretaries with legal experience), customer services, accounts and accountants, computer skills and reception skills.

Skills

More is now expected from employees in the commercial office area. Often staff will be expected to have more than one skill or to be multi-skilled. Employees themselves also have higher expectations of these roles. They are looking for career development, the opportunity to learn new skills and diversity in their roles. Accordingly salaries have been pushed in an upward direction for these roles.

Secretarial, word processing and reception roles have become less defined and more intertwined. Many employees prefer not to perform high word processing content roles, because of the dangers and high incidence of OSS (Occupational Strain Syndrome). It is important for people in these roles to keep in touch with continually changing office technology with training and up-skilling.

Office technology and more sophisticated use of technology has created great demand for systems operators and administrators.

IT and accounts staff, particularly accountants, are in high demand and those with experience are difficult to source.

Sales staff
The sales area is one of the most difficult for employers to staff at present. While many people are interested in these roles there are insufficient experienced people available, particularly those who may have specialist technical or industry experience. Demand for qualified marketers has also increased.

Telestaffing (or teleservicing, telemarketing and telesales) is a rapidly growing area of the employment market. There is increased demand for people with training or experience specific to telephone-based work. A sales or customer services background is important to most of these roles. More people are becoming interested in these roles and considering them as career options.

Opportunities
In general, the Auckland employment market offers many opportunities to skilled employees. There are plenty of positions available for people who have experience and the right attitude.

Christchurch

As with the Auckland and Wellington employment markets, the Christchurch employment market is experiencing a severe skill shortage in certain areas. Specifically these are: technical and information technology skills, accounting skills and legal administrative skills.

Secretarial and clerical
The Christchurch market currently requires more people with basic experience for general secretarial roles. As in Auckland, many employers prefer roles that offer more diversity and personal challenge than pure secretarial roles, therefore this gap needs to be filled. Again there is an intermingling of secretarial, word processing and reception roles, so that employees receive the diversity and challenge they seek from employment.

There is an insufficient pool of general and specialised clerical candidates to meet the current demand of employers. Many of the roles opening up on this area require basic rather than advanced skills.

Reception

Reception roles are increasingly being recognised as important frontline positions where contact with customers is made. Reception staff are expected to have highly developed communication and rapport-building skills.

Technology

Rapidly changing office technology has left the Christchurch employment market with a deficit of available employees to cope with change and upgrading technology. This is very evident in all computer-related roles – secretarial, systems operators, accounts and information technology.

Accountants

Accountants, both at graduate and more experienced levels, are in demand.

Sales

There are many opportunities for sales staff with planning and strategic skills, as well as the right personal attributes to match the culture of the employer company.

Opportunities

In general the Christchurch employment market has many opportunities for job-seekers, particularly those with computer related skills.

Optometrists

There are vacancies for optometrists in New Zealand but they are usually in the lower half of the North Island or in the South Island. Auckland has few vacancies because Auckland University runs the optometry courses, and the students prefer to stay in Auckland when they have qualified. I was told that some of the small urban and out of the way areas have difficulty in recruiting optometrists. Firstly you should contact the NZ Association of Optometrists and they will inform you what qualifications you need to be able to work in New Zealand. They will also answer any questions you may have.

New Zealand Association of Optometrists (Inc), PO Box 1978, Wellington. Tel: 64 4 473 2322. Fax: 64 4 473 2328. Website: *www.nzao.co.nz/*

Professional and technical

(Engineering, Architectural Construction, Scientific, Petro-chemical, Manufacturing, Computing, Sales/ Marketing)

There isn't much flexibility in this field of employment as there has in the past been an oversupply of architects, botanists, zoologists, geologists and geneticists flooding out from New Zealand universities.

Row Law Consulting informed me that applicants needed to be fairly rounded in experience with a degree in Engineering (BSc) with 5–7 years run of experience. Where they have had several disciplines covered in that experience, e.g. waste treatment and water supply, they will stand a better opportunity than those who are specialised. Work experience outside the UK is also an advantage as is experience in seismic codes.

Useful addresses

New Zealand Institute of Architects Inc, PO Box 2516, Auckland. Tel: 64 9 623 6080. Fax: 64 9 623 6081.

Website: *www.nzia.co.nz/*

Institute of Geological and Nuclear Sciences Ltd, PO Box 30-368, Lower Hutt, Wellington. Tel: 64 4 570 1444. Fax: 64 4 569 0600. Website: *www.gns.cri.nz/*

Institution of Professional Engineers New Zealand (IPENZ), PO Box 12–241, Wellington. Tel: 64 4 473 9444. Fax: 64 4 473 2324.
Website: *www.ipenz.org.nz*

Pharmacists

All pharmacists who intend working in New Zealand need to contact the Pharmaceutical Society of New Zealand to be registered. Address: 124 Dixon Street, Wellington. Tel: 64 4 385 9604. Fax: 64 4 382 9297.

There is a huge shortage of pharmacists in New Zealand. A registered pharmacist can expect to earn approximately $26–$30 per hour. There is a four week waiting period, after registration, before you can practise. Initial contact can be made by enquiring at the Provincial Pharmacy Services International office in Birmingham, UK.

Useful addresses

NZ Pharmacy Employment Ltd. Tel: 64 9 412 5480. Fax: 64 9 412 5483. Website: *www.pharmacy.net.nz/*

New Zealand Hospital Pharmacists Association. Website: *www.nzpha.org.nz/*

The Pharmacy Guild of NZ (Inc), Box 27-139, Wellington. Tel: 64 4 802 8200. Fax: 64 4 384 8085. Website: *www.pgnz.org.nz/*

Physiotherapists

Assessment of qualifications and registration is undertaken by the Physiotherapy Board of New Zealand who assess each application. The assessment process can take between four and six weeks.

The Board administers all forms of physiotherapy registration. Registration is a *legal requirement* for practising physiotherapy in New Zealand. Physiotherapists intending to work in New Zealand must complete formalities for registration *before* taking up employment. Write to the Physiotherapy Board and they will send you the necessary forms and information booklet. You will be required to pay an application fee of NZ$300.00 which is non-refundable.

Jobs can be found by looking in the newspapers and also through contacting New Zealand hospitals.

Useful addresses
New Zealand Physiotherapy Board, PO Box 734, Wellington. Tel: 64 4 471 2610. Fax: 64 4 471 2613. Website: *www.physioboard.org.nz/*
New Zealand Society of Physiotherapists, Box 27386, Wellington Tel: 64 4 801 6500. Fax: 64 4 801 5571. Website: *www.physiotherapy.org.nz/*

Podiatrists
All enquiries regarding registration should be made to the Podiatrists Board. Jobs can be found through the newspapers or by contacting the hospitals.

Useful address
Podiatrists Board, Box 10-140, Wellington. Tel: 64 4 499 7979. Fax: 64 4 472 2350.

Website: *www.regboards.co.nz/podiatrists*

Psychologists

Jobs can be found through contacting the hospitals and reading the newspapers for vacancies. Enquiries should be made to the Psychologists Board.

Useful addresses

Psychologists Board, Box 10–140, Wellington. Tel: 64 4 499 7979. Fax: 64 4 472 2350.
    Website: *www.reboards.co.nz/psychologists*
New Zealand College of Clinical Psychologists, PO Box 6366, North Dunedin Postal Centre, Dunedin. Tel: 64 3 474 5581. Fax: 64 3 474 5584.
    Website: *www.nzccp.co.nz/*

Quantity surveyors

There are good opportunities in New Zealand for quantity surveyors. Write direct to the Institute together with a copy of your CV.

Useful address

NZ Institute of Quantity Surveyors Inc, 108 The Terrace, PO Box 3635, Wellington. Tel: 64 4 473 5521. Fax: 64 4 473 2918. Website: *www.nziqs.co.nz/*
    Email: *karl/bale@nziqs.co.nz*

Real estate agents

You will need to gain a New Zealand registration, and details can be obtained from the Real Estate Institute of NZ (Inc). Jobs can be found by looking in the newspapers in the area of your choice, or by writing to the main agencies in New Zealand.

Useful addresses

Real Estate Institute of NZ (Inc), PO Box 1247, Wellington. Tel: 64 4 472 8942. Fax: 64 4 471 2262. Website: *www.reinz.org.nz/*

Real Estate Agents:

Harcourts Group Limited, PO Box 151, Wellington. Tel: 64 4 472 6209. Website: *www.harcourts.co.nz* (Harcourts have over 120 offices nationwide.)

Challenge Realty Services Ltd, (L J Hooker), 58–62 Johnsonville Road, Johnsonville, Wellington. Tel: 64 4 478 3109. Fax: 64 4 478 3106. (Offices throughout NZ.)

First National Real Estate, 143 Durham St, PO Box 567, Tauranga. Tel: 64 4 577 9683. Fax: 64 7 577 9674. Website: *www.firstnational.co.nz* (Offices throughout NZ.)

Valuers

It is necessary for overseas applicants to sit a law paper, and they must have been resident in New Zealand for 12 months. Job opportunities are limited. All applications and enquiries should be made to the New Zealand Institute of Valuers.

Useful addresses

Valuers Registration Board, 160 Lambton Quay, Private Box 5501, Wellington. Tel: 64 4 460 0110. Fax: 64 4 472 2244. Website: *www.linz.gov.nz*

NZ Institute of Valuers, PO Box 27-340, Wellington. Tel: 64 4 384 7094. Fax: 64 4 384 8473.
Website: *www.property.org.nz/*

Veterinarians

There are plenty of vacancies for veterinarians in New Zealand. You will need to register with the Veterinary Council of New Zealand. Jobs can be found in the newspapers and also through contacting the Veterinary Association.

Useful addresses

Patty Beckenham, Veterinary Association NZ (Inc), PO Box 11-212, Manners St, Wellington. Tel: 64 4 471 0484. Fax: 64 4 471 0494.
Website: *ww.vets.org.nz*

Veterinary Council of NZ, PO Box 10-563, Wellington 6036. Tel: 64 4 473 9600. Fax: 64 4 473 8869. Website: *www.vetcouncil.org.nz/*

PERSONNEL CONSULTANTS

A.P.S. Personnel, 611 Great South Road, Manukau, Auckland. Tel: 64 9 263 4322. Fax: 64 9 837 0824. (Engineering, office and secretarial, hotel and leisure staff.)

Adcorp NZ Ltd, for jobs via the web.
Website: *www.career.co.nz*

Advanced Personnel Services Limited, 829 Colombo Street, Christchurch. Tel: 64 3 365 4322. Website: *www.advancedpersonnel.co.nz/* (Office and secretarial, information and technology staff, executives, engineering, accountants, draughting, design engineers, computer systems/operators, labour hire, builders, tradesmen.)

Alectus Recruitment Consultants Ltd, Ports of Auckland Building, Quay St, Auckland. Tel: 64 4 366 3866. Fax: 64 4 498 0548. (Secretarial, reception, administration, promotional, accounts.)

Alpha Personnel Recruitment Limited, PO Box 99 256, Newmarket, Auckland. Tel. 64 9 524 2336. Fax: 64 9 524 2794. (Accounting, sales and marketing, secretarial, clerical, word processing, computer operators, data entry, advertising/media.)
Website: *www.alphajobs.co.nz/*
Email: *info@alphajobs.co.nz*

Sapphire Technologies, WestpacTrust Tower Building, 120 Albert St, Auckland. Tel: 64 9 373 2333. Website: *www.sapphirenz.com*

Cameron Mackay & Ellis, Castrol House, Level 5, 36 Custom House Quay, Wellington. Tel: 64 4 499 6688. Fax: 64 4 499 8665. (Executive and management.)

Candle NZ Ltd, 3–11 Hunter Street, Wellington. Tel: 64 4 473 9149. Website: *www.candlenz.co.nz* (IT recruitment.)

Clayton Ford Consulting Group, PO Box 10–083, Wellington. Tel: 64 4 473 6223. Fax: 64 4 471 2100. (Finance and banking.)
Website: *www.claytonford.co.nz*

Drake International Ltd, Tower Centre, Queen Street, Auckland. Tel: 64 9 379 5610. Fax: 64 9 377 3893. Website: *www.drake.co.nz* (General office, management, medical, industrial.)

Duncan & Ryan Associates, 135 Victoria Street, Wellington. Tel: 64 4 802 4888. Fax: 64 4 801 6656. Website: *www.duncanryan.co.nz* (Computers.)

Hawkins Associates, PO Box 10–013, Wellington. Tel: 64 4 499 9199. Fax: 64 4 499 9195.
Website: *www.hawkins4accountants.co.nz/*
Email: *hawkins.assoc@xtra.co.nz* (Professional and

technical.)

IDPE Consulting Group, Level 13, St John House, 114 The Terrace, PO Box 5288, Wellington. Tel: 64 4 472 2212. Fax: 64 4 472 2211.
Website: *http://idpe-consulting.co.nz* (Computers.)

Kelly Services (NZ) Ltd, Level 9, BDO House, 99–105 Custom House Quay, Wellington 6001. Tel: 64 4 499 2825. Website: *www.kellyservices.co.nz/* (Accounting, banking, WP operators, sales, secretarial, management, telemarketing, hospitality, marketing, clerical.)

Kelly Services (NW) Ltd, Level 10, Price Waterhouse Centre, 119 Armagh St, PO Box 13 418, Christchurch. Tel: 64 3 379 2963. (Secretarial, data entry, WP operators, medical, reception, spreadsheet operators, accounting, legal, sales and marketing, tradespeople, drivers, hospitality.)

Lacey Lee Simpson, PO Box 27144, Wellington. Tel: 64 4 382 9974. (IT recruitment.)

Lampen Group Limited, PO Box 2438, Auckland. Tel: 64 9 357 9800. Fax: 64 9 357 9801.

Mercury Consulting Group Ltd, 1 Grey Street, Wellington. Tel: 64 4 499 2624. Fax: 64 4 494 6880. Website: *www.mercuryrecruit.co.nz* (IT and computer professionals, telecommunications and electronic engineers.)

NZ Pharmacy Employment, Private Bag, Waitakere, Auckland. Tel: 64 9 412 5480. (Pharmacists, technicians, shop assistants.)

Rob Law Consulting Group, PO Box 10080, Wellington. Tel: 64 4 499 8800. Fax: 64 4 499 0955.
Email: *roblawauck@clear.net.nz*
Website: *www.roblaw.co.nz* (Engineering, architectural,

construction, scientific, petro-chemical, manufacturing, computing, sales/marketing.)

Rodgers & Partners, PO Box 391, Christchurch. Tel: 64 3 379 8909. Fax: 64 3 365 4494. Website: *www.rap.co.nz* (Executive and management.)

Select Appointments, Level 6, Clayton Ford House, 132 The Terrace, Wellington. Tel: 64 4 916 6740. Fax: 64 4 916 6754. Website: *www.selectappointments.co.nz/* (Secretarial, word processing, computer operators, reception.)

Sheffield Consulting Group, PO Box 10253, Wellington. Tel: 64 4 471 0122. Fax: 64 4 471 0413. Website: *www.sheffield.co.nz/* (Finance and banking.)

Stanford Recruitment Consultants, 294–296 Lambton Quay, Wellington. Tel: 64 4 472 0861. Fax: 64 4 499 4994. Website: *www.womens-business.org.nz/* Email: *Stanford.ltd@xtra.co.nz* (PAs, WP operators, admin, finance and accounting.)

Western Staff Services, 642 Great South Road, Ellerslie, Auckland. Tel: 64 9 525 5990. Website: *www.westaff.co.nz/* (Senior and middle management, office and clerical, sales and marketing, light industrial.)

Wheeler Campbell Consulting Ltd, 175 Queen Street, Auckland. Tel: 64 9 303 4500. Fax: 64 9 303 4501. Website: *www.wheelercampbell.co.nz* (Professional and technical.)

MEETING NEW ZEALAND QUALIFICATION REQUIREMENTS

Be kind to yourself – don't take the word of anyone unqualified who says that your qualifications will be alright.

Seek assistance from the New Zealand Embassy or Consulate before you leave home, and write to:

New Zealand Qualifications Authority Board, PO Box 160, Wellington. Tel: 64 4 802 3000. Fax: 64 4 802 3112. Website: *www.nzqa.govt.nz*

Make sure that you have got verification in writing *before* leaving home for distant shores. It is a lot less expensive, time-consuming and heart-breaking.

Teaching
Responsibility for assessing the qualifications of teachers trained overseas and for decisions as to their eligibility to teach in New Zealand state schools rests with the **New Zealand Qualifications Authority** (NZQA) and the **Teacher Registration Board** (TRB). Although teachers do not need to be registered, the New Zealand Immigration Service requires that immigrants wishing to teach in New Zealand meet the criteria for registration. Information on registration requirements and fees can be obtained from the **Ministry of Education**, PO Box 1666, Wellington, NZ. Tel: 64 0800 622 222 or 64 4 473 5544. Website: *www.teachnz.govt.nz*.

A fee for assessment of qualifications is charged by the NZQA. For more information contact: Support Officer, Qualifications Evaluation Service, New Zealand Qualifications Authority, PO Box 160, Wellington 6015, New Zealand. Tel: 64 4 802 3099. Fax: 64 4 802 3401. Website: *www.nzqa.govt.nz*.

Teaching positions are advertised in the *New Zealand Education Gazette*. Short-term teaching positions are usually advertised in local newspapers. The *Education Gazette* is available by writing to PO Box 249, Wellington, New Zealand. Tel: 64 4 917 3990. Fax: 64 4 917 3991. Email: *vacancies@edgazette.govt.nz*. Applications and enquires concerning the positions advertised in the *Education Gazette* should be made directly to the schools concerned.

Tutoring positions at polytechnics are also advertised in the *Education Gazette* and newspapers. University teaching positions are advertised in New Zealand and overseas newspapers and periodicals.

Medical

Nursing vacancies are usually advertised in the newspapers by the relevant hospital (Crown Health Enterprise). For further information regarding employment opportunities contact:

Nursing Council Ltd, Box 9644, 97 Courtenay Place, Wellington. Tel: 64 4 385 9589. Fax: 64 4 801 8502.

The address of some private nursing agencies:

Nightingale Nurses Ltd. Box 54 137, Plimmerton, Wellington. Tel: 64 4 239 9230.
Duty Calls Nursing & Home Care Ltd, PO Box 11-306, Wellington. Tel: 64 4 381 8666.
Website: *www.dutycalls.co.nz*

The Christchurch Nursing Bureau Ltd, Box 3957, Christchurch. Tel: 64 3 379 9732.

Geneva Health International, Hewlett Packard Building, 137–147 Quay Street, Auckland. Tel: 64 0 016 0200. Website: *www.genevahealth.com*

Doctors

The first step that you will need to take is to confirm your eligibility for registration as a doctor in New Zealand. All matters to do with registration and examination are administered by the **Medical Council of New Zealand**. Box 11-649, Wellington, NZ. Tel: 64 4 384 7635. Email: *nzma@namz.org.nz*. Website: *www.mcnz.org.nz* Contact should be made before you make any applications for employment.

Most vacancies for doctors are advertised in the *New Zealand Medical Journal* which is published by the New Zealand Medical Association (NZMA). Subscription to the *New Zealand Medical Journal* is free and automatic to NZMA members. A private subscription is available and NZMA offer a special subscription service for people only interested in the classified section.

Cost of the subscription within New Zealand starts from approximately NZ$255.15 and outside New Zealand from approximately NZ$280.00 – the cost depends on the type of postage used and where in the world the *Journal* is being sent to.

The New Zealand Medical Association regret to advise that they do not retain details of medical specialist training courses in New Zealand. You will need to obtain details about this type of training from either the Medical Council or the specialist medical colleges.

New Zealand Medical Association, 26 The Terrace, PO Box 156, Wellington. Tel: 64 4 472 4741. Fax: 64 4 471 0838. Email: *nzma@namz.org.nz*.

Royal NZ College of General Practitioners, Level three, 88 The Terrace, Wellington, PO Box 10440, Wellington. Tel: 64 4 496 5999. Fax: 64 4 496 5997.

Royal Australasian College of Physicians, PO Box 1634, Milton, QLD 4064. Tel: 61 7 3870 2505. Fax: 61 7 3870 2438.

Royal Australasian College of Surgeons, Surgeons Gardens, Spring Street, Melbourne, Victoria 3000, Melbourne. Tel: 61 39 249 1273. Fax: 61 3 9249 1219.

The New Zealand Medical Association advises that the employment situation for junior doctors in New Zealand is not very promising at the moment. Local medical schools are producing more graduates than the Area Health Boards can accept, and opportunities in general practice are rather limited by the intense competition that now exists in many cities. Should you decide to move to New Zealand and take up a position as a medical practitioner, the New Zealand Medical Association would welcome your application for membership.

The Auckland Medical Bureau at 272 Parnell Road, Auckland 1001. Tel: 64 9 377 5903 can arrange partnerships and the sale of medical practices.

SETTING UP A BUSINESS

Finding the right type of business can take time. Looking in the papers or/and contacting a real estate firm are the first steps to be taken. Write off for copies of New Zealand newspapers – see this chapter for addresses.

The Small Business Agency

The Small Business Agency runs workshops to help people who wish to run their own business. These come under the headings:

- Preparation
- Making a Start
- Management and Control
- Finance.

The addresses for enquiries are:

Small Business Agency (National Office), PO Box 11-012, Wellington. Tel: 64 4 475 3154.

Small Business Agency, Box 609, Whangarei. Tel: 64 09 438 2515.

Bizinfo, freephone: 64 0800 424946.

If you prefer to find empty premises and start up your own business, you should contact the real estate companies. Here is a small sample of shop and office space:

- Quality Office Space, Auckland City, 7,000 square feet ground floor modern fit out, $5.50 per square foot.
- Auckland City fringe office, studio 2 car parks, 1,050 square feet, $460 per week not including goods and services tax.

BUSINESSES
FOR SALE

**The Malvern Record
Newspaper & Copy Centre**
Darfield, South Island
Category: Service
Price: NZ $150,000 plus
stock at valuation

**The Fat Pigeon Garden
Cafe**
Ohakune, North Island
Category: Food + Beverage
Price: NZ $85,000 plus stock
at valuation

Mobi Scooter
Hamilton, North Island
Category: Industrial
Price: NZ $30,000 plus GST
if applicable

Clothing Manufacturing
Levin, North Island
Category: Industrial
Price: By negotiation

The Landscape Centre
Timaru, South Island
Category: Retail
Price: NZ $350,000 plus
stock at valuation

Tapu Store
Tapu, North Island
Category: Food + Beverage
Price: NZ $560,000 plus
stock at valuation

Challenger Motors
Henderson, North Island
Category: Industrial
Price: NZ $49,000 plus stock
at valuation

**Re-upholstery and
Furnishings**
Wellington, North Island
Category: Industrial
Price: NZ $130,000 plus
stock at valuation

Kapiti Hair Design
Paraparaumu, North Island
Category: Service
Price: NZ $25,000

Stone Centre
Taupo, North Island
Category: Industrial
Price: On application

Fig. 15. Some typical business opportunities for sale.

- Auckland City Office in the heart of the CBD – whole floor, 4,182 square feet. Large reception, fully partitioned, $11.50 per square foot.
- Quality serviced and furnished offices – central Auckland $450 per month.
- Auckland suburb, 4,673 square feet, high stud warehouse, 2 roller doors, $5.50 per square foot.
- Auckland suburb, 8,100 square feet of manufacturing space, 16 car parks, $5,500 per annum.
- Auckland City fringe live in/work 3,600 square feet office/showroom/accommodation.
- Auckland fringe showroom, 2,081 square feet, $29800 per annum.

Farming as a business

Pastoral agriculture is practised throughout New Zealand, with beef cattle predominating in the far north, dairying in Waikato (central North Island) and Taranaki (lower North Island), and sheep farming in the hills and in the south of the North Island. In the South Island, sheep farming is the main form of pastoral agriculture, with a sprinkling of beef cattle farmed in the high and hill country and wetter flat areas, and some dairying on the flat land of both coasts.

Livestock is rarely housed, but feeding of small quantities of supplements such as hay and silage can occur, particularly in winter. Grass growth is seasonal, largely depending on location and climatic fluctuations, but normally occurs for between eight and twelve months of the year. Stock is grazed in paddocks, often with movable electric fences, which allow rotation of grazing around the

FARMS FOR SALE

WELLSFORD/PORT ALBERT
100 acres, north facing, 30 rolling paddocks, all raced, good water and fencing, 2 brm character cottage, barn, yards and sand arena, 5km to Wellsford, tidy grazing block, ideal dairy runoff. $485,000 plus GST.

HUNTING OR BUSH BLOCK
176 ha, located between Te Puke and Rotorua with a good 4 brm house and ready supply of deer and pheasants. Suitable for a group of hunters or anyone wanting a weekend getaway. Offers in excess of $550,000 considered.

LAND TENDER
Okaihau Lifestyle Blocks/Runoff. Several options from 6ha upwards. Good strong country, natural water, 2 river frontage, several sheds and buildings. Tenders close 5 September 200X.

RODNEY TOMARATA
43 ha fattening and grazing block, nice balanced contour, well laid out, good water. Large 4bdrm home, native bush backdrop. HB shed, utility shed, calf rearing facilities. Top location. $650,000 + GST.

WELLSFORD
100 acres minutes to town and schools, well fenced into 30 paddocks, well raced plus 3 dams. Shed plus 2 horse pens, mare crush and 40 x 20 arena. Cute kauri cottage with sunporch. $485,000 + GST.

KAIPARA COAST HIGHWAY
First farm opportunity 23 hectares of flat pasture 4 b/r bungalow good farm building suit calf rearing etc. Tidal creek boundary with access to harbour. A lot of real estate for your dollar at $460,000 plus GST.

Fig. 16. Some typical farming enterprises for sale.

farm. Lambing and calving are carefully managed to take full advantage of spring grass growth.

For further information on farms and farming in New Zealand, contact:

New Zealand Dairy Board, Fonterra, Pastoral House, 25 The Terrace, Box 417, Wellington. Tel: 64 4 471 8300. Website: *www.nzmilk.co.nz*.

New Zealand Meat Board, Wellington. Tel: 64 4 473 9150. Website: *www.meatnz.co.nz*.

New Zealand Wool Board, Box 3225, Wellington. Tel: 64 4 472 6888. Fax: 64 4 473 7872. Website: *www.woolboard.co.nz*.

New Zealand Dairy Board, Private Bag 1992, Christchurch. Tel: 64 3 366 8416.

PAYING TAX IN NEW ZEALAND

Income tax is imposed by the New Zealand Government on income derived by a taxpayer in each income year. The tax year runs from 1 April to 31 March. The adoption of a balance date other than 31 March is approved where the business cycle makes it appropriate, or conformity with overseas balance dates is required, but the balance date is related backwards or forwards to the nearest 31 March for the purposes of applying tax legislation.

Income tax is levied and payable by every 'person' on all the income derived by that person during the income year. A 'person' is legally defined to include individuals, companies, local or public authorities and an unincorporated body of persons. Income tax is charged on most forms of income including business profits, employment income, royalties, interest, dividends and pensions. The current rates of tax are:

Income up to NZ$38,000 19.5%
Income over NZ$38,000 33%.

At present there is virtually no capital gains tax or wealth tax in New Zealand, but profits from certain speculative ventures and transactions in land or investments may in certain circumstances be liable to income tax.

A person, including a company, is assessable for income tax on all world-wide income derived while a resident of New Zealand. A **tax credit**, not exceeding the relevant New Zealand tax on the foreign source income, is allowed for foreign tax payable where such tax is similar in nature to New Zealand income tax.

A non-resident is assessable for income tax only on income with a source in New Zealand. Income with a source in New Zealand includes income derived from:

- any business wholly or partly carried on in New Zealand
- contracts made or performed in New Zealand
- service as an employee or agent in New Zealand
- the ownership of land in New Zealand
- investments in New Zealand companies or institutions
- money lent in New Zealand
- royalties deductible by the payer against New Zealand income.

Only in the first two instances is income apportionable between sources in New Zealand and sources overseas.

'Place of abode' test

The **permanent place of abode test** is the primary test of residence. An individual who is personally present in New Zealand for more than 183 days in total, over a 12 month period, will be deemed to be resident.

A person will be deemed not to be a resident in New Zealand where that person is personally absent for a period or periods in total of 325 days in any period of 12 months, provided that person is not resident in New Zealand by reason of maintaining a permanent place of abode in New Zealand, or is in the service of the New Zealand Government.

It is possible for a taxpayer to be resident in two countries. If this is the case, where a **double tax treaty** is in existence, the tie breaking provisions in the relevant tax treaty should be used to describe the taxpayer's residence for the purposes of the treaty.

Pay As You Earn (PAYE)

A pay as you earn (PAYE) system of collecting income tax is used for individuals. Income for PAYE purposes falls into two general categories – salaries/wages and other remuneration. PAYE is deducted from these at the time of payment.

At the beginning of each tax year, employees complete a tax code declaration form (IR 21). This becomes a tax deduction certificate when it is returned to the employee at the end of the financial year of when the employee leaves the job. The certificate will show the total amount of income the employee has earned, the tax deducted, any extra pay, tax-free allowances and the period of employment. The employee uses this information to complete a tax return at the end of the tax year (31 March).

Most salary and wage earners file at IR 5 tax return each year. The due date for the completed return to reach Inland Revenue is 7 June each year. You may think that because you are paying tax as you earn, you will not need to pay any extra at the end of the tax year. However, in most cases you will find that you do, unless you are in a situation where you can make deductions for allowable expenses, in which case you may be in the happy situation of being able to claim money back from the Inland Revenue.

PAYE deduction tables
Here is an extract from the weekly tax tables to give you some idea of the deductions you can expect from your weekly paypacket. Accident Compensation deductions are included.

Earnings	Tax payable (approx.)
$200	$33.63
$250	$44.78
$300	$55.93
$350	$67.08
$400	$78.23
$430	$84.92
$460	$91.61

$480	$96.07
$500	$100.53
$520	$104.99
$530	$107.22
$540	$109.45
$550	$111.68
$560	$113.91
$580	$118.37
$600	$122.83
$650	$133.98
$700	$145.13

Paying provisional tax

With business, farming and professional incomes, tax is not deducted at time of receipt but the taxpayer pays 'provisional tax'. A provisional taxpayer is any taxpayer who is liable for paying residual income tax of more than NZ$2,500. 'Residual income tax' is basically the amount of the tax assessed (including any New Zealand Superannuation surcharge), reduced by any tax deductions made from source deduction payment, tax paid overseas, tax paid by trustees, etc. Provisional tax is payable in three instalments. For taxpayers whose balance date is 31 March, payments are made in July, November and March each year. This means that you have to judge how much income you are going to make before you make it! If you underestimate you can be penalised.

Provisional taxpayers use the return form IR 3, which must reach the Inland Revenue Department by 7 July for the majority of taxpayers. Expenses are deducted from the gross business, farming or professional income and tax is calculated on the net income. Credit is given for the provisional tax already paid and for any rebates. If there is an overpayment the taxpayer will receive a refund or credit against future tax. In some situations interest is charged or paid on the under or overpayment of provisional tax.

Deductible expenses

For people in business, expenses which are incurred in producing income and are relevant and incidental to deriving that income may be claimed as a deduction from income. Expenses of a private, domestic or capital nature are not deductible.

Claiming exemptions

Income is exempt from tax in New Zealand only if provision is made in the Income Tax Act. Some of the more common items exempt from tax are: maintenance or alimony payments; some war pensions and service disability pensions; income derived from charitable and certain non-profit organisations and also lottery and raffle prizes. Rebates are deducted from the total tax payable.

Paying tax on your overseas income

New Zealand residents are liable for New Zealand tax on all income including income from overseas. Credit is allowed for any tax paid overseas, but this is limited to the New Zealand tax payable on that income.

Tax for non-residents

Non-residents are taxed in New Zealand only on income with a New Zealand source. If the income is interest, dividends or royalties, the person is liable for non-resident withholding tax (NRWT), unless the approved issuer levy is paid. NRWT is deducted by the bank or other paying institution.

Checking your residence status

For tax purposes, individuals are considered to be resident in New Zealand when they fulfil one or more of the following criteria:

♦ Individuals who have been in New Zealand for more than 183 days in any 12-month period.

♦ Individuals who have an enduring relationship with New Zealand. This means having strong financial, personal or other such ties with New Zealand. Each case is considered on its own facts.

♦ Individuals who are away from New Zealand in the service of the New Zealand government.

An individual ceases to be resident in New Zealand if they are:

♦ Absent from New Zealand for more than 325 days (about 11 months) in any 12-month period and during that time they do not have an enduring relationship with New Zealand.

Paying Goods and Services Tax

Goods and services tax (GST) is charged at 12.5% on supplies provided in New Zealand by a registered person in the course of a taxable activity.

Anyone with an annual turnover of NZ$30,000 or more must register for GST. Persons registered must charge and collect GST from their customers. GST-registered suppliers of goods and services pay GST on purchases and expenses made in the course of their business but may claim it back later. Registered persons must account for and pay all GST they have collected to the Inland Revenue Department.

GST is charged on the supply of goods and services. Some activities such as salaries and wages, hobby activities, and private sales of personal and domestic items are not taxable. GST is not charged on exempt supplies. Exempt supplies include all financial services, renting of residential property and the sale of donated goods and services by a non-profit organisation.

Paying company tax

Company taxation is also levied under the Income Tax Act, although companies in New Zealand are taxed in a different way from individual taxpayers. The main differences are that:

- A company does not get any of the special exemptions or rebates that individuals are entitled to.

- Certain dividends paid by a company are exempt in the hands of recipient companies.

- The rate of tax is different.

A company resident in New Zealand is assessable on all income, whether derived in New Zealand or elsewhere. A company is a New Zealand resident if any of the following criteria apply:

1. It is incorporated in New Zealand.
2. It has its head office in New Zealand.
3. It has its centre of management in New Zealand.
4. Control of the company by its directors is exercised in New Zealand.

Resident companies pay tax on their income at the flat rate of 33 cents in the dollar.

There are various types of companies that have specific methods of assessment. They are: overseas shipping companies, life insurance companies, mining companies and overseas contractors.

A company non-resident in New Zealand is only liable for tax on income derived from New Zealand. Non-resident companies are taxed at 38 cents in the dollar.

Dividends, interest and royalties paid to a non-resident company are subject to withholding tax at a rate specified in the double taxation agreement with the country within which the company is resident. Generally this is the final liability.

Paying tax on fringe benefits

This is a tax at 49% of the value of fringe benefits provided by an employer to an employee. It is payable by the employer on an annual or quarterly basis. Taxable fringe benefits include:

- The private use of a business motor vehicle by an employee.

- Low-interest loans.

- Free, subsidised or discounted transport and other goods and services.

- Employers' contributions to certain employees' superannuation funds and accident, sickness or death benefit funds and insurance policies.

The total fringe benefit tax collected in one recent tax year was NZ$331–393 million.

Can I hear you saying that they would tax the milk in a baby's bottle if they could get it out without the baby screaming!

Avoiding double taxation
Agreements to avoid double taxation have been entered into between New Zealand and Australia, Belgium, Canada, China, Denmark, Fiji, Finland, France, Germany, India, Indonesia, Ireland, Italy, Japan, Korea, Malaysia, Netherlands, Norway, Philippines, Singapore, Sweden, Switzerland, the United Kingdom and the United States. A visitor from one of these countries who receives income for personal services in New Zealand from an overseas employer should refer to the relevant agreement.

Bringing capital with you
Capital brought into New Zealand is free from tax, and there is no limit on the amount which may be brought into the country. However, income earned from investing that capital is taxable.

Setting up your pension

Pensions paid to New Zealand residents by countries with which New Zealand has a double tax agreement are generally exempt from tax in the country of origin and subject to tax in New Zealand. If a pension is taxed in the country of origin, credit is allowed in a New Zealand income tax assessment for the overseas tax paid, up to the amount of New Zealand tax payable on that income.

Getting family support

Family Support is provided to people with dependent children who meet income eligibility requirements. It ranges from approximately NZ$47 a week for the first child, to approximately NZ$60 a week per child for a second or subsequent child. Weekly Income New Zealand (WINZ) acts as agent for Inland Revenue in delivering Family Support to beneficiaries; income earners receive it through taxation. For further information contact – website: *www.ird.govt.nz*

BANKING AND FINANCE

Registered banks dominate the New Zealand financial system. The registration of banks in New Zealand is governed by the **Reserve Bank of New Zealand Act 1989**. This gives the Reserve Bank of New Zealand authority to register institutions providing certain criteria are met.

International banks operate as registered banks in New Zealand, either as a locally incorporated company registered bank or a branch of the parent bank.

Overview of banking

Ultimate control of banking in New Zealand lies with the

Reserve Bank of New Zealand. There are three categories of financial institutions which operate within New Zealand:

Registered banks
Most large financial institutions are registered banks. The registered banks are subject to the Reserve Bank's prudential supervision requirements. Their activities can vary from the provision of full retail and wholesale banking services, to specialised niche banking areas.

Savings banks
The traditional role of savings banks has been directed towards the collection of household savings and the provision of long-term finance on the security of residential property. The deregulation of the New Zealand banking system, which permits registered banks to undertake the functions previously performed exclusively by savings banks, has resulted in very few financial institutions being left in this category.

Other financial institutions
These consist of merchant banks and finance companies. Merchant banks operate primarily in the wholesale market and offer a wide range of financial services to corporate clients. This includes the management of investment portfolios, treasury management, underwriting of securities and advice on mergers and acquisitions. Finance companies lend primarily to individuals and businesses with security over assets purchased with the funding. Finance company receivables include consumer credit, leasing, floor plan and finance for real estate development. Finance company facilities are generally

short to medium term and at fixed interest rates.

The Reserve Bank of New Zealand (RBNZ)

The RBNZ acts as the central bank for New Zealand. As central bank the Reserve Bank is not acting in competition with the commercial banks. Its duties lie in overseeing the activities of the NZ financial markets.

The Reserve Bank's primary functions include:

◆ managing the money supply through the issue of Reserve Bank bills

◆ bank registration and prudential supervision of banks

◆ implementing the Government's monetary policy to achieve and maintain price stability

◆ providing banking services to the Government, other public sector entities, settlement banks and overseas central banks

◆ managing the foreign exchange rate

◆ advising the Government and other appropriate bodies on economic policy

◆ acting as Registrar for Government stock.

New Zealand banks

New Zealand no longer has total ownership of any bank. The main ownership is Australian with Australia New Zealand Bank, Bank of New Zealand, National Australia Bank (NZ) Ltd and Westpac Banking Corporation. The National Bank of New Zealand is British owned.

Fig. 17. A New Zealand bank cheque.

New Zealand currency

The decimal currency system was introduced in 1967. The New Zealand dollar became the monetary unit, replacing the pounds, shillings and pence system. We have $1 and $2 coins, $5, $10, $20, $50 and $100 dollar notes.

QUESTIONS AND ANSWERS

What does the Double Tax Treaty allow?

New Zealand has agreements for the avoidance of double taxation with 24 countries. The basic principle is that the country of source has the prior right to tax; the country of residence provides either a tax exemption or a tax credit.

Is the rental of property taxable?

Yes. Interest, rents and royalties form part of an individual taxpayer's income and will be assessed at the full rates. Individuals who are subject to PAYE (Pay As You Earn) may also be liable to make provisional tax payments if their residual income tax in relation to income other than source deduction payments exceeds NZ$2,500 in an income year.

UNDERSTANDING EMPLOYMENT CONDITIONS AND LAW

Signing a contract

The following is a summary of the provisions of the Contracts Act 1991:

> This Act removes monopolies over coverage and bargaining and gives employees the right to decide whether or not they wish to belong to an employees' organisation, such as a union, and the right to choose who, if anybody, they want to represent them. It aims to encourage bargaining outcomes that are relevant to the workplace and enables employers to negotiate either individual or collective employment contracts directly.

> In particular the Act provides for:

> *Freedom of association and voluntary membership of employees' organisations* – employees can determine for themselves whether or not they wish to join any form of employees' organisation, such as a union, and they are protected from undue influence in making that decision. No one, including employers, is able to compel any employee to join a union or to stop those who want to join from doing so.

> *Bargaining arrangements* – the nature of bargaining arrangements is negotiable with employers or their representative. In particular:

+ Every employer has an employment contract with every employee, either as an individual contract or as a collective contract.

- Employees and employers have the right to authorise another person, group or organisation to represent them in negotiations for an employment contract.

- Representatives must establish their authority to represent their employee or employer client and that authority must be recognised by the other party.

- Anybody may act as a representative, provided they have not been convicted of an offence punishable by five years or more in prison, within the last 20 years.

- Employees are required to formulate, together with their bargaining agent, an agreed procedure for the ratification of any settlement of a collective contract negotiated by the representative.

- Authorised representatives have rights of access to the workplace to assist the process of negotiation at any reasonable time.

- Authorised representatives may become party to an employment contract when the employer, employees and representative concerned all agree.

The bargaining arrangements give employers and employees the freedom to negotiate about what type of contract they want, and about the content of the contract, which may include any matter they choose. Thus a variety of contractual arrangements is possible, including individual or collective contracts and contracts which cover a single employer or a number of employers. Collective contracts will bind only those who agree to be included. The parties may agree to include a clause in a collective contract that new employees are permitted to join the contract, with the agreement of the new employee at the time the employment commences.

Joining a union

A new New Zealand government (Labour/Alliance) and a new President of the Council of Trade Unions (CTU), means that the falling membership of the CTU could be halted and improved on.

Mr Ross Wilson, the new President, said recently that top of his priority list was to bring all New Zealand's unions together into a single organisation. The CTU has a strength of 204,476 workers in 19 unions.

The new government has stated its intentions to restore the union's power which has steadily diminished since the Employment Contracts Act was introduced in 1991, which stated that workers were no longer forced to join unions.

Handling a personal grievance

An employee may claim a personal grievance against an employer for unjustifiable dismissal, other unjustifiable action by the employer, discrimination, sexual harassment, and duress in relation to membership or non-membership of an employees' organisation. All employment contracts must contain an effective procedure for the settlement of personal grievances. This can be the standard procedure as set out in the First Schedule to the Contracts Act 1991, or another procedure not inconsistent with the standard one. The application of the

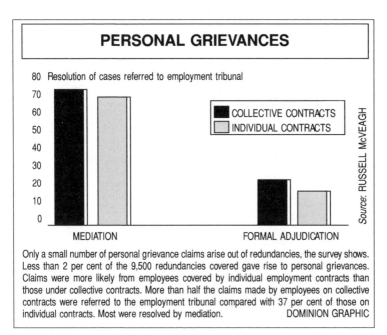

Fig. 18. Personal grievance claims.

procedures is not able to be frustrated by the deliberate lack of co-operation on the part of any person. Depending on the circumstances of each case, the remedy in the case of a proven grievance can include reimbursement for lost wages, reinstatement, and compensation for humiliation, loss of dignity and injury to feelings.

Knowing your rights

Certain other provisions, known as the Minimum Code of Employment, provide statutory minimum entitlements which apply to all employees. These include:

- Statutory minimum wage at two levels – an adult minimum wage applying to employees aged 20 and over, and a youth minimum wage applying to people age 16 to 19.

- Protection from unlawful deductions from wages.

- 11 paid public holidays where the holiday would otherwise be a working day.

- Three weeks' paid annual leave after 12 months' employment.

- Five days' special leave after six months' employment.

- Parental leave and employment protection.

- Equal pay for men and women.

- Access to procedures for resolving personal grievances and disputes.

Taking maternity leave

A woman is entitled to up to 14 weeks maternity leave, of which up to six weeks may be taken before the birth or, if agreed by the employer, a period before the adoption of a child under five years. Employers may not dismiss an employee for being pregnant or for applying for parental leave. Employees who are dismissed or given notice of dismissal for either of these reasons have a special right to go directly to the Employment Tribunal and ask for a temporary order to give them their job back, or cancel the notice of dismissal.

YOUR WORKPLACE ENVIRONMENT

Finding your niche

The old adage 'when in Rome do as the Romans do' applies in New Zealand, as it does in most places in the world.

Kiwis like to feel that new migrants fall in love with their country as soon as they set foot there. A word of advice – the last thing kiwis like to hear is 'how it is done at home, in England'. Don't complain at the kiwi differences, enjoy them!

Smokefree

Tobacco products consumption per adult has been falling to below the 1992 level to 1,579 cigarette equivalents per adult, among the lowest for developed countries. Door-step surveys of 10,000 persons showed that 27% of adults (28% of men and 26% of women) and 30% of 15–24-year-olds regularly smoked either manufactured or hand-rolled cigarettes.

Restaurants endeavour to limit smokers to a small area while cinemas and theatres are smokefree and so are all internal flights within New Zealand and all public transport systems. Most professional organisations prefer their employees not to smoke, and most office buildings are smokefree. If you happen to pass by at around 10.00 a.m., lunchtime or 3.00 p.m., you may well see groups of smokers congregated outside buildings for that life-giving puff. Some organisations will even prefer not to employ smokers, and the smokers who do work for them, especially in government departments, may be encouraged to quit the habit.

Working with computers

Most offices are highly computerised with Microsoft 6 being the most popular program because of its versatile office package, e.g. Schedulers for keeping up with diaries, and email for internal communications around organisations in the same building and in other branches.

Occupational Strain Syndrome (OSS) is a commonplace word among computer users, and most operators know of the necessary breaks and exercises that are recommended and the need for ergonomically correct desks.

Coping with accidents

A comprehensive system of accident rehabilitation and compensation insurance is provided for all New Zealanders under the Accident Rehabilitation and Compensation Insurance Act 1992. The Act has an emphasis on injury prevention, rehabilitation, risk management and compensation. It specifically acknowledges that risk management and rehabilitation are facets of injury and compensation cost control and that injury prevention, rehabilitation, risk management and compensation strategies need to be integrated.

Accident Rehabilitation and Compensation Insurance Corporation (ACC) is a form of compulsory insurance where the community as a whole, through the premiums paid, accepts responsibility for the accidents which inevitably afflict a proportion of its members. When you are employed, a proportion of the levy is paid by your employer and a proportion by you, the employee.

Note: it is not possible in New Zealand for an individual to sue for personal injury. Compensation may be sought through the ACC scheme.

Keeping safe and healthy

The Occupational Safety and Health Service is one of the five services to industry maintained by the Department of Labour. It is the primary authority responsible for setting occupational safety and health standards for all industries.

The role of the Occupational Safety and Health Service is to minimise the economic and social cost of workplace illness and injury. This involves administering and enforcing the Health and Safety in Employment Act 1992, developing occupational safety and health policy and providing health services to industry.

The service has extensive direct involvement with industry. It employs inspection staff with specific industry experience, as well as medical, engineering, scientific and technical personnel to provide advisory services. Recently its staff reported over 120,000 intervention activities in workplaces. Of these, approximately 60% of the total recorded activities related to the enforcement of legislation, while 40% comprised promotional and non-enforcement activities.

④

Education

EDUCATIONAL REFORM

In 1987 the then Government, the Labour Party, led by David Lange as Prime Minister and self-appointed Minister of Education, named a task force to review education and its administration. Since then nearly every aspect of the administration of education in New Zealand has been reviewed. The task force found that structures that had been in place for over a hundred years were in need of extensive reform as they were too centralised and too complex.

The basic aim of these reforms was to improve the quality of education for all New Zealanders, and their recommendations were that education should be based on choice, giving a range of options to both pupils and the institutions that provide education. The wishes and aims of parents and those in any education community needed to be recognised, and education needed to be culturally sensitive and provide equal opportunities and to practise good management.

THE SCHOOLS

The most significant changes were in the administration of primary and secondary schools, in partnership with teachers. Previously, this had been the responsibility of education boards and the regional offices of the

Department of Education. This responsibility was now decentralised to boards of trustees of individual schools who became accountable for meeting the objectives of their **charter** (an agreement between the school and the Minister of Education). Expenditure was made from bulk grants received from Government to run education institutions. The boards of trustees are now required to report to the Education Review Office, which reviews how well schools are meeting the objectives of their charter. The Education Review Office in turn reports directly to the Minister of Education.

Starting age

Most New Zealand students start their education at the age of five years, despite the legal starting age of six years. In 1990 100% of five-year-olds were in fact enrolled at primary school.

It will help your child integrate into the new school if you as parents make an effort to become involved. School camps, for example, take place in the summer months. The children, teachers and helpers spend 3–4 days away together at a camp, sometimes in the bush, in a relaxed situation, learning new skills. Parents are always needed to help out, in the kitchens preparing food, and also being involved in the various activities. It gives a greater understanding of the different roles the teacher is required to play.

Consider joining your own School Board of Trustees, and become involved with the committees when asked. There is no better way for you and your family to become familiar with the new lifestyle. I found that I made most of my friends from amongst the other parents I met at socials organised by the School Parent Teacher Association, and they still remain friends even though our families are now grown up.

The school curriculum

Primary/intermediate
In primary and intermediate schools the curriculum subjects cover oral and written language, reading, writing and spelling, mathematics, social studies, science, art and craft, physical and health education and music.

Intermediate school
At intermediate school the curriculum covers (in addition to the primary school curriculum) the skills of woodwork, metalwork, cooking and sewing.

Junior classes
The first three years of the child's education is spent in junior classes (Junior 1–3). Promotion is by age through the Standards 1–4 classes, and continues through Forms One and Two.

Secondary schools
Most secondary schools cater for students from Form Three to Form Seven, with average ages ranging from 13–18 years. Attendance is now compulsory until the age of 16, and education is provided free to the age of 19 years. The **core curriculum** subjects for secondary schools for Form Three to Form Four are language, social studies, mathematics, general science, health and physical education, music, art and craft, home economics. Optional

subjects may include economics, history, geography, French, Japanese and German. At Form Five to Form Seven levels, students have a wide range of subjects to choose from.

Old school tie
The old school tie attitude is still alive and well in some New Zealand private schools, despite the protests from those whose education was gained at the expense of the state system.

Private schools
Most of the private schools in New Zealand, even those previously well known and respected for their religious independence, have became part of the state education system by integration.

There are, however, still some registered private primary and secondary schools run by religious or philosophical organisations or private individuals. These schools aim to provide education that places more emphasis on religious beliefs, skills, attitudes and values.

Parents are prepared to pay for the right to educate their children in the way they believe. This attitude is not only related to religion, but also to academic and behavioural values.

Boarding schools
In New Zealand, attendance at a boarding school is not necessarily just for the rich. Because of the large rural communities, who quite often live in very isolated areas, many parents choose to send their children to boarding

schools, partly for the standard of education but also because of the need for their children to socialise. Most boarding schools also accept day pupils.

Dilworth School

A past Labour Party leader, Mike Moore, was educated at Dilworth School in Auckland. This school was founded under the terms of the will of James Dilworth. The trust deed requires 'that pupils be orphans or the sons of persons of good character and in straited circumstances'.

Correspondence School

This national school provides distance education for pre-schoolers, full-time primary and secondary pupils doing one or more subjects, and adult full-time or part-time students who wish to continue their education.

It offers over 800 courses from certificate to degree level. Subjects range from the new Bachelor of Business degree, real estate, hairdressing and agriculture, to plumbing and airline pilot's licences. There are over 350 tutors and 120 support staff, educating more than 25,000 students every year.

For further information on this form of education see the addresses at the back of this book.

Polynesian schools

Auckland is regarded now as the Polynesian capital of the world, and understandably, many schools in the Auckland area are either totally Polynesian or have a large percentage of Polynesian pupils. This means that many of the education programmes are orientated towards

Polynesian culture, and standards are modified to allow for language difficulties. Maori language and culture is taught widely in all New Zealand schools.

Education developments

The Ministry of Education has put into place a curriculum structure that established the essential learning areas, the skills needed and the values young children should learn at school. It set out the compulsory requirements from new entrants to school leavers.

The essential areas of learning are language, maths, science, technology, social sciences, the arts, health and physical well-being.

It was intended also to reinforce the values of individual and collective responsibility of honesty, reliability, respect for others and for the law, tolerance, fairness, caring and compassion, non-sexism and non-racism.

Reading problems

There are specialist teachers attached to schools throughout New Zealand who provide long-term assistance for children with serious reading problems.

Secondary school attainments

School Certificate

The School Certificate examination is taken by most pupils at the end of three years of secondary education. Except for part-time adult students, each candidate's course of study must include English, although the student is not required to sit the examination in that subject. A candidate may enter the examination in any number of subjects up to six and is credited with a grade for each subject. There are seven grades – A1 (highest), A2, B1, B2 (middle), C1, C2, and D (lowest).

School Certificate is broadly equivalent to the UK General Certificate of Secondary Education (GCSE) at grades A–E; the UK General Certificate in Education (GCE) at O level; the UK Certificate of Secondary Education (CSE) at grades one to three; and the Canadian or United States Grade 10.

Sixth Form Certificate
Sixth Form Certificate is awarded, on a single-subject basis to pupils who have satisfactorily completed a course of one year in one or more subjects. No more than six subjects can be taken. Each school candidate must study a course of English, though the candidate is not required to enter it as a Sixth Form Certificate qualification. Grades are awarded on a 1–9 scale, grade one being the highest.

Sixth Form Certificate is broadly equivalent to Canadian or United States Grade 11.

Higher School Certificate
Higher School Certificate is awarded to pupils who have been accepted for entry to Form Six and have since satisfactorily completed an advanced course of two years in at least three subjects. It is also awarded to pupils who have obtained an 'A' or 'B' Bursary qualification from the University Bursaries Examination.

Higher School Certificate, University Bursary or University Scholarship is broadly equivalent to UK GCE A levels; Canadian or United States Grade 12; in different Australian States, per 12 awards, Higher School Certificate, Senior Certificate, Matriculation, and Secondary School Certificate.

Bursary and scholarship examinations

The **University Bursaries Examination** is usually taken by secondary school pupils in Form Seven. It is a competitive examination for supplementary awards for study at a university. Subject scholarships are awarded on the basis of results in this examination and are administered by the New Zealand Qualifications Authority.

COSTS OF EDUCATION

Educating children can be costly, especially if they go to private school and then to university. Some estimates suggest it would cost NZ$132,927 to send a girl to private secondary school, independent boarding school, and to medical school. Five years' boarding is about $37,800 plus five years at a private school is around $81,625 and medical school is about $13,496 per year. Some sources suggest the costs could top $200,000 to become a doctor and as much as $50,000 to complete a Bachelor of Arts degree.

UNIVERSITIES OF NEW ZEALAND

New Zealand has seven universities: the University of Auckland, University of Waikato (Hamilton), Massey University (Palmerston Worth), Victoria University of Wellington, University of Canterbury (Christchurch), Lincoln University (Christchurch) and University of Otago (Dunedin).

Tuition fees		Per year
	NZ$	NZ$
State High		120.00*
Catholic School		8,500.00
Private School		16,325.00
– Registration fee	175.00	
– Enrolment fee	562.50	17,062.00
Boarding School		7,560.00
Exam fees – Form Five, five papers		75.00
– Form Seven, five papers		165.00

Sports gear

Sports uniform	65.00
Tennis racquet	200.00
Cricket bat	200.00
Hockey stick	200.00

Incidentals

Travel	500.00
Lunches	720.00
School trips	200.00

School clothing

Boy's basic per year	650.00
Blazer	147.00
Girl's basic per year	700.00
Blazer	140.00

Requisites

Stationery	80.00
Arts and craft	25.00
Schoolbag	50.00

Extras

Private music tuition one hour per week for 32 weeks	1,000.00
Music lesson half hour per week for 32 weeks	800.00
Instrument hire	200.00

Sports coaching

Tennis one hour per week for 32 weeks	1,200.00
Swimming one hour per week for 32 weeks	320.00

* Voluntary donation

Fig. 19. Approximate secondary education costs.

All the universities offer courses in a wide range of subjects in the arts, social sciences, commerce and science. Law and music courses are available at Auckland, Victoria, Canterbury and Otago universities. Most universities specialist in certain fields.

◆ The University of Otago offers courses in medicine, dentistry, surveying, home science, physical education and pharmacy.

◆ The University of Canterbury offers courses in forestry, engineering and fine arts.

◆ Lincoln University specialises in agriculture and horticulture and offers a wide range of commerce courses.

◆ The University of Auckland offers courses in architecture, planning, engineering, medicine, optometry and fine arts.

◆ Victoria University offers courses in architecture, public administration and social work.

◆ Massey University has courses in agriculture, horticulture, food technology and veterinary science as well as extramural tuition in a wide range of subjects for students.

Each university sets its own programmes, and each university council sets the dates for terms or semesters. All matters relating to management are the responsibility of the council of the institution which represents the interest of staff, students and the community. The council is also responsible for approving course regulations and for maintaining the equivalences of courses for degrees and other qualifications.

The university academic year runs from late February to early November each year. A university education is open to anyone meeting the entry criteria set by the individual universities.

Choosing the right university

It can be very difficult to assess which university would be the right one for you when you are living overseas, so here is a brief description of all seven to help you with this decision. The fees are for the year 2000, so it would be advisable to check they have not changed when you make your enquiries at the university of your choice.

When you have been accepted by the university of your choice you will automatically be passed on to the correct department for accommodation to be arranged.

Auckland University

The University of Auckland opened in 1883 and is the largest of New Zealand's seven universities. The University is in the centre of Auckland City, separated from the tower blocks of the central business district by historic Albert Park, where students can sit and relax in between lectures. To the south-east lie the trees and open spaces of the Auckland Domain.

The proximity of the University to the cultural and commercial amenities of New Zealand's largest city, attractive green setting and harbour views, bestow

<u>INITIAL APPLICATION FORM FOR A PLACE AT A NEW ZEALAND SCHOOL,</u>
<u>POLYTECHNIC OR COLLEGE OF EDUCATION</u>

THE PRINCIPAL

_____
(Name of Institution)

_____
(Address)
NEW ZEALAND

Dear Sir/Madam
I would like to study in New Zealand and should be grateful if you could:

a   allot me a place at your institution for_____
                                    (state year and form or programme in which you wish to study)
b advise whether you are able to arrange hostel accommodation, private board, or a place in a student flat
(indicate preference or delete if making your own arrangements for accommodation).
My personal details are as follows:

Name: _____
        (Family name)   (Personal names)
Address:_____

Telephone number: _____   Subjects being studied this year (indicate
                                          which subjects are taught in English):
Date of birth: _____   _____

Sex: _____   _____

Citizenship_____   _____
                                          I have made arrangements for accommodation
Present school and class: _____   with the following host (state if no accommo-
                                          dation arranged).
_____   _____

_____   _____
Previous Schools attended: I would like to study the following subjects at your
_____   institution (for secondary school students only)

_____   _____

First Language: _____   _____
                                          When I leave secondary school I intend to study
Number of years studying English: _____   further for (state the qualifications aimed at, e.g.
                                          Bachelor of Arts):
Examination results (attach certified copies   _____
of certificates for any public English tests
attempted and ALL public and school exam- _____
inations taken in the two previous years):   I attach a testimonial from the principal of my
_____   present school (to include comments on general
                                          ability, competence in English and ability to adjust
_____   to a new environment).

(Applicant's signature)_____   (Date) _____

Fig. 20. Applying for a place in education.

advantages enjoyed by few inner-city campuses anywhere.

Student accommodation
University halls of residence are available from NZ$150 to $185 per week, including two meals per day, but many students prefer to share private flats or houses, and there is a large selection of rented accommodation available at reasonable rates. Here students can expect to pay NZ$87 to $150 per week, plus a share of the food, telephone and electricity costs.

For further information contact the Accommodation and Conference Centre, 14–16 Mount Street, Auckland. Tel: 64 9 373 7599 ext 7691. Fax: 64 9 373 7552. Website: *www.auckland.ac.nz* or Auckland University International Office at Private Bag 92019. Tel: 64 9 373 7513. Fax: 64 9 373 7405. Email: *international@auckland.ac.nz*.

Lincoln University
Lincoln first opened its doors to students in 1878 as a small school of agriculture. A few years later Lincoln become Canterbury Agricultural College and a degree course in agriculture was added to the curriculum.

In 1961, Lincoln became a University College with close ties to the University of Canterbury and in 1990 it received independent university status. Lincoln University thus became New Zealand's seventh and newest university.

The University is situated in rural surroundings, 20km from Christchurch. The township of Lincoln is close by, and has a good range of shops and services.

Auckland University: Approximate International Student Fees

Degree	No. of years	Tuition fee NZ$
Faculty of Architecture		
Bachelor of Architecture Studies (BAS)	3	17,500
Bachelor of Architecture Studies (BArch)	2	17,500
Bachelor of Property (BProp)	3	12,500
Bachelor of Planning (BPlan)	4	15,000
Faculty of Arts		
Humanities – non laboratory based	minimum of 3	10,000
Social Sciences, Languages	minimum of 3	12,500
Performance, Geography, Psychology	minimum of 3	15,000
Faculty of Commerce		
Bachelor of Commerce (BCom)	minimum of 3	12,500
Faculty of Engineering		
Bachelor of Engineering (BE)	4	17,500
Faculty of Fine Art		
Bachelor of Fine Art (BFA)	4	15,000
Faculty of Law		
Bachelor of Law (LLB)	4	–
Law 1 (Legal System course for law intermediate)	–	see notes
Law 2 (Years 2-4)	–	12,500

Notes:
An LLB is made up two parts; Part 1 is made up of the Legal Systems paper and a variety of other subjects from the university's general degree programmes. The cost for the first year therefore depends on the choice of papers from the supporting degree. Part 2 only starts if the student has been admitted into this stage; the selection is based on academic merit.

Faculty of Music		
Bachelor of Music – Performance (BMus)	3	15,000
Faculty of Science		
Bachelor of Science (BSc)		
– Math, Computing, Information Science	3	12,500
– Other	3	15,000
Auckland Consortium for Theological Education (ACTE)		
Bachelor of Theology (BTheol)	3	10,000
Interfaculty Degree		
Bachelor of Technology	4	Yr 1-3 15,000
		Yr 4 17,500

Conjoint Degrees
In addition to the above listed single degrees it is possible to combine some of them.

Postgraduate courses
The Auckland University offers a wide range of postgraduate degrees and diplomas. For further information contact the International Office, University of Auckland, PO Box 92019, Auckland.
Email: *international@auckland.ac.nz*

Fig. 21. Auckland University tuition fees.

Lincoln now offers a wide range of single or multi-disciplinary research opportunities and has a tradition of commitment to its postgraduate students. Staff have expertise in the supervision and management of post-graduate programmes in commerce and management, primary production and natural resources, science and technology, and social sciences.

Close links with resource-based industries, government and private organisations and other bodies ensure that Lincoln University research programmes are relevant to society's needs. Students may receive advice and some supervision from skilled people employed by other organisations, and funding is available sometimes for collaborative programmes.

Farms
The University has five farms, as well as an orchard and a Horticultural Research Unit. The Research, Dairy and Arable Farms, together with the Horticultural Research Unit and the Sheep Breeding Unit, are adjacent to the campus.

Most field research work is done on the Research Farm and the Horticultural Research Area, but larger farm trials are carried out on the other units. Land and animals for research are allocated by a committee so that, as far as possible, every request is adequately accommodated.

Student accommodation
Accommodation is available in the halls of residence at a cost of about NZ$168 per week – this includes two meals a day. Self-catering halls of residence start from $90 per

Lincoln University: Approximate International Tuition Fees	
Undergraduate Courses	*NZ$*
B.C.M, B.Com (Tourism), B.Com (H & I.M), B.C.M, B.Com(H)	11,500
B.Com (Tran), B.Com (VPM), B.R.S, B.Com, B.R.S, B.R.M, B.Soc	11,500
B.Com (Ag), B.Com (Forestry), B.Com (Hort)	12,000
B.Agr, B.E, B.Hort, B.L.A, B.Sc	14,500
Cert F.S, Cert Nat. Res	13,000
Cert Wool	4,875
Honours	
B.P.R & T.M, B.Soc.Sc, B.R.S	11,500
B.Com	13,500
B.Agr.Sc, B.Hort.Sc, B.Sc	14,500
Undergraduate Diplomas	
Dip.F.M, Dip.Hort.Mgt.	13,500
Postgraduate Diplomas	
P.G.Dip.Agr.Eng, P.G.Dip.Agr.Sc, P.G.Dip.Appl.Sc	15,000
P.G.Dip.Hort.Sc, P.G.Dip.Soc.Sc, P.G.Dip.V&O	15,000
Masters Degrees and PhDs	
Animal and Food Sciences	28,500
Applied Management and Computing	17,000
Commerce	13,500
Environmental Management and Design	22,000
Human Sciences	16,000
Soil, Plant and Ecological Sciences	28,500
Note: All fees are subject to change.	

Fig 22. Lincoln University tuition fees.

week, which includes electricity, heating and telephone calls. Student flats start from $78 per week – this does not include electricity, heating and telephone calls. Family units are priced from $165 per week and also do not include electricity, heating and telephone calls. For further information contact the Accommodation Services, PO Box 84, Lincoln University, Canterbury, NZ. Tel: 64 3 325 3620.

Fax: 64 3 325 2960. Email: *taylor@lincoln.ac.nz*.

University of Waikato, Hamilton

Waikato University was established in 1964. There are currently nearly 10,000 students enrolled, including 250 international students. The spacious and picturesque campus is situated 3km from Hamilton City. Its facilities include well-equipped modern teaching buildings and laboratories which are grouped in a central academic area on an attractively landscaped campus covering 64 hectares. The campus also boasts a new recreation centre, extensive sporting grounds and a swimming pool.

The University region is steeped in Maori history and it includes four of the major tribal confederations: Tainui, Te Arawa, Mataatua, and Tairawhiti.

Student accommodation
There are five halls of residence costing roughly NZ$161 per week, per room – this includes three catered meals. Older students usually prefer to share a flat or house with other students, and there is a range of houses to choose from such as three- to five-bedroom houses on their own plot of land, or two-storied units/apartment blocks. You can expect to pay between $95 and $125 per week, per room; additional costs include electricity, telephone and food. For further information contact the International Students Office, University of Waikato, Private Bag 3105, Hamilton, NZ. Tel: 64 7 838 4439. Fax: 64 7 838 4269.

Otago University, Dunedin

Founded in 1869, the University of Otago is recognised internationally as a leader in many areas of research, and has first-class status as a teaching institution. The campus is one of the most beautiful and closely knit in New Zealand. The waters of the Leith River meander through the grounds, which contain an attractive blend of historic and modern buildings. The University is ringed by the halls of residence and these are surrounded by the distinctive Victorian and Edwardian houses and modern flats which are used for student accommodation. The University is only five minutes from the centre of Dunedin.

Student accommodation
Accommodation is available in the halls of residence at a cost of about NZ$160 per week. Private board is also available for around $110 per week. Sharing a house or flatting on present room rates will cost about $85 per week, plus food, electricity and power. For further information regarding the University, its courses and accommodation contact Otago University at PO Box 56, Dunedin, NZ. Tel: 64 3 479 8344. Fax: 64 3 479 8367. Email: *international@otago.ac.nz*.

Canterbury University, Christchurch
Canterbury is located in Christchurch, the largest city in South Island. On the coastal edge of the Canterbury plains, the city is close to both the sea and mountains. Christchurch is commonly referred to within New Zealand as the 'Garden City' and is surrounded by beautiful parks, beaches, reserves and is renowned for its recreational and cultural facilities.

The University's modern and well-equipped facilities spread across a spacious suburban campus, close to the city centre. The campus buildings have a floor area of

155,000 square metres in a park-like setting of 76 hectares and are home to over 12,500 students. The University of Canterbury offers a wide range of subjects in a variety of flexible degree structures.

Student accommodation

First year undergraduate students will be assisted to find accommodation in private homes with New Zealand families (private board). There is no permanent university accommodation for overseas students, but it is possible to stay in the Ilam Flats for four weeks. The Manager may be able to extend this time during the period June to November to allow students time to find their own accommodation.

Only a limited number of students can be given the initial four weeks in the Ilam Flats, so early arrangements are essential. Accommodation for spouses is only available in Ilam Flats from mid-November to mid-February. It is important to apply for accommodation well in advance as you may have to wait a month or more for vacancies. To make your reservations please contact The Manager, Ilam Flats, University of Canterbury, Private Bag 4800, Christchurch. Tel: 64 3 348 3441. Bookings will only be accepted if you have been accepted for the course.

Accommodation in private board may cost in the region of NZ $160 per week. Private flats may cost up to $100 per week, depending on the number sharing the flat. This does not include food, telephone and electricity.

University of Canterbury

Application for Admission *ad eundem statum*

1. Mr
   Mrs
   Miss   First name(s)   Surname or Family Name
   Ms

2. (a) Date of Birth .... (b) Place of birth .... (c) Married or Single ....

3. (a) Country of Citizenship .... (b) Country of Permanent Residence ....

4. **(a) Degree course to be taken.** .... **(b) Major subject** ....

5. I hereby apply for admission to the University of Canterbury *ad eundem statum*: *(Cross out the lines which do not apply)*

   either   (a) at entrance level

   or   (b) with credits towards the proposed degree course to be taken

   or   (c) with the status of graduate
                   (Degree) .... (University) ....

6. **EVIDENCE:** I attach the following certificates (originals or certified copies) in support of my application.

   ....

   ....

   CERTIFIED COPIES: If copies of documents are sent, each copy must be certified as a true copy by a Justice of the Peace, Solicitor, Notary Public or an official of the institution that issued the original document and must bear the official stamp of that person. Uncertified photo copies will not be accepted.

7. **FEE:** I enclose the fee of $N.Z.60 (including G.S.T.) (or sufficient of some other currency to yield this amount)

   Method of Payment .... (e.g. cheque, money order, bank draft, etc.)

8. **COMPETENCE IN ENGLISH:** If applicable, complete the appropriate section.
   I have sat IELTS/TOEFL on .... I shall be sitting IELTS/TOEFL on ....

9. **CERTIFICATE OF IDENTITY:**

   I ....
          First Name(s)   Surname or Family Name

   of ....
          town   country

   .... hereby certify that I am the person named in the certificates or statements listed above
   (occupation)

   Dated this .... Day of .... 20 ....

   SIGNATURE   SIGNATURE
   OF APPLICANT ....   OF WITNESS ....

   Address ....   Address ....

   ....

This form should be sent with the other documents to:
THE REGISTRAR, UNIVERSITY OF CANTERBURY, PRIVATE BAG 4800, CHRISTCHURCH, NEW ZEALAND.
A separate application must be made for enrolment. If your application for admission is successful you will be sent an application form

Fig. 23. Application for admission to the University of Canterbury.

For further information on Canterbury University apply to the Registrar, University of Canterbury, Private Bag 4800, Christchurch. Tel: 64 3 366 7001. Fax: 64 3 364 2999.

Approximate tuition fees	Undergraduate	Postgraduate
Arts	$12,000	$15,500
Commerce	$13,000	$15,000
Science	$16,000	$18,000
Engineering	$18,500	$20,000
Forestry Science	$17,000	$20,000
Law	$13,000	$15,500

Tuition fees paid in advance of enrolment will be refunded if the student does not enrol.

Victoria University, Wellington
Victoria University is situated on an imposing 16 hectare site overlooking the capital and its harbour. It lies within easy walking distance of the city centre, which can be reached by the cable car, and the National Library and Parliament buildings (the 'Beehive').

Established in 1899 Victoria was until 1962 a College of the University of New Zealand. With a faculty structure similar to that of many British universities, it offers both traditional academic disciplines within a flexible degree structure and a range of specialist courses. Recently there has been a major expansion in areas such as management, marketing and information systems, Asian and Pacific languages, Maori studies, English as a foreign language, drama, public and social policy and criminology.

Victoria University: Approximate International Tuition Fees

Degree	No. of years	Tuition fee NZ$
Faculty of Architecture		
First Year Architecture	1	15,000
Bachelor of Architecture Studies	4	17,000
Master of Architecture Studies	1	19,500
Faculty of Arts		
Bachelor of Arts	minimum of 3	10,750
Bachelor of Arts with Honours	1	13,000
Master of Arts (Thesis)	1	13,000
Faculty of Commerce		
Bachelor of Commerce (BCA)	minimum of 3	12,000
Bachelor of Commerce with Honours	minimum of 3	15,000
Faculty of Engineering		
Bachelor of Engineering (BE)	4	12,000
Faculty of Fine Art		
Bachelor of Fine Art (BFA)	4	15,000
Faculty of Law		
Bachelor of Law (LLB)	4	11,000
Bachelor of Law with Honours	1	13,000
Master of Law	1	15,000
Diploma/ Certificate in Law	1	10,700
PhD Law	3	15,000
Faculty of Music		
Bachelor of Music	3	13,000
Bachelor of Music with Honours	1	13,000
Master of Music	1	16,500
Faculty of Science		
Bachelor of Science (BSc)	3	15,000
Bachelor of Science with Honours	1	16,500
Master of Science	2	20,000

Note: The above fees are subject to change.
For further information, Website: *www.vuw.ac.nz*.

Fig. 24. Victoria University tuition fees.

The campus provides opportunities to take part in a variety of activities, as well as welfare and support services. As a university within a city, its students also have easy access to the capital's many amenities.

Student accommodation
There are three halls of residence that offer full-time accommodation – these are very popular with first year students. The cost starts around NZ$180 per week.

Flatting is also very popular. Shared flats can cost anywhere from $90 per week not including living expenses. Private board is available, and the cost usually includes two meals per day with three at the weekend – from around $165 per week. Further information can be obtained from the International Students office, Victoria University, PO Box 600, Wellington. Tel: 64 4 471 5350.

Massey University, Palmerston North
Founded in 1927, Massey Agricultural College was named after a former Prime Minister of New Zealand, William Ferguson Massey. The College offered degree programmes leading to Bachelor and Master of Agricultural Science and students could also enrol in a variety of shorter courses in farm management and technology. Courses in horticulture were introduced after the war.

Massey College became a University in early 1964. Massey is the leading provider of extramural or 'university correspondence' courses in the southern hemisphere.

Massey is now New Zealand's second largest tertiary institution. It occupies a 40 hectare campus. The University farms 5,250 hectares of land of which 900 hectares surround the campus. This area has a full range of agricultural enterprises including dairy farms, sheep and cattle farms, a cropping unit, orchard and a deer facility. As well as operating as commercial enterprises the farms are an extension of the lecture theatre, providing facilities for student demonstrations and research.

Student accommodation
The University has halls of residence with places for a limited number of students. In recent years demand has often exceeded supply so an application must be made. These are available from the University Liaison Officer or Residential Services Office. The closing date for applications is towards the end of October.

A single room costs roughly NZ$160 per week and includes breakfast and an evening meal. Accommodation outside the campus can be found within the surrounding area of Palmerston North. For further information contact the Registrars Office, Massey University, Palmerston North, NZ. Website: *www.massey.ac.nz*.

STUDENT BUDGETING
If you have a typical student's income and costs, you will spend most of your money on accommodation and food. Use the budget form below to work out your budget. The sample budgets are based on Victoria University, and so could change with other universities.

An approximation of living costs
Halls of residence

$	185.00	Per week for a single room
$	150.00	Per week for a shared room
$	200.00	Placement fee and Activities fee
$	30.00	Per semester for communal laundry facilities
$	110.50	Per semester for uncovered off-street parking
$	15.00	Per semester for a lockable bike shed

Flatting

$	78.00	Per week, per room sharing with 4–6 people
$	156.00	Placement fee
$	10.00	Per week for telephone
$	15.00	Per week for electricity
$	25.00	Per week for transport

University costs

$	167.00	Student services fee
$	15,000.00	Tuition (approx.)
$	50.00	Textbooks per semester
$	310.00	Insurance travel, health, personal, per semester

Now fill in the form which follows to see what your budget will be.

How to prepare your budget
1. Work out your income for the academic year:

	INCOME
Savings from vacation work	$
Income tax refund	$
Other income: interest, dividends, trust loans	$
Gifts, allowances from parents/relatives	$
Student allowances	$
A or B bursary award	$
Other scholarship or awards	$
Income part-time jobs	$
Total income for academic year	$

2. Work out your likely expenses for the academic year:

Tuition fees	$
Students' Association fee	$
Student services levy	$
Textbooks, stationery	$
Hall of residence deposit	$
Hall heating and linen charge	$
Hall residents fee	$
Bond for flat and agent's fee	$
Deposit: gas, electricity, phone	$
Total fixed expenses	$ ____

Sample budget 'A'

This sample given below is based on minimum costs. The headings are the usual area of student expenses. There is a possibility that these costs will change from year to year.

This budget assumes that a student has a shared room in the halls of residence for the 32 weeks of the academic year, not including the May and August vacations or mid-year break.

Weekly expenses	per week $	32 weeks $
Hall board	185.00	5,920.00
Snacks	20.00	640.00
Entertainment, postage etc	30.00	960.00
Subtotal	235.00	7,520.00

Fixed expenses	
Students services fee	167.00
Tuition fee (approx.)	15,000.00
Building levy	56.00
Resources fee	210.00
Textbooks, stationery etc	400.00
Hall deposit	200.00
Subtotal	16,033.00

Periodic payments (not all essential)

Insurance	310.00
Holidays	500.00
Sports, recreation, hobbies	170.00
Subscriptions for clubs etc	40.00
Clothes, footwear etc	500.00
Health: dentist, doctor	300.00
Subtotal	1,820.00

Approximate total expenditure	25,373.00

Sample budget 'B'

This sample budget is based on minimum costs, assuming that a student shares a flat with at least two others for an average of 37 weeks, and that the flat is given up or sub-let over the summer vacation.

Weekly expenses	*Per week $*	*37 weeks $*
Rent	120.00	4,440.00
Food (communal)	60.00	2,220.00
Lunches, snacks etc	35.00	1,295.00
Telephone rental (share of)	10.00	370.00
Electricity (share of)	15.00	555.00
Local travel (academic year only)	25.00	925.00
Entertainment, postage, toiletries	30.00	1110.00
Subtotal	295.00	10,915.00

Fixed expenses (see example 'A')		16,033.00
Periodic payments (see example 'A')		1,820.00

Approximate total expenditure	28,768.00

Continuing education

All seven universities have centres for continuing educa-tion. A typical university education centre has a director-in-charge and a staff of lecturers in a range of academic disciplines. The courses are conducted by various methods – lectures, study conferences, seminars, school of varying lengths (both residential and non-residential) and correspondence courses. Most universities continue to offer the general public substantial continuing education programmes in the liberal studies area. There has been, however, a significant increase in programmes designed for specialist groups, especially occupational. Some of these are national in scope.

North Island

University of Auckland, Private Bag 92019, Auckland. Tel: 64 9 373 7513. Fax: 64 9 373 7405.
Website: *www.auckland.ac.nz*

University of Waikato, Private Bag 3105, Hamilton. Tel: 64 7 856 2889. Fax: 64 7 838 4269.
Website: *www.waikato.ac.nz*

Massey University, Private Bag 11–122, Palmerston North. Tel: 64 6 356 9099. Fax: 64 6 350 5603.
Website: *www.massey.ac.nz*

Victoria University of Wellington, Box 600, Wellington. Tel: 64 4 472 1000. Fax: 64 4 499 4601.
Website: *www.vuw.ac.nz*

South Island

Canterbury University, Private Bag 4800, Christchurch. Tel: 64 3 366 7001. Fax: 64 3 364 2999.
Website: *www.canterbury.ac.nz*

Lincoln University, PO Box 94, Canterbury. Tel: 64 3 325 2811. Fax: 64 3 325 2965.
Website: *www.lincoln.ac.nz*

Otago University, PO Box 56, Dunedin. Tel: 64 3 479 1100. Fax: 64 3 474 1607.
Website: *www.otago.ac.nz*

TRAINING AT A POLYTECHNIC COLLEGE

Over recent decades vocational education and training has moved away from the secondary to the continuing education sector, with training formerly provided by technical high schools now provided for by polytechnics. Polytechnics offer a diverse range of vocational and professional programmes and cover an increasing number of various levels of specialisation.

There are 25 Polytechnics in New Zealand. They are Northland Polytechnic, Unitech-Institute of Technology, Auckland Institute of Technology, Manukau Polytechnic, Waikato Polytechnic, Bay of Plenty Polytechnic, Waiariki Polytechnic, Tairawhiti Polytechnic, Hawke's Bay Polytechnic, Wairarapa Community Polytechnic, Taranaki Polytechnic, Wanganui Regional Polytechnic, Manawatu Polytechnic, Whitireia Polytechnic, Central Institute of Technology, The Open Polytechnic of New Zealand, Hutt Valley Polytechnic, Wellington Polytechnic, Nelson Polytechnic, Tai Poutini Polytechnic, Christchurch Polytechnic, Aoraki Polytechnic, Otago Polytechnic, Telford Polytechnic and Southland Polytechnic. For further details about these organisations write to the Association of Polytechnics in New Zealand, 10344, Wellington. Tel: 04 471 1162. Fax: 04 473 2350.

CENTRAL INSTITUTE OF TECHNOLOGY (CIT)

Over 5,000 students a year from all over New Zealand go to the Central Institute of Technology to study the wide range of courses offered. Most courses fall into the areas of health and science, management or engineering, including many unique sources such as dental technology, podiatry, computer and software engineering, interior design, medical radiation therapy and embalming and funeral directing. An international flavour is added to the campus by CITEC Training Solutions, a wholly-owned subsidiary of CIT that manages training programmes for overseas students, some coming from as far away as Hong Kong, Switzerland and Pakistan.

A variety of qualifications are offered including bachelor degrees, diplomas, awards, certificates and New Zealand certificates. Studies can take from a few weeks to four years full-time study. Most courses are available to school-leavers, although some educational prerequisites are required for some courses.

> *Note*: experienced professional people can acquire new skills at intensive short courses and seminars, and people seeking 'second chance' education can enrol in foundation or 'bridging' courses leading to either employment or further study.

The campus is located in Heretaunga in Upper Hutt, Wellington. For further information write to:

Central Institute of Technology, Somme Road, Heretaunga, Upper Hutt, Wellington. Tel: 64 4 527 6398. Fax: 64 4 527 6359.

ADVANCED VOCATIONAL AWARDS AND TRADE CERTIFICATION BOARD EXAMINATIONS

The New Zealand Qualifications Authority has responsibility for Trade Certification and Advanced Vocational

Awards, including the curriculum and examination of all three-stage technician certificates, five-stage New Zealand Certificate Courses and the examination of candidates sitting trade certificate or advanced trade certification qualifications. The New Zealand Diploma offers an advanced qualification for students who have completed a New Zealand Certificate in the same or a related area.

Attending technician courses

Both the five-year New Zealand Certificate and the three-year technician certificate are offered in a variety of vocational areas. New Zealand Certificate courses are part-time and require regular study at day-release and evening classes or intermittent periods of full-time study block courses.

Most subjects may be studied through the Open Polytechnic of New Zealand. Students may also study selected New Zealand Certificate courses full-time at a polytechnic. All New Zealand Certificates require students to complete not less than three years of suitable work experience.

Attending trade courses

Training for trade qualifications account for a significant percentage of the work of polytechnics. The New Zealand Qualifications Authority has approved a wide range of trade courses and prescriptions under which assessment, examination and certification are conducted. Education and training requirements for the various trades are listed in the respective prescriptions. They specify a mix of theory and practical training, to be obtained through education providers and through on-job experience. The completion of prescribed requirements leads to the issue of Trade Certificate and Advanced Trade Certificate qualifications.

5

Housing and Living

BUYING A HOUSE

Whilst writing this book my family and I rented a house in a Wellington suburb. It was high on a hilltop with delightful views of the surrounding hills and with a glimpse of Wellington Harbour. The views were great and so we thought was the house, for which we paid NZ$220 per week. It had a very generous sized lounge, with big windows facing the Harbour. It was 'U' shaped with a dining/kitchen facing the hills (at the back of the house).

The large attractive bathroom had all-day sun, with a separate toilet. The back bedroom which was only a single also saw the sun for most of the day, and overlooked the hills at the back. The middle (slightly larger) bedroom only saw the sun in the early morning and the large main bedroom had a small window that only caught the early morning sun, with a large window overlooking the Harbour which was totally sunless. The warmest place in this house was undoubtedly the bathroom, and on cold days I could often be found sitting in there warming myself! My eldest daughter had even tried it out for saxophone practice!

As a result of this experience, I would always check now to see how the sun affected a property.

The windows in this house were very badly warped and seldom fitted properly. This meant that when the wind blew – and that was fairly often – the curtains would billow without the windows being opened!

Also, the house wasn't insulated. Consequently the rooms that saw the sun only briefly were cold and damp-smelling, especially in the winter, with mildew on the walls.

Never mind the view!

During the two years I sold real estate (houses only) I viewed literally hundreds of houses, and here are a few very important tips to bear in mind when you are buying:

- Is the house insulated?

- Does it face the sun – never mind the view!

- Does it have heating? (Very important if you are buying in the cooler areas, i.e. from Auckland south.)

- If you are buying in Wellington, especially, ensure that it isn't in the path of the prevailing wind, never mind the view!

- Look for damp and mouldy patches inside and outside.

- Make sure that building permits have been obtained where alterations or additions have been made.

- A property which lies below the level of the road is not always desirable.

- Make sure that the house isn't sheltered from the sun by the surrounding hills – a great possibility in Wellington.

- Check that all windows open and close properly.

- Check the house foundations, especially older houses built on piles. (Engage a builder or surveyor to check this out for you.)

- If it has a weatherboard or wooden exterior, check to see that there are no rotten patches – a poke with a pencil will show weaknesses. (Again, it would be advisable to get an expert to check this out.)

- Make sure that the house is *above* ground level. A house that is level with the footpaths will probably let rain in under floors.

- Wellington has the most amazing selection of houses dotted around the numerous hills. Some of them appear to be hanging from sky hooks! Make sure they are not! A Building Inspector from the City Council will check out the foundations and retaining walls for you.

Rainy days are best!

Whilst selling real estate I acquired a client, a dear old lady, who had been looking for the 'right' place for some time, but was in no hurry. I rang her one day with news of a very nice property. The day was fine and sunny, a real estate agent's dream, and I conveyed the good news.

To my disappointment she said the day wasn't 'right'. I enquired why, and she said she would only go looking on rainy days! I was surprised at this response, and asked why. She told me that lots of houses looked good on warm, sunny days, but it took a special place to look good on a grey, wet day! I rang her the next 'bad' day, and along she came dressed in her gumboots and wet weather gear!

LIVING IN NEW ZEALAND

PROPERTY MARKET

NORTHERN

Whangarei $160,000: Huge home, multi-storey, mod. 3-bed, lounge, dining, conservatory, ensuite. Handy amenities.

Auckland-Avondale $295,000: Luxury home, 4-bed, double garage, internal access, open plan living.

Ak-Mt Albert $390,000: Wonderful family home on large section. 3-4 beds. large living, great location.

Ak-City $300,000: Fully furnished 1-bed and carpark. hotel managed. north-west corner. Offers over.

Ak-Parnell $475,000: Multi-level contemporary style property, quiet bushy location. 4-beds, office, 2-baths.

Ak-Remuera $610,000: Northern slopes, flat section, prime, private and peaceful location. 3-beds + sunroom, spacious living.

Tauranga $395,000: Waterfront home. 3-bed. study, ensuite, pathway to beach.

Mt Maunganui $299,000: Quality home, 4-bed, sep. lounge, ensuite, many extras here.

Rotorua $230,000: 4-bed, sep. lounge, dining, study, inground thermal pool.

Hamilton $212,000: Split level 4-bed, sep. lounge, dining/kitchen, inground pool.

CENTRAL

Hastings $295,000: 3-bed, sep. lounge, conservatory, executive home with great views. Self contained flat.

Napier $320,000: Country living almost in town. Some 4.72 hectares of land with a private, 4-bed Lockwood home. Swimming pool.

New Plymouth $180,000: Single level villa, circa around 1918, partially restored, indoor/outdoor flow. 3-4 beds, close amenities.

Wanganui $235,000: College estate. multi-storey, a grand home offering plenty. 3-beds, sep. lounge, sep. dining, office, 2 sep. toilets.

Palmerston North $235,000: Split level timber home, 3-beds, sep. lounge, large section, deck fenced.

Lower Hutt $275,000: Modern split level home, 3-beds, lounge/dining, lovely setting amongst quality residences. Master ensuite, harbour views.

Wellington-Hataitai $380,000: Multi-storey contemporary house, 4-beds, sep. lounge, study, conservatory, outstanding family home.

Wgtn-Khandallah $725,000: Multi-storey, both formal and informal living, indoor/outdoor entertaining, family room, big games room, 5-beds.

SOUTH

Nelson $348,000: 3-bed, sep. lounge. sep. dining, study, ensuite, close city centre with great views.

Blenheim $269,000: Fantastic view. great street appeal, lots of features, 2-beds, rumpus/family, sep. lounge & dining.

Christchurch-Avonhead $319,000: Immaculate sun catcher, two storey house with many extras. Beside stream. 4-beds, 2 lounges.

Chch-Fendalton $790,000: Gracious family home with original interior detailing. 4 living areas, stream boundary. 5-beds, ensuite.

Chch-Halswell $207,000: 3-bed. bungalow, tastefully done throughout, sunny living, nice kitchen and bathroom.

Timaru $285,000: Near new executive home, absolute impeccable presentation, 3-4 beds (ensuite), courtyard.

Queenstown $995,000: A lovely home in Tuscany style with five bedrooms and 2 bathrooms, triple garage. Two acres.

Queenstown $395,000: 3-bed. home nestled amongst a mature cottage style garden, large outdoor living with unsurpassed lake views.

Dunedin-Waverley $175,000: Modern 4-bed. family home situated on beautifully landscaped section. All day sun.

Dunedin-Mornington $89,500: Newly renovated home, 2-beds, modern kitchen, spacious dining and living.

Invercargill $399,000: Prime city real estate. One of the landmarks, beautiful brick character mansion with ballroom, Would be over $1 million anywhere else. 6-beds. 5 sep. toilets.

Fig. 25. Houses for sale – typical examples.

Who stole the third bedroom?

There have been many cases of people buying a house only to put it straight back on the market again. This may sound strange, but when people don't take the time to visit a property more than once, before buying, errors of judgment can occur.

One couple were in such a hurry to buy, the husband being a very busy man, that they only saw the property once and then bought it. Were their faces red when they couldn't find the all important third bedroom, as it was only a two-bedroomed house!

Single and double storey

Houses can be single or double storey. Double storey houses quite often have garages on the ground floor, with a laundry, rumpus room (games room), possibly a workshop and maybe one bedroom. All the living and sleeping areas are on the first floor.

- If the advertisement just says 'house for sale' with no mention of two floors, then you can expect this to be a bungalow, i.e. with everything on one floor.

- Units are semi-detached, or can be found in blocks of four or more, single or double storey, on small sections.

- Townhouses can be one or two storey, free standing or attached by a garage on a small section. Some real estate agents advertise townhouses as being 'joined' (semi-detached). Townhouses are usually slightly more upmarket than units.

AGREEMENT FOR SALE AND PURCHASE OF REAL ESTATE

FOURTH EDITION MAY 1991

This form is approved by the Real Estate Institute of New Zealand and by the New Zealand Law Society.

DATE:

VENDOR:

PURCHASER:

Address of property:

Legal description: *Estate:* FREEHOLD (unless otherwise described)

Area   *Lot*   *DP:*   *CT:*

Purchase Price: $ *(including chattels at $*

Delete one of these: Plus GST (if any).   OR   **Inclusive of GST** (if any)

If neither is deleted the purchase price includes GST (if any).

Deposit: $

Balance of purchase price to be paid or satisfied as follows:

LSP date: **GST date:**

Possession date: **Interest rate for late settlement**   **% p.a.**

Special conditions: *(if any)*   **SEE OVERLEAF**

Fig. 26. Agreement for sale and purchase of real estate.

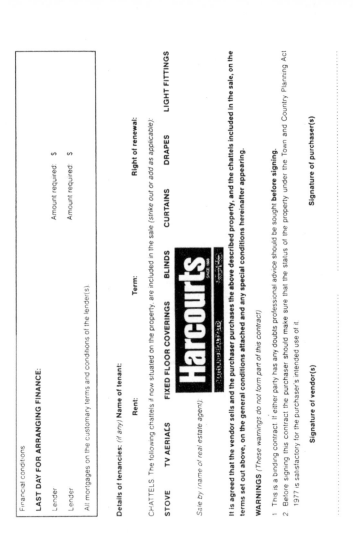

Financial conditions

LAST DAY FOR ARRANGING FINANCE:

Lender   Amount required: $

Lender   Amount required: $

All mortgages on the customary terms and conditions of the lender(s).

Details of tenancies: *(if any)* **Name of tenant:**

Rent: **Term:**   **Right of renewal:**

CHATTELS The following chattels if now situated on the property, are included in the sale *(strike out or add as applicable)*:

STOVE   **TV AERIALS**   **FIXED FLOOR COVERINGS**   **BLINDS**   **CURTAINS**   **DRAPES**   **LIGHT FITTINGS**

Sale by (name of real estate agent):

Harcourts
SINCE 1888

It is agreed that the vendor sells and the purchaser purchases the above described property, and the chattels included in the sale, on the terms set out above, on the general conditions attached and any special conditions hereinafter appearing.

WARNINGS *(These warnings do not form part of this contract)*

1 This is a binding contract. If either party has any doubts professional advice should be sought **before signing.**

2 Before signing this contract the purchaser should make sure that the status of the property under the Town and Country Planning Act 1977 is satisfactory for the purchaser's intended use of it.

Signature of vendor(s)   **Signature of purchaser(s)**

....

....

Fig. 26. Continued.

Villas

The older style homes, which are now referred to as 'villas', were built of wood, usually Kauri, which is now regarded as one of New Zealand's antique woods. They would typically have a corrugated iron roof which was painted.

They would also quite often have lovely ornate turn-of-the-century verandahs, reminiscent of Scarlett O'Hara, where the early settler families would sit and relax out of the heat of the day.

These homes today are keenly sought after and highly regarded as they look wonderful when renovated. They have the advantage of large spacious rooms with high ceilings, and make excellent family homes. They usually have separate laundries, a definite advantage, especially if you have lived in a house with the clothes dryer in the kitchen: when the day is wet and cold, and all the doors are closed, the rest of the house ends up streaming in condensation.

There are many of these old villas in Wellington, and they have been painted in very interesting colour schemes, with modern drapes, and they look quite wonderful. It would be great fun to renovate an old villa.

The quarter acre paradise

New Zealand has always been referred to as 'the quarter acre paradise'. This refers to the size of the sections of land once normal throughout New Zealand.

Some houses can still be found on the quarter acre sized section, mainly in less popular areas. However, in the popular areas people have been able to cut their sections in half, just retaining enough land around the original house, and perhaps using the back half of their land to sell to someone who could then build a small unit or townhouse type of property. Of course, if the access around the sides of the original house is not wide enough, then this cannot be done, as driveways have to be considered when this type of sub-division is undertaken.

It got to a stage when everyone was rushing to sell off part of their land, and so the sections got smaller and smaller. The Government finally stepped in to ensure that homes still had an adequate amount of land around them and stipulated that sections had to be a minimum of 690 square metres.

There is another special way of buying a home in New Zealand, and that is to choose your piece of land, and then find a house, usually an older type villa, that has been moved from its land, and stored in a builder's yard. It is then advertised for sale, the cost of removal to your land being included in the price.

It is not unusual to see a whole house – or a house cut in half with one half on one transporter and the other on another transporter –moving slowly along the road, usually at night or on quiet days, to its new site. Houses have even been shipped out by barge to someone who has chosen to live on one of the islands around this coast.

It is quite a sight to watch someone else's choice of wallpaper and curtains on full view going down the road, maybe half the kitchen with all its cupboard doors opening and banging shut, being driven down the main street of some small town.

Choosing building materials

The older style homes are quite often built of weatherboards with corrugated iron roofs. Modern houses are now being built of cheaper materials, i.e. sheets of composition materials which are then sprayed with fibre cement, and then painted, to give a Mediterranean look. Brick is used, but it is much more expensive; in lots of houses you will find perhaps one feature wall, usually the front door area, in brick. To build with brick would cost about NZ$130 per square metre against $110 per square metre for the sprayed finish. Wood, too, is now becoming too expensive to build with, and so this too is often used for a feature wall.

The insides of the houses comprise a 'shell' of wooden framework with sheets of plasterboard attached. Roofing materials can vary, with corrugated iron being the cheapest, followed by Decramastic (textured steel tiles) and concrete tiles with a baked enamel finish.

Real estate jargon

Section	Plot or piece of land
Gge	Garage
Corr	Corrugated
T/House	Town house
Pte	Private

Dble	Double
Brm	Bedroom
Lge	Large
Do up special	Handyman special for renovation
X-leasable	Section large enough to cut in half and sell half
Cnd	Condition
Mort	Mortgage
Redec	Redecorated
Qual	Quality
Ens	Ensuite
Incl	Include
Psn	Position
Spa	Jacuzzi
B and T	Brick building with tile roof
Sleepout	An outside room
Villa	Older style wooden house
Rumpus room	Play room
G V	Government valuation of the property
Crosslease	A half a section
Sep. Title	A cross-leased section with its own title
Back Section	A property built on a section behind other homes (no road frontage)
Bach & Crib	A holiday style cottage
Whiteware	Washing machine, dishwasher, fridge, cooker
Right of Way	A driveway which runs through other sections to give access to a back section
Woodburner	A wood burning fire which sometimes provides hot water
TLC	Tender loving care

HOUSING AND FURNISHING COSTS

Obviously there are always exceptions to the rules, and with house prices there aren't even any rules. Where you want to live, and how popular an area is, sets the prices for houses. In Auckland, for instance, a three-bedroom house in South Auckland would cost a lot less than a three-bedroom house in Remuera. So the prices quoted here are only for average homes in the middle price range areas.

In Wellington the cost would be approximately NZ$200,000. Prices in Auckland would be roughly around $260,000. In Taranaki the prices are less, with an average of $125,000. Manawatu around $130,000. In the South Island prices are usually less, and a house in Christchurch would be $170,000 and in Dunedin even less at $110,000. Obviously, if you are a cash buyer, then you are in an admirable position to barter, and you could end up with a really good buy. Real estate sales have slowed down over the last few years, and it is certainly a buyers' market.

If you write to a New Zealand newspaper and request a copy every now and then, you will be able to see at a glance how prices vary. See Chapter 3 for the addresses of newspapers, and the cost involved.

Furnishing your home

Furniture	*NZ$*
Lounge suite – two chairs and settee	2,000–5,000
Dining table and six chairs	1,500–4,000
Queensize bed	800–3,000
Children's bunks	500
Single bed	400–2,000

Baby's cot	300
Three-drawer dressing table with mirror	900
Six-drawer chest of drawers	800–1,500

Household goods

Woolrest fleecy underblanket (queen)	310
Blankets 100% wool	119
Duvets – single	159
– queen	249
Sheets – single	50
– queen	70
– cotton single	45
– cotton queen	49
Towels – hand	3–39
– bath	10–45

Electrical goods

Mitsubishi television 21″	449
Mitsubishi television 25″	899
Philips television 14″	392
Philips stereo	399–800
Philips stereo with CD, double deck, 2-way speakers	400–800
Philips AM/FM radio cassette	199
Panasonic microwave	599
Fisher and Paykel Autowasher	1,049
Fisher and Paykel A39	449
Fisher and Paykel A55	549
Kelvinator fridge freezer	1,549
Fisher and Paykel dishwasher	1,299
Fisher and Paykel fan oven	1,149
Sunbeam kettle – fast boil	70
Sunbeam toaster	90
Sunbeam iron – steam/dry	60
Sunbeam food processor	279
Red Devil vacuum cleaner	179
Breville cake mixer	229
Remmington hairdryer	100
Wall mounted towel rail	80
Electric blanket – single	100
– queen	159

Goldair fan heater	50
Kitchen	
Three piece stainless steel saucepan set	140
20-piece dinner set	120
Miscellaneous	
Steelcraft Calais Stroller	430
Victa two-stroke motor mower	599

In New Zealand, as anywhere else, it pays to shop around. Prices vary according to quality and the above prices are in the economy range.

I haven't forgotten to include the cost of wardrobes. In New Zealand most homes have built-in wardrobes.

Don't bring the kitchen sink!

It will probably be very hard to decide what you should bring with you. I can remember finding more and more belongings that I felt I just couldn't live without! My poor husband had to keep collecting yet another crate, with the strict instructions that this had to be the last! We did our own packing, and as the carrier was collecting the cases at 7a.m. my husband stayed up all night nailing down all the lids and painting names and addresses on the sides. We travelled here by sea and we were allowed a certain amount of luggage to be stored in the holds free of charge, so we took advantage of that!

Is it really worth it? For example, that lumpy old bed with the dip in the middle, that has always hurt your back, and that old wardrobe left to you by Grandma. Upgrade your bed: it could cost you as little as $800, and as I have already said, most homes here have built-in wardrobes.

You will need to change all the plugs on your electrical appliances when you arrive here, so you might as well give them to someone back home.

New Zealand power phase is 230 volts, 50 cycles. To ensure that your electrical appliances are compatible, consult an electrician in your own country, to save you the cost of bringing appliances to New Zealand that cannot be used.

Mortgage finance

Borrowing money on mortgage is a principal means of financing the building or purchase of houses and commercial buildings, and the purchase of farms. The main sources of mortgage finance for houses are registered banks and other institutions, i.e. saving institutions, finance companies and merchant banks.

RENTING

Rental costs

There is plenty of property to rent in all newspapers. Prices vary according to areas, and style of house you want to rent. You can rent a fabulous 'mansion' style place with five bedrooms and five bathrooms, swimming pool and four-car garage if you have NZ$1,500–$2,000 per week to spend. A medium-priced three-bed home for the average family will cost approximately $300 per week in Auckland, $225 per week in Hamilton, $180 per week in New Plymouth, $220 per week in Palmerston North, $340 per week in Wellington, $230 per week in Christchurch and $160 per week in Dunedin.

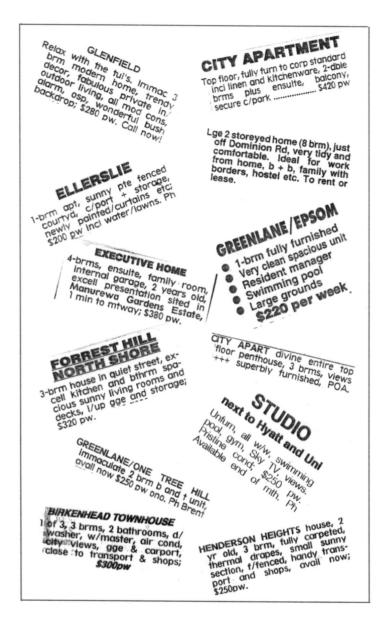

GLENFIELD
Relax with the tui's. Immac 3 brm modern home, trendy decor, fabulous private in/outdoor living, all mod cons, alarm, osp, wonderful bush backdrop; $280 pw. Call now!

CITY APARTMENT
Top floor, fully furn to corp standard incl linen and kitchenware, 2-dble brms plus ensuite, balcony, secure c/park .... $420 pw

Lge 2 storeyed home (8 brm), just off Dominion Rd, very tidy and comfortable. Ideal for work from home, b + b, family with borders, hostel etc. To rent or lease.

ELLERSLIE
1-brm apt, sunny pte fenced courtyd, c/port + storage, newly painted/curtains etc; $200 pw incl water/lawns. Ph

GREENLANE/EPSOM
● 1-brm fully furnished
● Very clean spacious unit
● Resident manager
● Swimming pool
● Large grounds
● **$220 per week**.

EXECUTIVE HOME
4-brms, ensuite, family room, internal garage, 2 years old, excell presentation sited in Manurewa Gardens Estate, 1 min to mtway; $380 pw.

CITY APART divine entire top floor penthouse, 3 brms, views +++ superbly furnished, POA.

FORREST HILL NORTH SHORE
3-brm house in quiet street, ex-cell kitchen and bthrm spacious sunny living rooms and decks, l/up gge and storage; $320 pw.

STUDIO
next to Hyatt and Uni
Unfurn, all w/w, swimming pool, gym, Sky TV, views. Pristine cond; $250 pw. Available end of mth. Ph

GREENLANE/ONE TREE HILL
immaculate 2 brm b and t unit, avail now $250 pw ono. Ph Brent

BIRKENHEAD TOWNHOUSE
1 of 3, 3 brms, 2 bathrooms, d/washer, w/master, air cond, city views, gge & carport, close to transport & shops; **$300pw**

HENDERSON HEIGHTS house, 2 yr old, 3 brm, fully carpeted, thermal drapes, small sunny section, f/fenced, handy transport and shops, avail now; $250pw.

Fig. 27. Properties to rent – typical examples.

Tenancy Agreement

Landlord's name:

Occupation:

Address (being an address for service, not a PO Box number):

Phone number:

Tenant's name:

Occupation:

Address (being an address for service):

Phone number:

Address of rented premises:

Furniture etc, provided by landlord (if any):

The Landlord and the Tenant agree that:
1 This tenancy shall commence on   /   /20
2 The rent shall be $ per week/fortnight.
3 The rent shall be paid weekly/fortnightly in advance.
4 The rent shall be placed at the following place or into the following bank account number:
5 The tenant shall pay a bond of $
6 The tenant shall not assign (transfer) or sublet tenancy without first gaining the landlord's written permission.
7 The tenant shall pay the solicitor's fee (if any) or the real estate agent's fee (if any) relating to the grant of this tenancy.
8 This tenancy is subject to the Residential Tenancies Act 1986.
9 Other conditions of this tenancy:

Dated: /   /20   (Landlord) ....

Signed: (Tenant) ....

Form supplied by

TEN∎NCY
services
A division of the Ministry of Housing

10 AiB/921

Fig. 28. A tenancy agreement.

If you are looking for a shared situation, you will pay around $80 to $120 per week, without costs, for a single room.

Bonds and fees

When you rent you will have to pay two weeks' bond, which is held by the Housing Corporation and returned to you when you leave the property, provided that it is left in the same condition in which you took it. If you find a property through the services of a real estate agent, then you will also have that fee to pay. It is usually one week's rent, i.e. if you are paying $200 per week rent, then you will pay $200 to the real estate agent.

REAL ESTATE AGENTS

Here are the names and addresses of the three largest real estate organisations in New Zealand.

Century 21

PB 1596, Palmerston North 5330. Tel: 64 6 356 4829.
PO Box 2506, Tauranga. Tel: 64 7 578 7000.
PO Box 21 087, Christchurch. Tel: 64 3 379 2121.
PO Box 68, Papakura, Auckland. Tel: 64 9 298 4209.
PO Box 35, Hamilton. Tel: 64 7 855 9013.
PO Box 2346, Rotorua. Tel: 64 7 347 7699.
PO Box 763, Invercargill. Tel: 64 3 218 6203.

Challenge Realty

PB 30 125, Lower Hutt. Tel: 64 4 569 9139.
PO Box 18, Greymouth. Tel: 64 3 768 4035.
PO Box 298, Wanaka 9192. Tel: 64 3 443 8511.
PO Box 21-158, Henderson, Auckland. Tel: 64 9 837 0726.
PB 1655, Dunedin. Tel: 64 3 477 4303.

Harcourts Group Ltd.

PB 5267, Dunedin. Tel: 64 3 477 5334.

PO Box 885, Tauranga 3015. Tel: 64 7 576 8770.

PO Box 33-114, Barrington, Christchurch. Tel: 64 3 332 1525.

PO Box 33-198, Takapuna, Auckland. Tel: 64 9 486 1029.

PO Box 10-777, Wellington. Tel: 64 4 473 7563.

PO Box 8054, Riccarton, Christchurch. Tel: 64 3 348 8784.

PO Box 396, Taupo 2730. Tel: 64 7 378 4170.

PO Box 610, New Plymouth 9999. Tel: 64 6 758 5206.

THE WEEKLY SHOPPING BASKET

500g butter	$2.00	1kg tomatoes	$7.95
1kg cheese	$7.57	lettuce	$2.25
500g margarine	$1.80	cauliflower	$0.99
750g weetabix	$1.89	1.5kg carrots	$0.79
2 litres milk	$2.96	1.5kg onions	$0.79
275g jar of jam	$1.79	1kg apples	$0.99
12 medium eggs	$3.15	200g instant coffee	$6.99
2 litre icecream	$2.79	100 tea bags	$2.89
1kg frozen peas	$1.00	8 toilet rolls	$1.79
500g frozen sweet corn	$1.10	small bottle bleach	$2.00
5 kg flour	$3.89	softly wool wash	$4.30
3 kg raw sugar	$2.49	1kg washing powder	$3.45
400g tin cat food	$1.54	large loaf of bread	$2.30
1kg beef top side	$7.89	pkt chocolate chip biscuits	$2.39
1kg rumpsteak	$8.77	1kg bacon	$10.95
1kg sausages	$2.49	bottle of white wine	$7.99
per kg no. 14 size chicken	$4.49	bottle of gin 1125ml	$26.95
per kg lamb roast	$6.99	bottle of vodka 1125ml	$28.95
per kg lamb chops	$5.79		
per kg pork shoulder roast	$6.45	*fish prices*	
2kg mince beef	$10.00	shrimps (kg)	$19.95
bottle of red wine	$13.95	salmon (kg)	$19.95
1.5lt lemonade	$1.68	oysters (doz)	$10.95
1kg banana	$1.39		

All prices fluctuate, these are only approximates.

QUESTIONS AND ANSWERS

Is the quality of New Zealand clothing good?

Yes, there is a very high standard, and a lot of emphasis on pure wool and cotton.

Are all the houses sold through estate agents?

No, there is some property on the market without the services of a real estate agent. Quite a lot of people try to sell their property themselves when first they decide, in order to avoid the real estate agent's fee.

6

Health and Welfare

HOW HEALTH CARE IS ORGANISED

The New Zealand health system is made up of public, private and voluntary sectors which interact to provide and fund health care.

Department of Health

The Department is the principal adviser to the Minister of Health on health issues. It administers relevant legislation, funds programmes and ensures the provision of essential services. It collects and disseminates information, liaises and consults on health matters, monitors and reviews health programmes and is responsible for ensuring that its work is underpinned by a focus on the Government's desired health outcomes.

Regional Health Authorities

In July 1993 four Regional Health Authorities were established as independent Crown Agencies with their own Board of Directors.

The primary objective of Regional Health Authorities is to ensure that the population in their regions receives optimum value from the health and disability support services funding, entrusted to the Regional Health Authorities within the parameters of Government policy. The RHAs purchase health procedures by way of tendering for services and contracting with health care providers, i.e. hospitals (CHEs), rest homes, etc.

Other care providers
Health care provided by general practitioners is also partially funded from the public purse, as are referrals to specialists and laboratory diagnostic services. Dental care is provided free to dependent children under 18 years of age. Eighty per cent of the cost of pharmaceuticals is met through public funding. A number of private hospital services are subsidised, and a range of private and voluntary organisations receive funding for services they are contracted to provide.

Accident compensation levies cover 4.2% of health care costs for services provided in the public and private sectors.

The private sector provides a wide range of health care options. Forty-five per cent of the population has private health insurance, meeting 3.5% of the total cost of health care.

An active voluntary sector incorporates a wide range of organisations which provide care, support, health education and research. Health care is also provided informally by families and relatives, and this is recognised through the growing provision of home support services in the public and voluntary sectors.

Health expenditure
General taxation funds an estimated 77% of the total costs of health care. This funding is primarily disbursed

through the Department of Health, which distributes funds to area health boards, and a wide range of health professionals and organisations providing services to the public. It also includes funding for health-related expenditure through other government departments such as Social Welfare, Defence and Police.

Over recent years governments have introduced a number of measures to curb health spending, while maintaining services. Area health board funding, which makes up nearly 70% of the Department of Health's budget allocation, has come in for particular attention.

A population-based method is used to determine funding for the boards. It takes into account the age and gender of the population in each region, by adjusting for the expected resource use of each age/ gender group, derived from national levels. Special health needs are also considered, through calculations based on socio-economic factors.

In 1992 the Government expanded the ability of the boards to charge each other for cross-boundary service provision. From February 1992, the boards began receiving revenue from inpatient and outpatient user charges.

Service statements have been developed by the Department of Health, in consultation with health service providers. These are designed to provide guidance to the area health boards on the content and structure of services provided by each board. The statements provide a national perspective on the key elements comprising a service, as well as the policy and legislative parameters for each service. Each board will design and provide the services in accordance with its own strategic and financial planning processes. These may reflect their assessment of local needs and resource priorities.

NEW ZEALAND'S HEALTH & WELFARE SCHEME
The Department of Social Welfare, which reports to the Minister in charge of the department, exists to assist Government to achieve its goals in meeting the welfare needs of New Zealanders.

These social security goals fall broadly into three groups:

1. To ensure that all the people of New Zealand receive an adequate income.

2. To provide and deliver welfare services and support to the community.

3. To allocate and deliver resources and support to community groups and organisations and enhance their ability to deliver Social Services.

The **New Zealand Income Support Service** provides for:

- National Superannuation
- Unemployment Benefit
- Domestic Purposes Benefit
- Invalids Benefit
- Sickness Benefit
- Widows Benefit.

Reciprocity Agreements

United Kingdom

The **Social Security (Reciprocity with United Kingdom) Act 1983** provides for reciprocity in a comprehensive range of benefits. The general principle of the convention is that people migrating from one country to another will be taken into the social security scheme of the receiving country, and paid benefits under the laws and conditions applicable to other residents of that country (not the home country).

In essence, if you have lived for the last ten years in the country with the reciprocal agreement, you will be automatically entitled to receive **income assistance**. If you do not live in a country with a reciprocal agreement you will need to have lived in New Zealand for ten years before you qualify.

Reciprocal agreements are also in place for citizens of Australia and the Netherlands (in some categories only).

For further information call:

Income Support Service
International Affairs Office
Free phone: 64 0800 552 002.

Superannuation

The benefit rates are approximately:

	Net NZ$
◆ single person living alone	225.55 pw
◆ single person sharing	208.20 pw
◆ married couple	347.00 pw

In 1987 the Labour Government decided, on the advice of the Minister of Finance, Roger Douglas, to discontinue tax incentives for personal insurance and superannuation savings. Prior to this, a person was allowed a tax rebate of NZ$1,400 on personal superannuation, and $1,200 on subsidised superannuation. The Government chose not to replace this with another scheme, and many people saw this as a disincentive to save.

The New Zealand Government is facing the same problem as many other countries, i.e. the increasing population of elderly people, which in turn places a big burden on the working population. The question now being asked is whether the New Zealand Government can continue to make superannuation payments indefinitely.

It is very obvious when you take the National Superannuation payment, and consider the cost of living (see chapter on Housing and Living Costs), that some extra savings must be made in order to able to retire with some dignity. There are many superannuation and insurance companies operating in New Zealand, and it certainly pays to shop around for the best deals.

Given below are some of the better known financial consultants and superannuation schemes:

Financial consultants
Money Concepts, 109 Molesworth Street, Thorndon, Wellington 6001. Tel: 64 4 473 0876.
Website: *www.moneyconcepts.co.nz*

Money Concepts, 169 Princess Street, Dunedin 9001. Tel: 64 3 477 5660.

Tower Trust Ltd, Box 2949, Wellington. Tel: 64 4 495 0995. Website: *www.towertrust.co.nz*

Superannuation schemes

Forsyth Barr Frater Willliams, Box 97, Auckland. Tel: 64 9 303 2473.

AMP, PO Box 1499, Wellington 6015. Tel: 64 4 384 6369.

Tower Retirement Investment Ltd, PO Box 1086, Christchurch 8015. Tel: 64 3 365 4065.

Tower Retirement Investment Ltd, PO Box 742, Nelson 7016. Tel: 64 3 548 7025.

Unemployment benefit

The reciprocal agreement applies for citizens of the United Kingdom and Australia, which means that should the situation arise you would receive unemployment benefit. Citizens of other countries need to have lived in New Zealand for 12 months before they become eligible.

For further information contact Work and Income New Zealand, PO Box 12-136, Wellington. Tel: 64 4 916 3300. Fax: 64 4 918 9779. Website: *www.winz.govt.nz*.

Domestic purposes benefit

The domestic purposes benefit is paid to:

- ◆ a parent caring for children without the support of a partner
- ◆ a person caring for someone at home who would otherwise be hospitalised
- ◆ an older woman alone – only in some cases.

The amount the beneficiary receives depends on:

* age
* whether they are married or have a partner
* number of children living with the recipient
* how much income they earn.

For further information contact Work and Income New Zealand, PO Box 12-136, Wellington. Tel: 64 4 913 0300. Fax: 64 4 918 9779. Website: *www.winz.govt.nz.*

Sickness benefit

This is for people who can't work and have had a drop in their earnings either because they are temporarily sick or injured, or because they are pregnant. The reciprocal agreement applies in this section also for Britain and Australia.

For further information contact Work and Income New Zealand, PO Box 12-136, Wellington. Tel: 64 4 916 3300. Fax: 64 4 918 9779. Website: *www.winz.govt.nz.*

Widow's and bereaved families benefit

The widow's benefit is paid to a woman whose husband or partner has died. The benefit helps those who have children to support or who have spent a number of years married or raising children – if the recipient does not have children, in order to qualify they must be over 50 years old. If the recipient has remarried then they are no longer entitled to receive this benefit.

For further information contact Work and Income New Zealand, PO Box 12-136, Wellington. Tel: 64 4 916 3300.

Fax: 64 4 918 9779. Website: *www.winz.govt.nz*.

HEALTH SERVICE CHARGES FOR THE PATIENT

Visiting the doctor

The cost of a visit to a doctor in New Zealand varies depending on the doctor and possibly the area where you live. If you are on a low income and qualify for a **community services card**, you will pay a subsidised rate. If you do not, the approximate costs are as follows:

- senior citizen $30.00
- adult $60.00
- child under 5   free
- child 5–18 $30.00

If you just require a repeat prescription, then the charge (without seeing the doctor) will be $6. On top of this you will have to pay the cost of the drugs prescribed; each pharmacy has its own charges, depending on the drugs needed.

Visiting the dentist

There is no free dental treatment in New Zealand, and the cost of keeping your pearly smile can be horrendous. The figures shown are approximate examples, as treatments can vary, and so can the dental costs. It certainly pays to check around first before making an appointment.

Procedure	*Typical fee*
Examination, X-ray and polish	$180.00
Normal filling	$200.00
Root filling	$1,500.00

Some private health schemes do cover dental treatment, so it would pay to check around before taking out cover if this would be a priority for you.

For further information contact the Dental Council of New Zealand, PO Box 10-448 Wellington, New Zealand. Tel: 64 4 499 4820. Fax: 64 4 499 1668.

Your state of health

Public health care in New Zealand is undergoing several changes, timed it seems with Government mood swings. It was decided in 1991 that hospitals should be run as businesses (that means paying tax). Several smaller community hospitals were closed down.

Waiting lists exist for many operations, and for some life-threatening situations, families have had to raise many thousands of dollars to send the patient overseas for treatment.

The benefits of private health schemes are quite obvious in such a situation. You then can have the special care you need without having to mortgage your home to get medical treatment. The schemes also pay a percentage of your visits to your doctor.

Medical insurance companies

These are a few medical insurance companies:

Medic Aid, 46 Smithfield Road, Wanganui 5001. Tel: 64 6 347 1895.

Southern Cross, PB 99-934, Newmarket, Auckland 1031. Tel: 64 9 356 0900. Website: *www.southerncross.co.nz*

Southern Cross, PO Box 27-145, Wellington. Tel: 64 4 384
4199. Fax: 64 4 385 0771.
Website: *www.southerncross.co.nz*
Southern Cross, PO Box 1316, Dunedin 9015. Tel: 64 3
477 6365.
Southern Cross, PO Box 922. Ivercargill 9515. Tel: 64 3
218 3106.
Southern Cross, PO Box 1091, Hamilton 2015. Tel: 64 7
839 5108.
Aetna Health, PO Box 6772, Auckland. Tel: 64 9 302
8720.
AMP General Insurance, AMP Building, PO Box 1093,
Wellington. Tel: 64 4 498 8000.

Typical costs of operations
Here are some typical costs for 'everyday' type surgery in
a private hospital:

Tonsils (child)	$ 1,590
(adult)	$ 1,795
Varicose veins	$ 2,170
Knee replacement	$12,520
Ingrown toenails	$ 710
Mastectomy	$ 1,930
Cardiac bypass	$21,445
Hip replacement	$11,585
Hysterectomy	$ 3,910

Hospital charges
Reciprocal agreement exists for citizens of England,
Scotland, Wales and Northern Ireland, as well as citizens
of Australia to receive free hospital treatment for
emergency cases. This of course does not cover a pre-
known medical state, where you would have to pay for

treatment. Accidents are also covered in the A.I. Act under ACC (the Accident Compensation Corporation).

For citizens of other countries where a reciprocal agreement is not in force, the costs can be large, e.g.:

	Excluding GST (12.5%)
Outpatient (flat rate)	$188–$300
Overnight stay (minimum)	$457–$3,704

On top of this will be the cost of treatment you may require. Surgical costs can be from $3,700 per day for intensive and critical care. X-rays, blood tests, CT scans, operating costs and pharmacy costs are extra.

Eligibility for free treatment

+ Those granted permanent residence or admitted as refugees by Immigration services.

+ Cook, Nuie and Tokelau Islanders.

+ Residents of Great Britain and Northern Ireland, including any premature births and complex maternity cases, but not including normal maternity care or those with a pre-existent condition.

+ UK Royal Navy personnel.

+ US Antarctic Expedition personnel.

+ Those in possession of an extended work permit of two years or more. (The passport must be sighted for evidence of the permit.)

Not eligible for free treatment

+ All other nationalities not mentioned previously, including citizens of the Commonwealth nations,

Ireland, Japan, Fiji, Western Samoa, Tonga, New Caledonia, Tahiti, Kiribati and Vanuatu.

◆ NZ citizens or their dependants who have not themselves lived in NZ. Ordinarily, once a New Zealander, always a New Zealander, but those born to New Zealanders overseas must live in New Zealand to qualify.

◆ Those born in NZ or Australia, but now resident elsewhere (apart from NZ) or who have come here specifically for treatment.

◆ Diplomats.

◆ Fullbright scholars, except those from UK or Australia.

◆ Seamen from overseas ships. (Shipowner pays.)

◆ Those on temporary permits (i.e. student/work/ visitor).

Work permits and visitor permits are normally issued for a maximum of one year only.

THE ACCIDENT COMPENSATION CORPORATION
We have a scheme here in New Zealand whereby everyone has $1.24 per $100 deducted from their earnings, and the employer also pays a proportion, i.e. from $1.18 to $5 per person per week depending on the type of work done; dangerous occupations will pay more.

In the event of an accident, the Accident Compensation Corporation pays for the treatment to the injured person; if that person is unable to work any more, then they are paid a percentage of their earnings up to a limit of around $86,000.

Some say that the scheme is good, but there have been many occasions when a person has been badly injured by, say, a car accident, and they are the innocent party. Under normal circumstances they could have sued that person, but Accident Compensation Corporation has taken away the right of a person to sue. So instead of a good lump sum payout, which might have paid for special equipment to help the injured person, the victim now has to be content with a weekly payment relative to the size of their earnings at the time of the accident subject to a maximum limit of approximately $86,000 per annum.

Example
In 1990, just to give you an illustration, I was driving along a secondary road, and whilst waiting to turn right was hit from behind. The resulting damage was whiplash resulting in a permanent weakness to the right shoulder/neck area. I claimed Accident Compensation. After being examined by a specialist – 12 months after the accident – I was awarded $12,000. Since then the terms of Accident Compensation have been changed, and people can no longer receive lump sum payments.

SUNSHINE CAMPS
The first health camp in New Zealand was organised by Dr Elizabeth Gunn in 1919. Dr Gunn was the school doctor for the Wanganui area; she believed that if delicate and undernourished children could be taught the basics of hygiene and nutrition and receive the benefit of rest and

fresh air, many of their ailments would be cured. With the help of a local farmer, volunteer teachers and equipment hired from the army, Dr Gunn organised the camp at Turakina, near Wanganui. The camp was run along military lines with a bugle wake-up call in the morning, regimented eating and sleeping times, toothbrush drill, marching and flag saluting. After six weeks of camp-life the children flourished.

The success of Dr Gunn's health camps aroused public interest in the idea and by 1929 'sunshine camps', financed by private donations, were being run in several areas. 1929 also saw the first issue of health stamps by the Post Office with each stamp sold contributing one penny to the health camp fund. The first permanent camp was established at Otaki in 1932. By 1936 the movement was growing rapidly and a **National Health Camp Federation** was formed to oversee the burgeoning number of camps. In 1937 the King George V Memorial Fund raised 175,000 pounds sterling to establish permanent camps throughout the country.

The tradition of health camps that Dr Gunn established continues today. There are now seven permanent health camps at Whangarei, Pakuranga, Rotorua, Gisborne, Otaki, Christchurch and Roxburgh. Four to six-week camps are held for children aged five to 12 years. The children are usually referred by teachers or doctors. Health camps today also help children with psychological or behavioural problems. As well as the games, schooling and health education that have always been part of the health camp regimen, children are now taught anger management, learning skills and life skills such as basic cooking and general personal hygiene. The Ministry of Education runs a special school in each camp where children with education problems can be given extra attention to develop positive attitudes towards school-work and learning. New Zealand Post continues to issue health stamps every spring, raising up to NZ$100,000 a year for health camps and child health generally.

QUESTIONS AND ANSWERS

Is alternative medicine available in New Zealand?

Yes, very definitely. There is a very strong interest in acupuncture, aromatherapy, chiropractors and reflexology. There are also experts on herbal remedies.

Is dental treatment covered by the Health Department?

Only for children who are still at school. Everyone else must pay. Private health insurance can cover this.

Do I have to pay for medical treatment if I have an accident?

No. This type of treatment, whether in the hospital or from a doctor, is covered by Accident Compensation.

7

Living Under the Law

HOW THE LEGAL SYSTEM WORKS

New Zealand has inherited the British tradition of an independent judiciary, seen as a protection against unnecessary intrusion by the state into the lives of citizens. The Judicature Act 1908 and the Constitution Act 1986 contain a number of key provisions, designed to ensure judicial independence. Judges (including those who sit in the Court of Appeal) are appointed by the Governor-General, not the government. Neither Court of Appeal nor High Court judges may be removed from office except by the Sovereign or by the Governor General on grounds of misbehaviour or incapacity upon an address of the House of Representatives. District Court judges may be removed from office by the Governor-General, but only on the grounds of inability or misbehaviour.

The salaries of judges are determined by the Higher Salaries Commission under the Higher Salaries Commission Act 1977. Salaries may not be diminished during a judge's commission. No person may be appointed a judge unless he or she has held a practising certificate as a barrister or solicitor for at least seven years. The retirement age is 68, although former judges may be reappointed as acting judges for two years, or one year if the judge is 72 years of age when reappointed.

The court system

At the head of the hierarchy of courts of New Zealand is the Judicial Committee of the Privy Council. Below this is the Court of Appeal followed by the High Court, and the District Courts. All courts exercise both criminal and civil jurisdiction.

The Judicial Committee of the Privy Council

The Privy Council is the final appeal tribunal for New Zealand. Appeals to the Privy Council may be brought by leave of the court appealed from, or by special leave of the Privy Council itself. Leave is granted as of right from any final judgement of the Court of Appeal, where the matter in dispute amounts to the value of NZ$5,000 or more, or directly or indirectly involves some claim to property, or some civil right exceeding that value. The Privy Council has a discretionary power to grant special leave in criminal cases. Such leave is not often granted in criminal appeals from New Zealand.

The Court of Appeal

The highest appeal court in New Zealand, the Court of Appeal, has existed since 1846 and is constituted by the Judicature Amendment Act 1957.

Its primary function is to settle the law of New Zealand and to reconcile conflicting decisions of the other courts. It hears and determines ordinary appeals from the High Court. Certain other proceedings in the lower courts may, by order of the High Court, be removed to the Court of Appeal. The court does, however, also have some original jurisdiction.

The High Court

The High Court of New Zealand was first established (as the Supreme Court) in 1841. It has all the jurisdiction which may be necessary for a court to administer the laws of New Zealand.

The High Court exercises jurisdiction in cases of major crimes, Admiralty proceedings, the more important civil claims, appeals from lower courts and tribunals, and reviews of administrative actions. The High Court also has inherent jurisdiction to punish for contempt of court. It consists of the Chief Justice and 32 other judges, as prescribed by the Judicature Act 1908.

Specialist courts

These consist of the **Employment Court**, the **Family Courts**, **Youth Courts**, **Maori Land Court** and **Maori Appellate Court**.

Tribunals

Over 100 tribunals, authorities, boards, committees or related bodies exist to deal with other disputes, largely between individuals, on matters such as environmental planning, economic issues, scientific and technical matters, censorship, welfare and benefits, taxation, occupational licensing and discipline, activity licensing (e.g. shop trading hours) and company registration.

Jury service

Every person between the ages of 20 and 65 years (inclusive) is eligible for jury service, with some exceptions. Those who are not appropriate to serve on a jury because of their occupations are ineligible. A person may also be excused if jury service would cause serious inconvenience a or hardship, or if it is against a person's religious beliefs to serve on a jury. Also precluded are people with recent prison records and those who have been imprisoned for more than three years.

LEGAL AID IN NEW ZEALAND

The Legal Services Act 1991 brought together in one statute the civil and criminal legal aid schemes and aligned them as far as possible. It also gave statutory recognition to the **duty solicitor scheme** and to **community law centres**. The Act established a new administrative structure – the **Legal Services Board** and **District Committees**. The Board is responsible for the legal aid budget. Its role is, however, wider. It can, for instance, investigate other ways of providing legal services to the public and set up pilot schemes.

Community Law Centres and Neighbourhood Law Offices

These offices and centres are set up to provide legal advice to people who cannot afford to go to a law firm. They are funded from a variety of sources and central government.

THE RISING CRIME RATE

When I came to this country in 1972, everyone was still talking about a 'big' murder case a few years earlier, when a man named Arthur Allen Thomas was convicted of murdering two people. He has since been acquitted.

New Zealand was in those days a very 'safe' country. People used to leave their house doors unlocked, and in fact some had never had a house key! People used to leave their cars unlocked when out shopping: there was never a problem with stealing.

Today, unfortunately, New Zealand has caught up with the rest of the world, and its crime rate is much increased. The sad thing is that the nation has become 'accustomed' to crime. New Zealanders today hardly bat an eyelid when hearing of people 'going berserk' and murdering several family members (this has happened about three times over the last two or three years). What has happened to this once 'safe' country?

According to *Statistics New Zealand*, in the year 2000/ 2001 total recorded crime dropped by 1.9%. Seven and a half thousand more crimes were solved than the previous year. There were 10,500 fewer burglaries, and more were solved; but violent offending increased by 8.6%. Speeding offences rose from 124,170 to 176,684, and the road death toll for the year ended 30 June 2002 was 430, the lowest in nearly four decades.

Traffic offenders

New Zealand is a panel-beater's dream. I had never seen so many cars with body damage until I came to New Zealand. The trouble, of course, is with the drivers – not the cars! The attitude of drivers here has to be seen to be believed. They drive very aggressively, hoot behind you when you obey the speed limits, and drive up right behind you to make you hurry. This is probably one of the worst features of some drivers here. Nor will they let you in when you are trying to get into the main stream of traffic from a side road; the game seems to be to see how many drivers you can block! Cutting close in front is another favourite game.

Consequently the police have a big job to keep an eye on traffic offences. Drink drivers have recently been blitzed by the police department, with road blocks to check on drunks, who are then asked to blow into a little bag; if the crystals in the tube change colour, they can tell roughly how much drink has been consumed.

The penal system

New Zealand's penal system has evolved to protect the community from offenders both through deterrence and reformation, with increasing emphasis on rehabilitation in recent years.

The main sources available to the courts for dealing with offenders, other than by imprisonment, are fines, reparation, supervision, community services, periodic detention and community care. On conviction for murder a mandatory sentence of life imprisonment is imposed. The death penalty for murder was abolished in 1961. Capital punishment was removed as a penalty for all crimes (latterly treason and mutiny in the armed forces) in 1989.

The most common violent offences by males receiving custodial sentences were aggravated robbery (18% of violent offenders and 9% of all prison inmates) and injuring and wounding (13% of violent offenders and 7% of all inmates).

The most significant major offence groups represented for females were property offences (40%) and violent offences (34%). A smaller proportion of female prisoners were incarcerated for drug offences (16%) and six females were in custody for traffic offences. The most common violent offences for which female offenders were given custodial sentences were murder (25% of all violent offenders and 8% of all inmates) and injuring and wounding (26% of violent offenders and 8% of all inmates).

Nearly half (48%) of the cases which resulted in a custodial sentence for some offence other than a traffic offence related to Maori offenders, 43% to European offenders and 7% to Pacific Islanders, according to the New Zealand Statistics Department.

The police

On 1 July 1992 the New Zealand Police and the Ministry Transport's Traffic Safety Service merged to concentrate resources and target serious traffic offences.

The national administrative and operational control of the New Zealand Police is vested in a commissioner who is responsible to the Government through the Minister of Police. For operational purposes, New Zealand is divided into six police regions, each controlled by an assistant commissioner.

Regional commanders are responsible for the general preservation of peace and order, for the prevention of offences, and for the detection of offenders in their areas of command. Policing is maintained by a system of mobile patrols and foot 'beats', coordinated by communications network.

The police are responsible for enforcing the criminal law principally the **Crimes Act** and the **Summary Offences Act**, but also various other statutes such as the **Arms Act**, **Sale of Liquor Act**, **Gaming and Lotteries Act**, **Misuse of Drugs Act** and **Transport Act**.

The summary prosecution of criminal offences investigated by the police is undertaken in the District Court by trained police prosecutors. Police in country districts in some cases hold additional appointments such as registrars and bailiffs at District Courts, probation officers and honorary fishery officers.

The ordinary police are not armed. The **armed offenders squads** are a group of specially equipped and trained officers who deal with offenders with weapons. About 200 members throughout the country perform armed offenders squad duties on a part-time basis.

The **special tactics group** is made up of selected members of armed offenders squads who are specially trained to deal with any acts of terrorism. The only act of terrorism in New Zealand was in 1985 when a team of French saboteurs entered the country illegally by sea.

'The Rainbow Warrior' – 10 July 1985
On a peaceful winter's night in July 1985, two frogmen slipped into the cold waters of Auckland Harbour. They attached two explosives to the hull of *The Rainbow Warrior*, the flagship of Greenpeace, and hurried away. There was a party on board, a birthday celebration attended by 30 people. The first explosion was felt and

lights went out and the ship started to list, everyone got off the ship except for the photographer Fernando Pereira; he decided that he had time to rescue his camera equipment. The second explosion came, and the ship went down with Fernando.

LAW FOR DRIVERS

These are some key New Zealand laws to know:

- The legal drinking age is 20 years of age.

- Traffic travels on the left-hand side of the road.

- Cyclists must wear safety helmets.

- Motorcyclists must wear crash helmets and always display their lights.

- The wearing of seat belts in vehicles is compulsory.

- Speed limits: 100 km/h for cars, motorcycles, vans and light vehicles; 90 km/h for buses, heavy motor and articulated vehicles; 80 km/h for school buses and any vehicles towing trailers.

The major cause of accidents on the roads is excess alcohol and exceeding the speed limit.

Vehicle inspections

All vehicles using the roads must be inspected regularly to ensure their mechanical and structural fitness. They are inspected every six months, but vehicles first registered since 1 December 1985 and less than three years of age may be inspected every twelve months. Most lightweight vehicles are required to have a 'Warrant of Fitness' which can be issued at approved garages or at Testing Stations.

Old-fashioned courtesies
Petrol stations in New Zealand are very much serve yourself, but you can still get service. I was astonished whilst on a trip to England recently to find that my dear old Mum, who is in her 80s, had to fill up her own car with petrol.

Importing your car
There are costs involved in bringing your car into New Zealand, and these costs depend mainly on the country in which your car was manufactured.

◆ If, for instance, your car was manufactured in the United Kingdom you will be charged a duty based on the price paid for that car of 20% (less depreciation).

◆ For cars manufactured in any other country, there will be a duty based on the price you paid for the car, less depreciation, of 35%.

◆ First time immigrants will *not* be charged duty if they have owned the car for twelve months before coming to New Zealand.

In some circumstances – even with the depreciation formula being applied – this valuation based on price paid will make the all-up cost of the vehicle to the importer thousands of dollars higher than the equivalent used vehicle in New Zealand. This situation is related to the reduction of car prices as a result of large numbers of secondhand cars being imported into New Zealand.

Collectors of Customs have authority to apply a method of valuation based upon the New Zealand market price of the vehicle where it can be established that the normal method of valuation will result in a substantial disadvantage to the importer.

This information is only a guide, and confirmation should be sought two to three months before shipping, by writing to:

The Collector of Customs –

PO Box 29, Manurewa, Auckland 1730. Tel: 64 9 275 1970.
PO Box 2218, Wellington 6015. Tel: 64 4 473 6099.
PO Box 440, Napier 4015. Tel: 64 6 835 5799.

Popular new car prices (approx.) all inclusive of GST (12.5%)

Alfa Romeo 146 1.6l TS	$37,995	Land Rover Defender 90	$53,800
Audi A3 1.8 Turbo	$54,900	Mazda 323 Astina Ltd	$29,195
BMW 318is Convertible	$82,000	Mercedes Benz E240 Classic	$103,700
Chrysler Neon LX	$28,490	MGF VVC	$59,000
Citroen Xsara 1.8 SX	$36,500	Mitsubishi L200 Petrol	$28,450
Daewoo Nubira SE	$25,500	Musso E32 Petrol	$51,040
Daihatsu Charade LsiA	$18,800	Nissan Pulsar LX Hatch	$27,195
Fiat Bravo 1.6SX	$27,995	Peugeot 406 VS	$63,000
Ford Mondeo LX 1.8 TDS	$31,900	Porsche 911 Carrera Coupé	$208,000
Holden Vectra GL 2.2 Sedan	$32,995	Renault Laguna 2.2 TD RXE	$50,000
Honda Prelude Vti-R	$42,000	Rover 416 Sli	$36,500
Honda Civic Lxi	$27,000	Saab 9-3 SE 2.0 Turbo	$67,200
Hyundai Lantra 1.6 GLS	$28,900	Subaru Impreza WRX 2.0	$46,990
Jaguar Sovereign 4.0 V8	$155,000	Suzuki Baleno GS	$18,950
Jeep Wrangler Spt Htop	$41,990	Toyota Starlet XL Hatch	$48,990
Kia Sportage 2.0 4WD DLX	$32,995	VW Passat 1.8	$69,950
Lada Niva 4WD	$14,495		

Petrol prices in New Zealand are approximately $1.12 per litre for unleaded petrol.

Secondhand car prices (approx.)
Here are some typical examples:

1992 Alfa Romeo 33S P4WD	$17,000	1994 Mercedes Benz C280	$39,995
1997 Audi A4 Quattro turbo	$37,995	1993 Mitsubishi Galant Viento	$14,999
1992 BMW 535i	$29,990	1994 Nissan Sunny Salon	$13,999
1993 Citroen Xantia 2.0i	$18,000	1991 Peugeot 205 Gti	$15,000
1994 Daihatsu Charade hatch	$8,999	1992 Porsche 928 GTS	$79,999
1995 Fiat Punto turbo	$15,990	1996 Renault Laguna	$25,999
1992 Ford Laser XL 1.6	$6,995	1990 Range Rover Vogue SE	$25,999
1991 Holden Commodore	$15,990	1994 Saab 900S	$23,999
1991 Honda Accord Ascot	$11,999	1998 Subaru Legacy	$19,999
1995 Hyundai Sonata 3.0 V6	$16,499	1992 Suzuki Alto	$6,995
1990 Jaguar xj40 Sovereign	$34,995	1993 Toyota Corona	$14,999
1995 Land Rover Discovery	$32,990	1994 VW Golf	$20,990
1995 Mazda Lantis X 5dr	$18,995	1992 Volvo 940 GL	$16,999

Those are just a few advertisements taken at random. If you would like to see more, write to one of the newspaper offices and ask for a current issue to be sent to you.

The New Zealand Herald, Box 32, Auckland.
The Dominion, Box 1297, Wellington.
The Otago Times, Box 517, Dunedin.
The Christchurch Star, Box 1467, Christchurch.

The cost of one newspaper to the United Kingdom would be about NZ$12.55 airmail and $4.05 sea mail. Send your money with your request; payments may be made by cheque or credit card.

New intending residents

An immigrant, i.e. a person coming to New Zealand to take up permanent residence for the first time, is allowed duty and GST free entry of a motor vehicle, motorcycle and motor scooter under the conditions set out below. It is possible for more than one vehicle to qualify under this concession. To benefit you must be able to comply with all of the following requirements, supported by full documentary evidence:

◆ You are coming for the first time to New Zealand to take up permanent residence (that is, you have never lived in New Zealand).

◆ You must have personally owned and personally used the vehicle for at least one year before the date of your departure for New Zealand or the date on which the vehicle is surrendered for shipping, whichever is the earlier.

◆ You must be importing the vehicle for your own personal use and not for sale, gift or disposal in any other way.

◆ You must be prepared to give a written undertaking that if you sell or dispose of the vehicle within two years of the date of its importation, you will pay an amount equal to the duty and GST which would otherwise be payable.

The terms of the above concessions are legal requirements as set out in the Tariff of New Zealand. Unless you can satisfy the Customs that all these requirements have been complied with, full duty and GST will be payable. If you require an assessment of the amount of duty and GST payable on your car, please obtain a copy of Customs Notice No. 6. *Private Motor Vehicle Imports.* This Notice explains how you should calculate the value for duty and how to determine the charges payable on the vehicle.

Steam cleaning

The Ministry of Agriculture and Fisheries require that all used vehicles entering New Zealand are steam cleaned to prevent the introduction of animal and plant diseases and pests, except used vehicles from Australia if on inspection at the port of entry they are found to be clean.

To avoid delay in New Zealand, vehicles may be steam cleaned immediately prior to shipment and a **Certificate of Steam Cleaning** produced to the Agriculture Quarantine Service on arrival. An inspection of the vehicle is required before release to ensure that cleaning has been adequate. This will be carried out at an approved area.

Vehicles not steam cleaned before loading, or found to be contaminated on arrival, will be cleaned in New Zealand and reinspected before release. The cost of having your car steam cleaned here is approximately NZ$44 which includes Goods and Services Tax.

We shipped our car out to New Zealand – it took approximately five weeks to arrive.

Left-hand drive vehicles

Under the Customs Import Prohibition Order (No. Two) 1952, there is a restriction on the importation of left-hand drive vehicles. Before shipping a left-hand drive vehicle to New Zealand you must obtain approval to import from the Ministry of Transport, Land Transport Division, 1 Queen Street, Private Bag 106 602, New Zealand. Tel: 64 0800 108 809.

Registration and licensing of vehicles

All vehicles using public roads need to be regularly licensed:

Vehicle	Annual fee (approx.)
Cars	$217.05
Motorcycles	$263.80 (60cc or less)
	$275.05 (over 60cc)
Rental cars	$242.55
Vans	$217.05
Tractors (non road use)	$ 21.30

Note: for further details about registration in New Zealand: Email: *info@tregistry.co.nz*.

Fig. 29. A New Zealand driving licence.

The 'infernal' combustion engine

Cars are one of the biggest threats to the global environment. The transport sector is estimated to be responsible for 40% of New Zealand's greenhouse gas emissions. New Zealand has the second highest rate of cars per capita in the world, with petrol consumption increasing by 4% a year. Because of the relatively small population and spread of the towns and cities, it is not always possible to use public transport, hence the high use of private vehicles.

GETTING THROUGH CUSTOMS & EXCISE

New Zealand is relatively free of pests and beasties, and intends to keep it that way! Its geographical isolation has provided a natural barrier against many of the world's more serious agricultural pests and diseases. Strict quarantine laws are in place to prevent this, and are enforced by uniformed officers who carry out inspections at seaports and airports.

There are heavy penalties for concealing dutiable goods from customs, for making false declarations, and for presenting false documentation such as false receipts.

People who knowingly bring restricted items into New Zealand and do not declare them will be prosecuted and will be subject to severe penalties and forfeit of goods.

Prepare to be checked

If you are bringing camping gear, tramping shoes, farm work clothing etc you must declare these to the MAF people at the Customs counter at the airport. They can then be carefully inspected to ensure they are free from any harmful substances.

Only recently two Russian cargo ships were suspected of carrying Asian gypsy moth eggs, which would have been laid whilst the ship was in an overseas port. The MAF had to inspect every inch of one of the vessels where some eggs were found on a packing case, and the other ship was not allowed into New Zealand ports because it wasn't considered to be 'clean'. If the eggs got into New Zealand they would very rapidly establish themselves in this country; since there are 'ideal' breeding conditions, these moths could devastate New Zealand's forests.

You might think there would be no harm in bringing in your favourite pot of jam or honey, a cutting from your special rose bush, and you might even think that your family goldfish wouldn't cause a tragedy. It would – **these things would be destroyed on your arrival**. So why not find them a good home *before* you leave? The same applies to the cat and the canary – *don't* think you can smuggle them in.

Prohibited goods

The following are prohibited, and you will need special **CITES certification** to bring them into New Zealand:

- Ivory in any form, that includes jewellery, ornaments, etc.

- Eggs and egg products, dried egg powder, instant meal products and egg cartons.

- Freshwater fish including salmon and trout, except canned.

- Honey including pollen, honeycombs, beeswax.

- Meat and meat products, fresh or cooked, including small goods except canned products.

- Popcorn (unpopped).

- Leis and Lei materials (Pacific island garlands).

- Plants live, dried, including pot plants and plant cuttings (except with correct certification).

- Straw packaging. Straw handcrafts may be allowed after examination and treatment.

- Animals, domestic pets, birds, fish, insects and fertilised eggs.

- Biological cultures and organisms.

- Clam shells and coral in any form, including jewellery, curios and souvenirs.

- Turtle and tortoise shells, including jewellery, souvenirs, hand crafts and curios.

Restricted goods

The following items are restricted and *must* be declared on arrival, when they will be examined:

- Coconuts including unprocessed product and husks.

- Dairy products, cheeses, milk, milk powder, butter, milk-based baby foods.

- Saltwater fish, fresh, dried and frozen, all species.

- Fruit, fresh, dried, frozen or cooked.

- Herbs and spices in any form, including when used in medicines.

- Honey from Niue.

- Mushrooms, fresh or dried.

- Noodles and rice including processed and instant meal products.

- Nuts, unprocessed and raw.

- Vegetables, fresh, dried, frozen or cooked.

- Bamboo, cane, rattan, basketware and mats in any form.

- Bulbs, corms, rhizomes and tubers.

- Cut flowers, dried flowers and leaves.

- Pine cones and pot pourri, including natural and decorative products.

- Seeds in any form, including commercially packaged.

- Animal remedies, including vaccines, pet and stock foods.

- Artefacts, including wooden carvings, figurines, shields, drums, spears and masks.

- Camping equipment, including clothing and footwear.

- Clothing, equipment and footwear used on farms or where animals are present (including slaughter houses) and shearing equipment.

- Feathers, bones, horns and tusks in any form.

- Furs, skins and hunting trophies.

- Saddles and riding equipment, including clothing, footwear and grooming equipment.

- Soil and water in any form, including religious items.

- Stuffed animals and reptiles.

- Wool (unprocessed) and animal hair, including yarns, crafted rugs and apparel.

Remember, by complying with these regulations you are helping New Zealand to protect its $8 billion horticultural industries which could be devastated by dangerous pests and diseases.

All fresh fruit, vegetables and living plant matter *must* have an **International Phytosanitary Certificate** (IPC) before they can be brought into New Zealand. Such goods arriving without the necessary documents will be destroyed or shipped to their country of origin at the passenger's expense.

For further clarification on these matters, you could contact the New Zealand Immigration Office or Embassy nearest to you, or contact:

The Ministry of Agriculture & Fisheries, Ray Emery Drive, Mangere, Auckland 1701. Tel: 64 9 275 5668.
The Ministry of Agriculture & Fisheries, Box 2526, Wellington 6001.
The Ministry of Agriculture & Fisheries, Box 54, Kaitaia 0500. Tel: 64 09 408 0900.

Bringing in animals

If you are from the United Kingdom, Norway, Sweden, Hawaii or Australia, and your dog or cat has been born in that country, then there are no quarantine requirements, only health tests which must be done before coming to New Zealand.

If, however, you are from a country other than the above, then there are strict quarantine requirements. Your animal will have to be quarantined in England for six months plus two months residency, or in Hawaii for four months, with two months residency, before being allowed into New Zealand. For further clarification or any further queries please contact one of the Ministry of Agriculture and Fisheries offices given above.

Bringing in drugs

Do not import drugs into New Zealand. The importation of drugs could result in your imprisonment. Be extremely wary of carrying packages or baggage for strangers.

QUESTIONS AND ANSWERS

What protection is there for a potential secondhand car buyer?

A motor vehicle securities register is administered by the Department of Justice; this is called **Autocheck**. A consumer considering buying a vehicle can phone the register toll free to check if any security interest is registered against the vehicle.

Can I drive in New Zealand on an overseas licence?

A valid driver's licence can be used for one year in New Zealand; the owner must then take a written and oral test in order to obtain a New Zealand driver's licence.

8

The Government
and the Economy

NEW ZEALAND'S CONSTITUTION

New Zealand's constitutional history can be traced back to 1840. Under the Treaty of Waitangi, the Maori people exchanged their sovereignty for the guarantees of the treaty and New Zealand became a British colony. New Zealand is today an independent state, a monarchy with a parliamentary government. Queen Elizabeth II has the title of Queen of New Zealand.

The constitution is concerned with the legislative, executive and judicial organs of government, their composition, powers and duties, and the relationship of these organs. New Zealand's Constitution Act 1986 brings together in one statute the most important provisions, and clarifies the rules relating to the governmental handover of power. It deals with the main components of New Zealand's statutory constitutional provisions: the Sovereign, the executive, the legislature and the judiciary. The Act and its provisions are safeguarded by the requirement of a special procedure to make amendments. The Electoral Act 1956 is the only other New Zealand constitutional statute to have such a provision.

A number of United Kingdom Acts (referred to as 'Imperial Acts') are still in force as part of the law of New Zealand. Some are historic constitutional Acts, such as the Magna Carta and the Habeas Corpus Act 1679. These Acts are listed and defined in the Imperial Laws' Application Act 1988.

A parliamentary monarchy

A British colony since 1840, national sovereignty was established by the Statute of Westminster in 1947; however, New Zealand remains a monarchy. The Governor-General, Queen Elizabeth II's representative, summons and dissolves Parliament, and assents to legislation.

The Parliament is made up of 120 members of the House of Representatives, elected under a mixed member proportional (MMP) voting system. General elections are held every three years.

National leaders

Governor-General	Hon Dame Silvia Cartwright
Prime Minister	Rt Hon Helen Clark
Deputy Prime Minister	Hon Dr Michael Cullen
Leader of the Opposition	Hon Simon William English

The seat of Government is the **Beehive**, situated in Central Wellington, the capital of New Zealand.

The Maoris

The Treaty of Waitangi

The **hapu** and **iwi** are the indigenous tribes and sub-tribes of New Zealand and their peoples now comprise about 14.5% of the population. In 1840 they signed a compact agreeing to exchange their governance for the guarantees of the Treaty of Waitangi. This treaty established the modern nation of New Zealand.

While the treaty has always been recognised and valued within Maori society, it could not be enforced in the courts as it has never been incorporated into statute law. In a landmark Court of Appeal case (*New Zealand Maori Council v Attorney General, 1987*) the special relationship between the Maori people and the Crown was interpreted by the Court as requiring the partners to act reasonably and with the utmost good faith towards each other. A number of Acts of Parliament now require the Crown to have regard to the principles of the Treaty of Waitangi, or to Maori interests or a Maori perspective.

Waitangi Tribunal

This tribunal considers claims from any Maori who considers he or she, or any group of Maori of which he or she is a member, is prejudiced by any legislation, policy or practice by or on behalf of the Crown which is inconsistent with the principles of the Treaty of Waitangi.

In the year 1991–92 the major report completed was that concerning the Te Roroa claim in the Dargaville area. Beginning 30 June 1992 hearings and conferences were held on 17 claims. Some of the areas under examination were the Ngai Tahu fisheries, Crown Forest assets; Tainui (Waikato River dam); railway lands; geothermal claims; Waikareao Estuary and Wellington Tenths.

The Crown and the Governor-General

The Governor-General is the representative of the Sovereign in New Zealand and exercises the royal powers derived from statute and the general law (prerogative powers). The powers of the Governor-General are set out in the Letters Patent 1983, and it is for the courts to decide on the limits of these powers. The Governor-General's main role is to arrange for the leader of the majority party in Parliament to form a government. Almost all the powers of the Governor-General are now statutory.

The Crown is part of Parliament and so the Governor-General's assent is required before bills can become law. The Governor-General is required, however, by constitutional convention and by the Letters Patent, to follow the advice of ministers. In extraordinary circumstances the Governor-General can reject advice if he or she believes that a government is intending to act unconstitutionally. This is known as the 'reserve power'.

The Sovereign appoints the Governor-General on the Prime Minister's recommendation, normally for a term of five years.

How Parliament works

Parliament consists of the Sovereign and House of Representatives. The members of the House, which has one chamber, are elected by universal suffrage in accordance with the Electoral Act 1956. Each Parliament has a term of three years, unless dissolved earlier. The Governor-General has the power to summon, discontinue and dissolve Parliament. The Queen and the Governor-General act on the advice of their Ministers.

The Constitution Act provides for Parliament to have full power to make laws; a Bill passed by the House becomes law when the Sovereign or Governor-General assents to it. The Act cancels the power of the United Kingdom Parliament to make laws for New Zealand.

The Constitution Act reaffirms the constitutional principles about parliamentary control of public finance; the Crown may not levy taxes, raise loans, or spend public money except through an Act of Parliament.

The judiciary

The judiciary is the third branch of government. The Constitution Act includes mechanisms to preserve the independence of judges, an important principle of the New Zealand Constitution. The judiciary interprets Acts passed by Parliament and also reviews actions of the Executive to ensure that it is acting within the law.

New Zealand Bill of Rights 1990

New Zealand has a Bill of Rights, but the Act of 1990 is not entrenched as 'higher law'. Thus the judiciary cannot strike down laws which are inconsistent with it. Where a legal provision is ambiguous, the Courts are required to interpret that provision consistently with the rights and freedoms contained in the Bill of Rights Act.

The Bill of Rights defines basic human rights. It applies to actions of the legislative, executive and judicial branches of government and to the activities of the public services.

Other sources of the Constitution

Included among other sources of the Constitution are the prerogative powers of the Sovereign, other statutes such as the State Sector Act 1988, the Electoral Act 1956 and the Judicature Act 1908, relevant English and United Kingdom statutes as defined in the Imperial Laws Application Act 1988, decisions of the Courts and conventions such as the democratic nature of the New Zealand constitution.

Political parties

There are two dominant political parties, the National and Labour parties. The Labour Party formed the Government between 1984 and October 1990, and the National Party from October 1990 until the elections of late 1993. In the 1993 general election when the National Party was returned people were not only asked to vote for their member of parliament, but whether or not they favoured MMP (mixed member proportional) system rather than the FPP (first past the post) system. The MMP won by a small margin. At the next election in 1996 parliamentary members were elected by MMP. Third parties have also been elected to Parliament in recent years in very small numbers, and a few members have left the main political parties to sit as independents.

Public service

The state sector is responsible for carrying out the policies of the Government. It comprises government departments and ministries along with the parliamentary, education, social welfare, housing, health and defence services, and a number of statutory organisations. The role of the public service is defined in the State Sector Act 1988, the Public Finance Act 1989 and the Official Information Act 1982, as well as in a large number of specific statutes.

Voting in elections

Persons 18 years and over have the right to vote in parliamentary elections. Enrolment as an elector is compulsory, but voting is not. To qualify for enrolment persons must:

- be at least 18 years old

- be New Zealand citizens or New Zealand residents

- have lived continuously in New Zealand for at least a year at some time

- have lived continuously for one month in the electorate they are to be enrolled in.

The conduct of polls is the responsibility of the Department of Justice. It is controlled by a returning officer in each electorate, who arranges voting facilities and staff, conducts the election, supervises the counting of votes, and declares the result.

Voting is by secret ballot. A preliminary count of ordinary votes is available for each electorate on election night, and final results are normally available a fortnight later, once special overseas votes have been received and counted. But the outcome of the voting is generally clear by the following day.

A CHANGING ECONOMY

Despite the problems of being a small population separated by a tremendous distance from most of the rest of the world's population, New Zealand has become a significant trading economy. The trade has always been based on farming, but in recent years New Zealand has been forced to diversify its markets and products. At present Australia is its largest export market, followed by Japan, the United States of America and the United Kingdom.

An exporting nation

New Zealand depends much on its export earnings. The following list summarises its key export business:

Principal exports	Year ended 2001	2002
	NZ$ (million)	
Meat & edible offal	4,182	4,429
Fish, crustaceans & molluscs	1,374	1,402
Milk powder, butter & cheese	5,790	5,891
Wood & wood articles	2,192	2,380
Aluminium & articles thereof	1,295	1,176
Casein & caseinates	624	699
Mechanical machinery & equipment	1,321	1,394
Principal imports		
Mechanical machinery & equipment	4,111	4,371
Vehicles, parts & accessories	3,667	4,389
Petroleum & products	3,486	2,822
Electrical machinery & equipment	3,390	2,801
Textiles & textile articles	1,738	1,657
Plastic & plastic articles	1,337	1,313
Iron & steel articles	929	1,011

Export oddities

The Government has been promoting a drive for an export-led economic recovery, and this has led to many New Zealand businesses developing new and unique overseas trade opportunities. The following are a few of the more enterprising examples taken from information published by the Department of Statistics:

- Seagram (NZ) Ltd are providing South Korea with 100,000 litres of malt whisky from its Dunedin-based Wilsons distillery.

- Hills Hats Ltd in Porirua won a contract to supply 36,000 woollen berets to the United Nations Peace Keeping forces.

- Orange roughy fish roe, once a waste product of orange roughy processing, is being marketed by a Wellington firm as an alternative to caviar. It has been successfully tried out in restaurants and will soon be available on Air New Zealand flights. Companies in New York, Sydney and Melbourne are interested in importing the roe which compares favourably with Russian lumpfish roe at a fraction of the price.

- Suttons Moss Ltd on the West Coast is exporting $1 million worth of sphagnum moss to Japan and Taiwan.

- Southern Alpsocks, manufacturers of outdoor socks, sold a consignment of 5,000 pairs to a Canadian outdoors wear chain. The firm said that New Zealand outdoor wear products had a high reputation in Canada and that they plan to use the socks' origin as a selling point.

- Deer velvet exports for 1991 topped $50m, mostly to South East Asia.

- Trial exports of opossum meat to Taiwan and Hong Kong have proven promising. If trade takes off, a return of $10 per carcass is expected.

- Tikaland Products have developed small but thriving niche markets in Australia, Britain and Germany for their canvas backpacks and cycle panniers.

- Riverland Estate Winery in the Kumeu valley supplied 120,000 bottles of sparkling kiwifruit wine to an importer in Florida. The wine is like an Asti but drier, suiting the American palate for dry wines.

- A Palmerston North entrepreneur is importing live ostriches for farming in New Zealand. Ostriches produce edible meat, feathers, oils for cosmetics, and soft leather suitable for making bags and leisure wear. The birds will be slaughtered in New Zealand and sent overseas for processing.

- Earnest Adams Ltd made an initial export sale of 54,000 microwave pies to supply 500 supermarkets throughout Taiwan. The mince and beefsteak pies are the first of the type available in Taiwan.

- Christchurch boat-engine manufacturer CWF Hamilton received an order for six twin jet engines to power rescue boats for the Italian Coast Guard.

- The largest-ever shipment of hydrogen peroxide, 800 tonnes valued at $1m and manufactured by Du Pont New Zealand, was exported to South America.

Agriculture

Farming and horticulture are major industries, providing a high proportion of New Zealand's export earnings.

Traditionally farming has centred on sheep and cattle to produce sheepmeat, beef, wool, dairy produce and hides, although in recent years new types of livestock have included deer, goats and fur-bearing animals such as fitch.

Horticulture has always provided well for the home market, but since the 1970s horticultural produce has become an important export earner.

Meat

Meat industry products are New Zealand's second largest export income earner, accounting for about 18% of merchandise exports. New Zealand's main meat exports are lamb, mutton and beef. About 80% of these products in 1997–98 were exported overseas. The domestic market purchases over 99% of the pigmeat and poultry produced in New Zealand.

Export marketing

New Zealand is a major exporter of sheepmeat, accounting for 54% of the world export trade; it is a small player in the global market for beef, accounting for about 6.4% of all the world beef exports.

New Zealand's major meat markets include the United Kingdom, Germany, France, Saudi Arabia and the United States for lamb; the United Kingdom, South Korea and France for mutton; and the United States, Canada, Japan, South Korea and Taiwan for beef.

Wool

New Zealand sheep are largely dual purpose meat/wool animals and their wool is predominantly strong; 75% of the clip is greater than 33 microns in diameter. This contrasts sharply with Australian wool, of which 99% is less than 33 microns. New Zealand is by far the largest producer of strong wools: it contributes a quarter of the world total and two and a half times as much as either the former Soviet Union or China, the next most significant producers. When the quantity of strong wool entering world trade is considered, New Zealand's share becomes even greater. Over 70% of traded strong wools are estimated to originate in New Zealand.

Net domestic consumption of wool in New Zealand is amongst the highest in the world on a per head basis. In 1997–98 the largest importers of New Zealand wool were China, the United Kingdom, India, Germany and Belgium.

New Zealanders love to luxuriate in pure wool products; the babies lie on pure sheepskin rugs, and customers look for the 'Pure New Zealand Wool' labels when purchasing clothing. Beds often have pure sheepskin underlays, and pure wool blankets. The shops and offices usually have wall-to-wall carpets, and so of course do private homes.

Wool product exports

The most important wool product exports from New Zealand are floor coverings and yarns. It is estimated that 34% of New Zealand wool is used in machine-made carpets, 12% in handknotted and hand-tufted carpets, 44% in apparel, and 10% in other uses, primarily upholstery and bedding. Total export earnings from wool products were $25.5 million in 1997–98.

Dairy produce

Dairy product exports constitute over 20% of total merchandise trade receipts for New Zealand, and, with the exception of milk and some dairy products for local consumption, the industry is primarily geared towards overseas markets – which account for between 90 and 95% of all milk produced on an annual basis.

Overseas marketing

The international market for dairy products is characterised by its small size relative to total world milk production, with only about 5% of production entering international trade. Because of this the market is especially vulnerable to shifts in climatic, commercial and political forces. Marginal production changes in the major producers can trigger massive shifts in supplies of, and prices for, products on the international market.

The major dairy exporters are the European Union, New Zealand, Australia, and to a lesser degree the United States of America and Canada. These five exporters supply between 90 and 95% of dairy products traded on the international market. Relatively smaller quantities are exported by the Nordic countries and from Eastern Europe.

The dairy industry has been working to diversify its markets for many years. Today, New Zealand's major markets vary for different products. There has been reduced access to both the United Kingdom and the European Union butter market; Britain, however, remains New Zealand's most valuable market for butter.

The old Soviet Union countries are important purchasers of New Zealand butter, as is the Middle East and North Africa, both of which have recently risen to prominence as markets for New Zealand produce.

The Dairy Board's export earnings from dairy products in 1998 were $4.6 billion, over 20% of total New Zealand merchandise exports.

Grape growing and wine production
The major grape growing regions are Gisborne, Hawkes Bay, Marlborough, Auckland and Poverty Bay. Perhaps you may have seen these names on wine labels at your own supermarket.

The area planted in wine grapes has doubled since 1990 to 12,665 hectares. In 1990 wine exports were valued at NZ$244 million. Chardonnay and Sauvignon are the major white grape varieties, and the major premium red grape varieties are Pinot Noir and Cabernet Sauvignon.

The key export markets for New Zealand are the UK, Australian and the US.

Jane Hunter and Hunter's Wines
Leading international viticulturist and managing director of Hunter's Wines (NZ) Ltd, Jane Hunter has successfully led Hunter's Wines since the death of her husband Ernie Hunter in 1987. Jane grew up in the Riverland area of South Australia where her parents owned vineyards. Jane married Ernie Hunter, an Irish immigrant, in 1984. Ernie had pioneered the overseas marketing and promotion of New Zealand wines and had established Hunter's Wines

at Blenheim in the early 1980s.

Since taking over Hunter's Wines, Jane has expanded the winery's operations – 40,000 cases of wine are now produced annually, three times the amount produced in 1987. Twenty per cent of the winery's produce is exported to Britain, Ireland, Switzerland, Canada and Australia.

Hunter's wines have earned an international reputation. Jane Hunter has been billed as one of the five best female 'wine makers' in the world, and her wines have been requested by the King of Sweden and the Prince of Thailand. The winery has won many international awards ranging from number one chardonnay in the world for its 1986 vintage, to the 1991 sauvignon blanc being awarded the Marquis de Goulaine trophy for the best in its class at the 1992 London International Wine and Spirit Competition. More recently the winery has concentrated on producing dry white wines and promising red wines. If you haven't done so already, try some!

Forestry

Forests cover about 29% or 8.1m hectares of New Zealand's land area. Of this about 6.4 million hectares are in natural forest and the rest is planted in production forest. Of the total planted production estate, about 91% is radiata pine (pinus radiata) and 5% douglas fir. Hardwoods comprise about 3% of New Zealand's planted production forests. The most important hardwood plantation species are eucalyptus originating from Australia.

Many of the earlier plantation forests were developed by the state, but the impetus for development and ownership has moved increasingly to the private sector over recent decades as the industry's capital and infrastructure has expanded. This led to the planting of 52,000 hectares of new forest in 1998. The volume of wood available for export is expected to increase dramatically, with about a 74% increase between 1996 and 2010. This projected increase assumes 60,000 hectares of new plantings occur each year.

Exports
Forest products are important earners of overseas funds. In one year recently exports of forest products were valued at about NZ$2,242m. Australia was the largest customer, taking 31%, mainly in sawn timber, paper and paperboard, panel products and wood pulp. The rest is taken by smaller customers, of which the largest was Korea at 11%.

Fisheries
New Zealands 200 nautical mile Exclusive Economic Zone (EEZ) is, with an area of 1.3 million square nautical miles, one of the world's largest. There are about 1,000 species of marine fish known in these waters, of which about 100 are commercially significant.

For a number of years the Government has limited foreign fishing in New Zealand waters to the tuna fisheries. Foreign charter fleets used to dominate the deepwater fisheries. There has been a significant investment by the seafood industry in new vessels with 63% of the total catch been taken now by New Zealand vessels.

Exports

The New Zealand fishing industry is export orientated, with more than 80% of the commercial catch being sold overseas. Significant exports were:

Commodity exported	Quantity tonnes (000)	Value NZ$m
Finfish or wetfish	261.6	746.1
Rock lobster	2.9	111.2
Shellfish	73.5	268.4

The principal export markets were Japan, $283.4m, United States, $195.5m and Australia, $130.6m.

Energy and minerals

New Zealand depends on a sustained supply of energy and mineral resources to fuel the economy, maintain industry and commerce, and sustain the well-being of its citizens. New Zealand is not self-sufficient in a number of key energy and mineral commodities; the shortfall is made up by imports.

The importance of oil security was highlighted during the 1990–91 Gulf crisis, when measures were taken to boost local oil production. This was done in conjunction with International Energy Agency emergency procedures. While the crisis did result in price rises, these were not as great as in some other countries nor were there any problems with continuity of supply. International oil markets are now more flexible than they were in the 1970s, with less risk of major disruptions to imported oil supplies. Thus, while oil supply security is still an important issue, it is unlikely to be as crucial as it was in the 1970s.

Unless significant new oil and gas discoveries are made, New Zealand's long-term self-sufficiency in hydrocarbons is expected to decline after 2005 as known oil and gas reserves run down.

Electricity

New Zealand is fortunate to have many rivers suitable for generating cheap hydro power. Hydro electricity was first used in New Zealand in the gold mining industry and the first generating station supplying the public with electricity was installed in Reefton in 1887 by the Reefton Electric Lighting Co. The first general government operated station was the Lake Coleridge scheme opened in 1914. The first thermal station was Meremere which was opened in 1958.

The winter of 1992 was quite severe, with record snow falls, and hard frosts. Unfortunately the hydro lakes were also quite low after a dry summer and autumn, and so everyone was encouraged to 'switch off' – and even shower together! – to save electricity.

The possibility of 'wind power' is now being looked into as a real alternative to hydro. In Wellington recently, high on a hill overlooking the Harbour, a propeller was erected on top of a tall pole, to test the viability of wind power.

Natural gas

Almost a third of the gas produced in New Zealand is used by electric power stations at New Plymouth, Huntley and Stratford. Another third is used to produce synthetic petrol at Motunui and 13% goes to produce methanol at Wairata. Industrial and commercial users consume the rest. Not all areas can receive gas for residential use.

Geothermal energy

Geothermal steam is used for electricity generation in the Wairakei and Ohaaki geothermal power stations. It is also used for direct process industrial heating, and for commercial and household heating. Geothermal waters are also used for recreational purposes and tourism.

Although geothermal systems are found throughout New Zealand, only those in the area between Lake Taupo and the Bay of Plenty (15 high temperature fields), and in Northland (Ngawha field) have the potential to provide a significant energy resource.

Whilst travelling from Tauranga in the Bay of Plenty, to Lake Taupo, you will pass through Wairakei Thermal Area; you will see signs as you approach, warning you of the danger of steam blocking your visibility as you drive through. The children always used to play 'spot the geyser' and look for areas where steam would just be pouring out of the earth, as there are many such locations in the Taupo area. The sheer delight of plunging into a thermal 'hot pool' is something indescribable. There are several of these in commercial areas throughout the Bay of Plenty, Rotorua and Taupo areas. In Rotorua many of the motels have their own thermal hot pools.

Minerals

New Zealand's mineral resources are diverse, but mining is generally small scale. Gold, ironsand, clays and sand and gravel for construction are the main minerals mined. Total yearly production of non-metallic minerals recently was valued at about $208m, while the value of metallic minerals totalled about $5164m.

New Zealand has in the black sands of the west coast beaches a large potential resource, stretching from Westport in the South Island and from Wanganui to Muriwai in the North Island. New Zealand Steel Ltd has two mining operations in the North Island. Titanomagnetic slurry is pumped to ships moored offshore for export to Japan.

Manufacturing

Small firms make up a big slice of the manufacturing sector. Companies with fewer than 50 employees produce 85% of manufacturing output and represent two-thirds of the manufacturing workforce. Here is a quick overview:

Aluminium
New Zealand Aluminium Smelter Ltd's Tiwai Point smelter has an annual production capacity of 244,000 tonnes of ingots.

Chemicals
A number of policies affecting the use of industrial chemicals have been modified to give greater protection to the environment. Timber treatment chemicals such as PCP are no longer used in New Zealand, but their accumulation in and around major mills poses environmental problems.

Electronics
The main consumer products are whiteware, plus a few niche market products. Strong growth has been enjoyed in the agricultural technology, health, commercial/industrial and professional radio and communication sectors.

Engineering

The most significant contribution to growth in engineering has been the government's decision to commission two ANZAC frigates, in partnership with the Australian Government.

Motor vehicles and components

New Zealand no longer has a motor vehicle assembly industry. All vehicles are imported in a fully built-up state. Imports of popular cars include: Nissan, Ford, Mazda, Mitsubishi, Toyota and Honda.

Tyres

To protect the two tyre manufacturers in New Zealand there is a tariff levy of 15% on all imports.

Paper

The Kinleith Mill operated by NZFP Pulp & Paper Ltd produces kraft linerboard, sack kraft and market pulp. Most of this is destined for overseas markets.

Software

New Zealand software manufacturers are in the forefront of export growth. Concerted efforts are under way to increase software exports to Australia.

Carpets

The two main manufacturers which produce wool-rich carpets are Feltex Carpets and Cavalier Bremworth, both based in Auckland.

Footwear

New Zealand has a long established footwear manufacturing industry. Shoe exports have risen dramatically in recent years. Australia is the main destination of New

Zealand footwear exports.

Assistance to industry

The Government's business development policy is aimed at assisting regions to identify and capitalise on their own opportunities for development. As part of this policy the Government provides targeted assistance through its **Business Development Programme**.

The object is to encourage businesses to become more innovative and internationally competitive. Currently the programme comprises a network of 21 Business Development Boards, three grant schemes, and the 'ExcelleNZ' quality products:

Business Development Board, Box 1041, Napier 4015. Tel: 64 6 835 2044.

Business Development Board, Box 7040, Auckland. Tel: 64 9 308 9141.

Business Development Board, Box 960, Hamilton 2015. Tel: 64 7 834 0100.

Business Development Board, Box 7045, Wanganui 5031. Tel: 64 6 345 0949.

Beyond 2000

The shape of New Zealand society today, as in the past, is the outcome of the interaction of global trends with uniquely local circumstances. There have been strong, interconnected and highly influential changes in the world that we live in. For example:

◆ awareness about globalisation, the effects that this places on the society, the economy and the government

- strengthening of the Information Technology industry which has provided new opportunities for both acquiring information and exploiting a global market

- shifts towards more service-based businesses

- changes in export requirements from the diverse number of trading partners New Zealand now has.

Running alongside these significant economic alterations are changes within New Zealand's social and demographic environments. These three factors all play a significant part in the shaping of New Zealand's future.

Statistics have shown for over a decade that New Zealand has been characterised as an aging population. However, New Zealanders are also becoming more educated. The knowledge economy may be creating more opportunities in employment for those who are now involved in the education systems.

Globalisation will challenge the identity of New Zealanders. The results could change current economic and social policies and processes, blur international lines and characteristics and open up networks and access to information.

The effects of these complex and interrelated changes on New Zealand fall beyond the social and economic capital base, to impact on social and economic progress and wellbeing. As the Government is in a current stage of change following the election of a new Labour lead alliance, new polices and practices will soon come into place. For a closer look at the changing economy go to the New Zealand Immigration Service Website: *www.immigration.-govt.nz.*

9

Women in New Zealand

THE STORY OF AN EARLY WOMAN SETTLER

According to family historian Anne Folkema, Jane Udy was pregnant with her fifth child when she landed on the beach at Te Whanganui a Tara (Port Nicholson) in February 1840.

Pito-one pa (Maori Meeting House) lay to the west; Hikoikoi was the mouth of the river estuary to the east, with the Waiwhetu Owhiti (Maori) settlements on the opposite bank. In between, assorted temporary dwellings housed the Europeans who had arrived on the ships *Aurora* and *Oriental.*

Jane Udy gave birth to Thomas Clemence on 25 May under an awning, hastily erected after the family's second cottage built of flax and grasses burnt to the ground.

Jane's husband Hart Udy was a builder, and was in great demand to build homes for the new settlers. It was said that there were only six builders in Wellington in 1840, so times were fruitful for Hart Udy and his family. His eldest son Hart Junior began working with him in 1844, when he was only nine. Jane Udy eventually became a mother of nine children, and ran the farm and home that they owned. Poultry and dairy products often contributed to household income, while other farm produce increased self-sufficiency. In this way the family built up sizeable savings.

However, the family's position in the Hutt Valley was not a straightforward one. Issues of land had not been settled, and in 1845 the Udys were stripped of their possessions by an unidentified Maori party.

In May 1846 a military outpost was attacked and six soldiers were killed. The Udys remained, hiding in the dense bush beside the river, or taking refuge in the Wesley Chapel.

Yes, the early settlers were a strong and determined breed. The women had to work long hard hours utilising what they could; they would have known 'luxuries' before they set sail for New Zealand, and upon arrival had to learn to live off the land and by their own wits.

When I came to New Zealand in 1972 things had settled down somewhat! I found the women very capable and able to turn their hand to just about anything.

I soon learned new skills, and find that I can now make a very good attempt at just about anything. I have learned how to bottle fruit, and can cook for any number of unexpected visitors, I can sew, having made several ball gowns, suits, dresses – you name it! I had always thought that Christmas mincemeat only came in jars off the shop shelf; upon coming to New Zealand I learned how to make my own mincemeat, and believe me I could put any bottling firm out of business if I so chose!

CENTENNIAL SUFFRAGE 1893–1993

Universal suffrage was gained in New Zealand in 1893, and the Government designated 1993 as Suffrage Centennial Year. It established a $5 million Trust Fund to contribute towards projects which will:

- enhance the status and advancement of women
- commemorate the centenary of women's suffrage in New Zealand
- publicise the positive contributions women have made to New Zealand's political, economic, social and cultural life.

The Trust's objectives are to stimulate activities which close the gaps between women and men, and Maori and non-Maori women, and to focus on projects which will help women achieve greater confidence, skills, opportunities and recognition.

In addition to community initiatives funded by the Trust and private sponsorship, all government departments will fund and organise activities and projects aimed at improving the situation of women.

A unit within the Ministry of Women's Affairs is servicing the Trust and coordinating centennial activities.

Women today

Women make up nearly 51% of the population and have adopted a saying, born out of television advertising, that 'girls can do anything'. Women can now be found in many job situations that only a few years ago would have been thought impossible.

- Lynne runs a haulage business in Auckland: she concentrates on house moving, and plays an equal role with her employees. She comments that other women's attitudes have been the hardest to take.

- Megan works as a 'melters tapper' at a steel mill in the South Island. Her working partner, a male, says that she is better than some of the men, and certainly more dependable in the dangerous job they do at the furnace face.

- Helen has worked as an overhead crane driver at a steel mill, doing the dangerous job of moving huge pots of molten metal from one spot to another. She says that she had to prove herself, and now the men respect her. It's a fine line she says; you mustn't be seen to be doing the job *too* well!

- Joan is a pilot with a commercial airline. She says that she has found most hostility from other women. One passenger was heard to say to her husband upon boarding the aircraft that she didn't fancy a woman driver!

- Carol has worked at a South Auckland Steel mill for six years as a crane driver. Initially she was ignored, but now she is accepted as one of the best.

- Women comprise 22% of the lawyers in New Zealand. They are generally paid less than men and fewer of them are partners in law firms.

- Racing is a big industry in New Zealand, with even the smallest of towns having race tracks. Only a few years ago it was a male dominated scene, but now half New Zealand jockeys are women!

◆ Penny Jamieson was the first woman to be consecrated as an Anglican bishop; the ceremony was performed in Dunedin in 1990.

◆ Dame Catherine Tizard was the first female Governor-General in New Zealand, a position she held from 1990 to 1996.

Women at work

Women's increasing participation in the labour force has been one of the strongest employment trends in the post-Second World War period. Women now comprise almost half of the labour force. Since 1991, the number of women in paid part-time work has increased 55% to reach 287,934. Meanwhile, 516,378 women were in full-time jobs. However, women received less income than men, with the median income for women in the year to March 2001 being NZ$14,500, compared with NZ$24,900 for men.

Young women are more likely than young men to be studying and more likely to have a post-school qualification. Nineteen per cent of women aged 20 to 29 have a degree or higher level qualification, compared with 14% of men. The most common field of study for women with a post-school qualification is health (22% compared with 5% of men), while engineering and related technology is the least common (2% compared with 33% for men).

EQUAL PAY?

Paid employment is the main source of income for women aged under 60 in New Zealand. According to figures published by *Statistics New Zealand* in 2001, the average ordinary time weekly earnings for females was $572.50 and male's weekly pay was $751.15.

The positions of women and men in the distribution of market income are starkly and diametrically opposed. Women are concentrated in the lower income groups, men in the higher. In spite of this, the relative position of women has improved slightly, with a 3% increase in the proportion of women in the top two income groups, and a 3% decline in the number of men in these groups.

The reasons for the disparity in earnings are many, including women's lower labour force participation, their fewer average hours of paid work, greater likelihood of intermittent participation in paid work, and younger average age in the workforce, lower levels of education and different occupational distribution. A recent study suggests that these factors can explain at least two-thirds of gender differences in pay, leaving one-third unexplained.

Women of all ages are more likely than men to rely on income from welfare benefits and pensions. Benefits made up over 20% of the incomes of women under the age of 35 in 1988–89, compared with 5% of men's income in the same age group. For women aged 35–59, 14–15% of their income came from benefits compared with 2% of male income in the same period. Over the age of 60, 72% of women's incomes is derived from social welfare payments, compared with 49% of men's incomes. Maori women are particularly dependent on welfare payments; benefits were the sole source of income for 47% of Maori women in 1981, compared to 25% of non-Maori women.

The Equal Pay Act 1972

The Equal Pay Act 1972 sought to remove discrimination in rates of remuneration based on the sex of employees. The Act has been interpreted as providing for equal pay rates for men and women doing the same work, although it does allow for special rates to be paid to employees on the basis of 'special qualities'. A difficulty lies in distinguishing whether payments are for special qualities or represent discrimination. The fact remains that women continue to earn significantly less than men.

While the pay gap between male and female earnings closed by seven percentage points (72% to 79%) between the passage of the Equal Pay Act 1972, and its final implementation in 1977, it rose to only 81% in the next 15 years.

Despite the Equal Pay Act the distribution of market income is heavily weighted in favour of males as noted above. In all occupational groups male full-time employees receive higher median incomes than their female counterparts. This is so even in occupational groups which are predominantly female, such as clerical work. Even though 74% of clerical workers are female, they earn on average only 73% of the average male clerical worker's pay. In the service and sales occupation groups, men's full-time median incomes were respectively 73% and 69% higher than women's.

In the higher paid occupational groups the gaps are not quite as large. Male full-time managers and administrators have a median income which is 48% higher than their female co-workers, while for male professional and technical workers it is 39% higher. This is probably a reflection of the higher education qualifications which are required for these occupations, which attract some measure of higher reward. However, even where qualifications are equal, women do not earn as much as men. For example, in 1986 only 17% of women with tertiary qualifications earned over NZ$20,000, compared to half all men with similar qualifications. Nearly half of all women with tertiary qualifications earned $10,000 or less compared with only 15% of men. A lack of qualifications has a significant impact on the incomes of Maori women, whose full-time earnings in 1986 were over $2,000 less than that of all women. Of this difference, 30% has been attributed to lack of qualifications.

Recent figures show average ordinary time weekly earnings for in the region of NZ$720.00. In comparison women earned approximately NZ$550.00.

CURRENT ATTITUDES IN NEW ZEALAND

Thankfully the New Zealand male isn't as 'crass' as his Australian counterpart, who so often likes to refer to all women as 'Sheilas'. Perhaps this is an inordinate fondness for women named 'Sheila', or even a huge memory lapse!

The modern New Zealand male is more sensitive, and in many cases the male has taken over the traditional female role in bringing up the family whilst the woman pursues her career, or perhaps finishes her studies. There are, however, still pockets of males who continue to denigrate the female into the 'house help' role. Some New Zealand males still retain the 'settlers' mentality of hard living and hard drinking, rugby and racing.

The attitude of some men towards females, who compete for jobs in a male dominated workforce, especially in manual work areas, is that expressed by Arthur Daley of the TV series *Minder*, i.e. 'her indoors', or the well worn phrase 'the little woman at home'. We can only hope that such labelling of women will soon be a thing of the past. Here in New Zealand we are working towards that. Let's hope we are the first to achieve this, as we were with votes for women.

'Women Should Not Imitate Men'
A recent article in a Christchurch newspaper by General Eva Burrows of the Salvation Army said:

> 'In seeking equality, women should not imitate men. They must remember the feminine factor, they have their own psyche, gifts and talents. We can be equal but different. This world is very aggressive, competitive and masculine. It needs the feminine touch. You despoil your characteristics if you try to lead in a masculine way. Women should not be limited to a life in the home, it was right for them to take their place in all the professions.'

LIFE FOR RURAL WOMEN

According to the recent report *Status of New Zealand Women*, rural women continue to form only a small percentage (14%) of the total female population. This includes women living in rural settlements as well as those living on farms. (The term 'rural' is defined as those areas outside centres of population of 1,000 or more people.)

New Zealand women have traditionally been well organised. For example the **Country Women's Institute** cements social bonds; the **Women's Division Federated Farmers** (WDFF) acts as a lobby group within Federated Farmers (the major association of New Zealand farmers) and between farming women and the rest of society; and since 1980 **Women in Agriculture** (WAG) has developed a support network for women moving into non-traditional roles and employment in agriculture.

What a rural survey showed

A survey carried out recently by rural women's organisations showed that:

♦ Women who live on farms do 80% of the household duties.

♦ 60% of farms have only one unpaid worker (usually paid in kind with housing, food etc) and 70% have no paid employees.

♦ 80% of farm women work with the stock but most do not decide what will be done or how it will be done.

♦ Only 30% of farm women regard themselves as farmers. Almost half regard themselves primarily as homemakers, but are expected to assist on the farm as required at short notice, usually for no pay.

♦ 40% of farm women work in paid employment off the farm, and 30% believe that this is essential to supplement farm income. Women are more likely to work off the farm than men, but are constrained by a lack of job opportunities in rural areas. Some farm women have taken up paid work in towns and return to the farm only at weekends.

'For home and country'
The **Federation of Country Women's Institutes of New Zealand** has four aims: to unite women to promote the international motto – 'for home and for country'; to foster handicrafts, choral, drama, and other cultural activities; to encourage participation in community and national affairs; and to promote international understanding and goodwill through the organisation, **Associated Country Women of the World** (ACWW).

Women's Division Federation Farmers (WDFF) began life in 1925 with 16 members. A Mr L H McAlpine, an organiser for the Farmers Union, helped start this organisation. He had been shocked to learn of the conditions facing many rural women – primitive houses, bad roads, isolation, loneliness, illness and lack of help of any kind. The **Emergency Housekeeping Service** was established and still exists today, now known by another name, **Home Care**.

During the war years, as well as knitting socks and sending parcels to the troops, the WDFF raised 5,000 pounds sterling to buy a Spitfire aeroplane for the defence of Britain. This very large sum was raised in just one month from donations and the collection of scrap metal. In the 1950s an education bursary was established and since then there have been many grants and bursaries for rural people to take up education opportunities.

Today, the WDFF is concerned to establish a national rural health task force to monitor the impact of the health reforms in rural areas; promote rural equity issues on special education funding; and regenerate interests in neighbourhood support groups to fight increasing crime levels in country areas. They are also promoting the role of rural women in small business and tourism ventures to diversify their economic bases. Among other occasions in their celebrations of the women's suffrage centenary, WDFF organised Project Tree – a nationwide kowhai tree planting scheme.

WOMEN'S SOCIAL OPPORTUNITIES

A survey done by the Hillary Commission for Recreation and Sport showed that women do less vigorous physical activity than men. A total of 32% of males and 24% of females get the quality and quantity of exercise necessary for aerobic fitness, whereas over 40% of women and less than 40% of men do moderate physical activity. Most of the difference was due to doing housework, done by 93% of women but only 59% of men.

Until age 11, boys and girls were equally active, but male activity increased slightly after the age of 11 (by 2%) and female activity decreased (by 10%). There was a marked difference in girls' and boys' preferred physical activities: girls favoured dancing, horseriding and netball, while boys preferred cricket, rugby union, skateboarding and soccer.

It was found that women were less likely to run or jog than men (27% female, 41% male) but more likely to swim (29% female, 26% male). Walking was equally popular with both sexes. Women were more likely to do fitness exercises at home or go to a fitness class, and were more likely than men to exercise alone.

The three most popular exercises for women were swimming, cycling and aerobics, and for men swimming, snooker/pool and cycling. Young men under 18 play rugby and tennis, and young women play tennis. Older men and women play golf and lawn bowls.

Clubs for women

There are many types of clubs for women, ranging from the Church groups, such as 'Young Wives'. I joined such a group when I first arrived, and met a good range of people, and still retain contact with them, even though I am no longer a 'young wife'. There are also professional clubs, for females only, and **Toastmasters** which is usually a male and female organisation. The best way to find out about the range of clubs available to you is to contact the Citizens Advice Bureau nearest to you, and they will give you a complete run down.

◆ Citizens Advice Bureau, 305 Queen Street, Auckland. Tel: 64 9 377 3314.

And don't forget the YWCA which is alive and well in all the main areas.

If you enjoy outdoor sports, there are always golf clubs to join, and outdoor bowls is another very popular sport. If you feel a little more energetic there are plenty of tennis clubs, squash clubs and swimming and also athletic clubs.

THE COST OF LOOKING GOOD

A visit to the hairdresser for a cut, shampoo and set costs in the region of $78–$98 for women and $58–$68 for men, depending upon the standard of hairdressing salon. To have highlights or a permanent colour with a set would cost up to $113, a tint would be $63, a semi permanent would start around $53 and a perm would cost around $98–$153.

Correct dress is advisable for a career woman, and a suit would cost in the region of $300–$600. Casual wear is the order of the day for holidays and weekends, and after work occasions, and there are lots of shops to tempt you. They range from the low-priced casual wear shops, many of which are Australian, to the small boutiques, which are usually privately owned, and stock the more unusual lines of clothing, to the larger department stores like **Kirkaldie & Stains** in Wellington and **Smith & Caughey** in Auckland, where you can choose from a large range of clothes to suit all occasions. **Farmers** is a cheaper range department store with branches throughout New Zealand; there you can buy anything from a plant pot to a new coat.

If you live in the north of the North Island, you will find you can probably survive the 'winter' with a lightweight coat or raincoat. But if you live in the lower half of the North Island, or in the South Island, you will need a warm winter coat. This will typically cost somewhere between $200 and $500.

Shoes can cost between $100 and $200 for New Zealand made, to $150–$300 and even more for imported ones.

Perfume is quite expensive, due largely to the high import cost. A few price comparisons:

Estee Lauder

White Linen	100ml	$ 93
	50ml	$ 72
	25ml	$ 49
Oscar de la Renta	30ml	$ 80
Eau de Toilette	2fl. oz	$130
Opium	30ml	$ 89
Chanel Allure	30ml	$130

Makeup prices are as follows:

Revlon

Night cream	$ 50
Day cream	$ 40
Foundation	$ 35
Blusher	$ 30
Lipstick	$ 19.70

Estee Lauder

Cleanser	$ 50
Toner	$ 46
Night repair cream	$155
Moisturiser	$130
Makeup base	$ 72
Foundation cream	$ 70

These are just a few examples of the prices you can expect to pay in New Zealand. These are by no means the only cosmetics you can buy here, as all the cosmetic companies are selling very well in New Zealand.

SOME FAMOUS NEW ZEALAND WOMEN

Jean Batten

Born in Rotorua in 1909, died in Jamaica in 1982 of an untreated dog bite. Jean Batten was one of the world's pioneer women aviators, establishing a string of world records in the mid-1930s. Her tally as a record-holding solo pilot includes four world records for any type of plane, and another five important records. During the war she worked as an ambulance driver in France and in a munitions factory in Dorset, having failed the eye test for the Air Transport Auxiliary of the RAF.

Katherine Mansfield

Born in Wellington in 1888 and died in Fontainbleau in 1923. Katherine Mansfield is New Zealand's best known and respected author. Her work has earned her an international reputation as one of the finest short story writers in English. Her work has been translated into 20 languages.

Malvina Major

Born in Hamilton in 1943. She was awarded an OBE in 1985 and a DBE in 1991. Malvina Major has one of the finest lyric soprano voices in the world, particularly suited to the music of Rossini, Bellini, Donizetti and Mozart. She received wide acclaim for her international performance in Rossini's *Elizabetta Regina d'Ingliterra* at London's Camden Festival and in 1960 made her international debut at the Saltzburg Festival as Rosina in the *Barber of Seville*.

Kiri Te Kanawa

Born in Gisborne in 1944. She studied under Sister Mary

Leo from 1959 to 1965. Kiri left New Zealand at the age of 21 to study at the London Opera Centre. Upon graduating, Kiri joined the Royal Opera House, Covent Garden, making her debut in 1971 as Xenia in *Boris Godonov* by Moussorgsky. She is world renowned and especially remembered for singing at the wedding of Prince Charles and Lady Diana Spencer.

Kate Sheppard
Born in Liverpool in 1848, and died in 1934. Kate was a very able leader, and between 1888 and 1893 she organised five petitions to Parliament calling for women to be included as voters in general elections. Rejected one after the other, the petitions gained more signatures, until the fifth in 1893 carried the names of 31,872 women, about a third of the adult female population at that time. On 19 September 1893, as a result of determined campaigning, the Electoral Bill received the Governor's consent.

Yvette Williams
Born in Dunedin in 1929. Yvette jumped a record-breaking 6.24 metres in the long jump, making her the first New Zealand woman to win a gold medal at an Olympiad. She won four gold British Empire Games medals and set a world record for the long jump between 1950 and 1954. She has won many other events, and was named New Zealand Sportsman of the Year (an award won by a woman only once before) in both 1950 and 1952.

Annelise Coberger
Born in Christchurch in 1971. Her Bavarian grandfather, Oscar Coberger, had been his region's ski champion. He

emigrated to New Zealand in 1926 and opened the country's first ski shop at Arthur's Pass. With such an illustrious parentage it is no wonder that Annelise was so keen on skiing. At 18 years she won the prestigious German junior slalom championships. In 1991 with an international ranking of fifth in the slalom event, she climbed from a world ranking of 86th to be placed 24th. In the 1991–92 northern winter she won her first World Cup.

Amy Block

New Zealand's most notorious woman was undoubtedly Amy Block, the confidence trickster. She spent her life fabricating a series of personalities and complicated scenarios in order to gain money. She spent nearly half her career in prison from 1884 to 1909. When not in prison she obtained work as a cook or housekeeper defrauding her employers of money and possessions. She created a variety of personas, including Miss Crisp, Mrs Merry, Mrs Chanel and Charlotte Skevington. Her greatest coup was in 1908 when she posed as Percy Carol Redwood, passing herself off as a wealthy young man (the nephew of a Bishop!); while taking a holiday in Port Molyneaux, she courted a landlady's daughter. They married with 200 guests attending the wedding. Her fraudulent behaviour was her undoing, and she was put on trial for false pretences in 1909.

QUESTIONS AND ANSWERS

How many women in New Zealand own farms?

Fewer than five per cent of farms are owned by women with sole titles. Most of these come through inheritance as a widow or daughter, rather than by independent purchase.

What pre-school care is there for children?

Kindergartens and playcentres are very popular in all areas. Full-time kindergarten care for the working mother would cost around $100 per week.

Leisure Opportunities

In 2002, 1,955,700 people travelled to New Zealand to holiday or visit family and friends.

AROUND AND ABOUT THE NORTH ISLAND

The Bay of Islands

Starting in the 'winterless north' there are so many beautiful beaches you would find it hard to choose which was the best. The **Bay of Islands**, with Paihia the most popular holiday resort, is the most beautiful holiday spot. From here you can go on the 'Fullers Cream Trip' on a modern catamaran – *The Big Cat* – and cruise around all the beautiful little coves in luxury, dropping off at Russell, an old settlement across the harbour from Paihia. There are lots of game fishing launches which can be privately hired, or you can just pay to go for a trip on one and catch the 'big one'.

Accommodation is covered in this area by bed and breakfast, motels, hotels, luxury lodges and resorts. For comprehensive and up-to-date information on location and prices for these accommodation options go to *www.purenz.com*. Information can also be obtained from New Zealand Tourism Offices overseas.

The Coromandel Peninsula

Travelling south through Auckland, the next notable holiday favourite with New Zealanders is the **Coromandel Peninsula**. Here you will find many beautiful secluded shores, with bush and grass verging onto the beaches. At Hahei Beach, named after a legendary Maori explorer, you will find two Maori Pa sites at the southern end, and beyond that two 'blowholes' which can provide a spectacular sight at high tide. A two hour return walk at the northern end of the beach leads to a large sea-formed cavern known as Cathedral Cave.

Accommodation is covered in this area by bed and breakfast, motels, hotels, luxury lodges, resorts and holiday homes. For comprehensive and up-to-date information on location and prices for these accommodation options go to *www.purenz.com*. Information can also be obtained from New Zealand Tourism Offices overseas.

The Bay of Plenty

South once more, we reach the **Bay of Plenty**, renowned for its wonderful long expanse of white sands. Mount Maunganui is the most popular holiday spot, especially for the young people, who find lots to do during their summer holidays, from bungy-jumping to white water rafting. This is the place to go if you are looking for a hectic New Year's Eve, with bands and open air concerts all the rage. Tauranga, the main city of the Bay of Plenty, lies across the harbour from Mount Maunganui. There is a harbour bridge for easy access. Here you will find an excellent selection of shops and facilities. A big feature of this area is the Hot Water Sea Pool complex at Mount

Maunganui. Here you can luxuriate in wonderful temperatures all year round. There is nothing nicer on a cold miserable day than to go along to the Pools. To lie in the lovely hot water at night to look at the stars is a great experience.

Accommodation is covered in this area by bed and breakfast, motels, hotels, luxury lodges, resorts, holiday homes and homestays. For comprehensive and up-to-date information on location and prices for these accommodation options go to *www.purenz.com*. Information can also be obtained from New Zealand Tourism Offices overseas.

The Lakes

Inland now to the Lakes, to Lake Rotorua first. Here you will be able to sightsee to your heart's content, as this is the place to be for the traditional Maori Concert Parties, and Maori Hangi's, the Maori way of cooking. A hole is dug in the ground, lined with stones, and a fire lit. The stones heat up, and when they are hot enough, food wrapped in sacks is lowered into the pit. These are then covered and the food left to cook for many hours. The results are delicious. Rotorua is a land of thermal activity with hot water geysers and hot mud pools – many of the motels in this area have their own thermally heated spa pools. The imposing Tudor Towers, set amongst beautiful gardens, is the place where the early settlers used to flock to 'take the waters' with a bathhouse built for rheumatic people. The fishing is excellent here, the lakes and streams abounding with big fish. At the Rainbow Springs visitors centre you can feed large trout by hand in the pools which run through this area – no fishing is allowed here though!

Accommodation is covered in this area by bed and breakfast, motels, hotels, luxury lodges, resorts, holiday homes, homestays and backpackers. For comprehensive and up-to-date information on location and prices for these accommodation options go to *www.purenz.com*. Information can also be obtained from New Zealand Tourism Offices overseas.

Lake Taupo

Lake Taupo lies in the centre of New Zealand's central volcanic plateau. Here is the world famous Wairakei geothermal hydroelectric power establishment. Lake Taupo itself is a very popular retreat for many a 'top person' or movie star wanting a peaceful fishing holiday. This is where you always catch 'the big one'! Here also are thermal hot baths, the AC Baths being a very popular venue. There is also an old historic hotel, De Bretts Thermal Resort, with two large thermal mineral outdoor pools, freshwater pools and 12 private minerals pools. Here the early settlers used to come to soak their rheumatic limbs in the comforting waters.

Taupo also makes a good stopping off point for the ski fields just 90km south, at Tongariro National Park.

If you are a golfing fan, you can play a round on the internationally famous Wairakei Golf Course, or maybe the Taupo Golf Course further into town would suit you. Lake Taupo itself offers a variety of attractions with yachting, water skiing, jet boating and rowing.

Accommodation is covered in this area by bed and breakfast, motels, hotels, luxury lodges, resorts, holiday parks, and homestays. For comprehensive and up-to-date information on location and prices for these accommodation options go to *www.purenz.com*. Information can also be obtained from New Zealand Tourism Offices overseas.

Mount Egmont

We can cross now to the west coast and New Plymouth, with Mount Egmont National Park on the doorstep, an ideal environment for the tramper, or we can take it easy and use the Mount Egmont daily shuttles.

Golfers have a choice of nine golf courses; bowlers are very welcome in all the clubs; and fishing enthusiasts will be well satisfied with the rivers and streams.

Accommodation is covered in this area by bed and breakfast, motels, hotels, luxury lodges, resorts, holiday parks, homestays and backpackers. For comprehensive and up-to-date information on location and prices for these accommodation options go to *www.purenz.com*. Information can also be obtained from New Zealand Tourism Offices overseas.

Sightseeing in Wellington

South to the capital Wellington, where there is sightseeing in abundance: you can either go around at your own pace, or join one of the city tours – either of these is certainly a 'must' to explore the steep hills, narrow crowded streets, Parliament, a quaint cable car, art galleries, a zoo and the Botanic Gardens to mention a few.

Accommodation is covered in this area by bed and breakfast, motels, hotels, serviced apartments and back-packers. For comprehensive and up-to-date information on location and prices for these accommodation options go to *www.purenz.com*. Information can also be obtained from New Zealand Tourism Offices overseas.

DISCOVERING THE SOUTH ISLAND

From Wellington you can cross to the South Island by sea or air. By sea you can cross with your car at around $190 for the car each way, $59 per adult $35 per child each way. The alternative is to cross by sea at a cost of $59 and catch the Mount Cook Landline Coach to your destination. The coach will meet the ferry and take you to Christchurch for $132 per person. To fly across to, say, Christchurch from Wellington will cost around $250 one way by Air New Zealand or Ansett.

In the South Island the scenery is equal to anywhere in Switzerland, with the majestic mountains begging you to go skiing (in the winter of course!).

Picton

Why not stop awhile in Picton, where you will alight from the ferry? Picton is the principal centre of Marlborough Sounds, a breathtakingly beautiful scenic reserve with regular launch cruises in and around the bays in Queen Charlotte Sound. You can also take a fishing trip and a moonlight cruise during the summer months.

Accommodation is covered in this area by bed and breakfast, motels, hotels, luxury lodges, resorts, holiday parks, homestays and backpackers. For comprehensive and up-to-date information on location and prices for these accommodation options go to *www.purenz.com*. Information can also be obtained from New Zealand Tourism Offices overseas.

Christchurch

Christchurch has a lot to offer, with lovely parks and reserves, and the Avon River idling through gives a peaceful restful feeling – even though Christchurch itself is a very busy tourism centre. You can make your base here whilst you visit all the places of interest, as Christchurch is fairly central, and has excellent transport facilities.

Accommodation is covered in this area by bed and breakfast, motels, hotels, luxury lodges, resorts, holiday parks, homestays and backpackers. For comprehensive and up-to-date information on location and prices for these accommodation options go to *www.purenz.com*. Information can also be obtained from New Zealand Tourism Offices overseas.

Queenstown

Queenstown is a must, even out of the ski season. There is windsurfing, water skiing and fishing to be had – not forgetting the excitement of white water raft trips and exhilarating jet boat rides on the nearby rivers. Ride on horseback along the original goldmining trail to the historic town of Moonlight, or by mini-coach to the beautiful Skippers Canyon, also steeped in goldmining history. For the more leisurely minded, a trip on the *SS Earnslaw* on Lake Wakatipu is a delight. The scenery is wonderful.

Accommodation is covered in this area by bed and breakfast, motels, hotels, luxury lodges, resorts, holiday parks, homestays and backpackers. For comprehensive and up-to-date information on location and prices for these accommodation options go to *www.purenz.com*. Information can also be obtained from New Zealand Tourism Offices overseas.

Franz Josef

Up the west coast of the South Island you will pass through Haast Pass, Fox Glacier and then onto Franz Josef. This is a small tourist centre near the northern boundary of Westland National Park. Franz Josef is a tranquil settlement nestled amongst the splendid native forest of the coast under the massive peaks of the Southern Alps. There are many safe, pleasant walking tracks in the surrounding bush and foothills of the mountains. Of particular interest is the Franz Josef Glacier, which is a short walk or drive from the town.

Accommodation is covered in this area by bed and breakfast, motels, hotels, holiday parks and backpackers. For comprehensive and up-to-date information on location and prices for these accommodation options go to *www.purenz.com*. Information can also be obtained from New Zealand Tourism Offices overseas.

Nelson

Moving on northwards still, passing through Hokitika, Greymouth until you reach Nelson. Nelson has the reputation of being one of the sunniest spots in New Zealand. It is sheltered by the hills, and has fine mountain, river and lake scenery. There are golden beaches – Tahuna, Rabbit Island and Cable Bay. At Tahuna there is a children's playground, skating rink and golf course.

Accommodation is covered in this area by bed and breakfast, motels, hotels, luxury lodges, resorts, holiday parks, homestays and backpackers. For comprehensive and up-to-date information on location and prices for these accommodation options go to *www.purenz.com*. Information can also be obtained from New Zealand Tourism Offices overseas.

SKIING IN NEW ZEALAND

The skiing season in New Zealand extends from June to late October at ski areas in the North and South Islands. Many fields also have snow-making equipment to ensure reliable snow depth and quality. New Zealand has 12 commercial ski areas, 12 club ski fields and one commercial cross-country ski area.

In the North Island the main skiing centre is Mount Ruapehu in the Tongariro National Park. There are two commercial ski fields, Whakapapa and Turoa, and one club field (Tukino) at Ruapehu, with the Manuganui ski club area in Mount Egmont in Taranaki (New Plymouth).

In the South Island the commercial ski areas are Coronet Peak, the Remarkables (Queenstown), Cardrona, Treble Cone (Wanaka) Ohau, Mount Dobson (Aorangi), Porter Heights, Mount Hutt, Mount Lyford (Canterbury), and Rainbow Valley (Marlborough). There are ten smaller ski club fields in the South Island.

The Waioru Nordic Ski Area on the Pisa Range near Wanaka offers 24 kilometres of cross-country skiing. Glacier skiing on the Tasman and Fox Glaciers, with access via ski-planes, is also available, while guided heliskiing and ski touring open up the Ben Ohau Ranges, the Harris Mountains, the Two Thumbs Range, the Mount Cook/Tasman Glacier area, Mount Hutt and Queenstown in the South island and the Ruahine Ranges in the North.

Winter skiing holiday packages

There are a variety of package holiday specialists that are listed on the website for Tourism New Zealand at *www.purenz.com*. Skiing is such a large part of the New Zealand winter that these companies can cater to your specific needs and at your level of budget. Whether you want to go skiing, snowboarding or heliskiing on one mountain or many they will provide you with a package deal to suit you. Both Air New Zealand and Ansett offer competitive deals in the winter season but these prices vary seasonally. So the best idea if planning a skiing holiday in New Zealand is to go to the Tourism New Zealand site and have a look at the package deals on offer and also check your local papers for hot deals. Information can be obtained and your holiday booked from New Zealand Tourism Offices overseas.

Transportation

By bus

There are two main bus passenger operators that provide daily scheduled services through the country. **Newmans Coach Line** provide services in the North Island and around the major tourist routes in the South Island, while **Intercity Coachlines** operate the largest network throughout both islands.

Travelling by coach is an easy way to see New Zealand in comfort. All accommodation, meals and baggage are taken care of and the driver or guide often provides a commentary, pointing out all the significant sites and stories relating to historic events or Maori legend. Most destinations have several departures daily. You can book in advance but this is not usually necessary.

Newmans Coach Lines have timetables for both the North and South Island. They offer a **Stopover Pass**, which means that you can travel for up to three months over a selected route travelling whenever and wherever you want. The North Island pass takes you from Auckland to Wellington via the main cities for around $95 for adults. The South Island pass travels from Christchurch to Queenstown via Milford Sound for around $132 for adults. For more information about this service contact Newmans Coach Lines on Tel: 64 9 913 6200. Fax: 64 9 913 6121.

Intercity Coachlines have three different comprehensive packages: a **North Island pass**, a **South Island pass** and a **New Zealand pass**, and within each pass there is a variety of different travel routes to cater to your plans, giving total flexibility as to when and where you want to go. For more information contact Intercity Coachlines on Tel: 64 9 913 6100. Email: *info@coachnet.co.nz*.

Renting a car

Discover New Zealand for yourself. All international car rental businesses are available in every major city. Budget, Hertz, Avis as well as a few local companies offer comprehensive motoring on New Zealand's uncongested, good quality roads.

Rent-a-Dent has branches all through New Zealand. They supply quality rental vehicles and competitive prices. They have cars, station wagons and campervans for hire. Cars start from $59 per day and a mini coach from $95 per day. These prices include unlimited kilometres, and GST (Goods and Services Tax of 12.5%), but not insurance. For further information contact the Auckland branch at 105 Cook Street. Tel: 64 9 309 0066.
Website: *www.rentadent.co.nz*.

Two-wheel rentals

You can also tour New Zealand on two wheels. Mike Vinsen, a licensed motor vehicle dealer at 300 Great North Road, Grey Lynn, Auckland, Tel: 64 9 827 6619, has motorcycles, mopeds and scooters for rental, with helmets and riding gear also available.

BACKPACKING AND FARM HOLIDAYS

Backpacking

Backpacking is a very popular form of holidaying. There are hostels in most tourist towns and cities, where you would expect to pay an average of $20 per night for single accommodation, $15 for shared. These prices include Goods and Services Tax. All hostels have self cook kitchens, laundry facilities and common areas where you can meet and exchange information with fellow travellers. You do not have to be a member to stay at any of the hostels, and no institutional rules apply. Linen and blankets are available for hire, though some hostels supply these free.

Discount cards
Discounts have been arranged for many backpackers' hotels, from film developing and tandem parapenting, to cheap fruit and vegetables. Many hostels have VIP cards so you can take advantage of these discounts.

Some discount cards give excellent travel discounts – 50% off Air New Zealand and Ansett New Zealand domestic fares, 30% off Intercity Coaches and Trains, 10% off Kiwi Experience-Backpackers Adventure Travel, and 10% off Fiordland Travel (South Island). These specials are available on the **VIP Backpackers Discount Card** which can be purchased for $20 and is valid for 12 months. For further information write to: Back Packers Accommodation Council of New Zealand, level 15, Price Water House, corner of Hobson and Wyndham Streets, Auckland, New Zealand. Tel: 64 9 377 4714.

Farms and homestays
Farms and homestays are a popular way of spending a holiday. What better way to get to know the New Zealanders than by staying in their homes with them as a host or hostess? Tourism New Zealand has 59 farmstays listings. To view these go to their website at: *www.purenz.com.*

It may be the perfect opportunity to get away from city life and take a walk in the clean country air or you may want to join in with the farm's day-to-day running or you may like to try a traditional New Zealand home cooked meal. Many farmstays are close to an abundance of outdoor activities like skiing, horse riding, and fishing. Homestay accommodation tends to find something to suit everyone.

Farm homestays mean living on a typical working farm, varying in size from 100 to over 10,000 acres, often running upwards of several thousand sheep. In addition you can find dairy farms, orchards and properties with horticulture.

Country homestays are usually based on a few acres in the country, handy to a major city or town. They usually run some sheep, and possibly other animals such as deer and goats. Quite often country home hosts are retired farmers, or they may work in a nearby town or city. These are referred to as 'lifestyle blocks'.

To get a run down on prices for homestays go to *www.purenz.com* and contact the places of your choice through their internet sites or phone numbers.

It is advisable to book your farm or homestay as far in advance as possible to secure the properties of your choice, especially from November through to February. A holiday can also be booked through your local travel agent. Bookings and information can also be obtained from New Zealand Tourism Offices overseas.

YOUTH HOSTELLING

Youth hostelling is a very popular way to see New Zealand. For information contact New Zealand Youth Hostel Association, Auckland. Tel: 64 9 309 2802. Fax: 64 9 303 9525.

The traveller must be aware of the fact that New Zealand is no longer free of crime, and you must always keep in mind the following:

- Do not travel alone.
- Do not hitch hike.
- Do not give lifts to strangers.
- Do not leave valuables in cars.
- Do not place yourself in an isolated situation.
- Always be aware of dangerous situations just as you would at home, and in the rest of the world.
- Do not place your trust in a smiling face.

VISITING NEW ZEALAND'S ISLAND NEIGHBOURS

The beauty of living here in the Pacific Ocean is the number of idyllic islands available for the holiday of a lifetime. If you dream of two weeks basking in the sun on a 'Robinson Crusoe' type island, then you will be able to take your pick.

Vanuatu (formerly the New Hebrides)

This is a chain of more than 80 islands, only three hours' flying time from Auckland. This diverse country's features include active volcanoes, coral islands and wide sandy bays with luxuriant tropical vegetation. The time zone is one hour behind New Zealand.

The population are Melanesian inhabitants born in Vanuatu and called ni-Vanuatu. The country's population is about 130,000. The official languages are English, French and Bislama (pidgin English). Summer is from November to March with an average of 28 degrees Celsius and winter from April to October with an average temperature of 23 degrees Celsius. Dress is casual, but not *too* brief: tropical clothes for men's evening wear and light dresses or skirts for ladies. The cost of a seven day stay is around $939 per person to $2,000 per person.

Fiji
Fiji is 300 islands of beaches, reefs, corals, forests, rivers and peace! If you are a lover of *Treasure Island*, *Robinson Crusoe* or *Mutiny on the Bounty* this is the place to be! Here you can see the water though which Captain Bligh sailed after the mutiny; you can picnic on deserted islands, see old cannibal ovens, and let fish nibble your toes.

Fiji has something for everyone, with accommodation from extreme luxury to affordable budget. It is a paradise for backpackers, not only because of the wide range of affordable budget accommodation ranging from $5 upwards, but also because of the friendliness and genuine hospitality of the people. Seven days here will cost between $950 and $2,200 per person, depending on the time of year.

Norfolk Island
An interesting aspect of Norfolk Island is its colourful past filled with some of history's more notable seamen, such as Captain James Cook and the *Bounty* mutineers.

From its early days as a convict settlement, the island has become an historian's paradise with its old buildings as from the penal days to the early homes of the Pitcairn settlers (*Bounty* descendants).

There is something to do all the time here, without repeating yourself too often – bush walks, snorkelling, fishing, surfing, diving, horse riding, gun clubs, golf, tennis or bowling, just to mention a few. There is a wide range of accommodation available, and seven days here would start from $1,100 per person.

Tonga

The kingdom of Tonga is an archipelago of some 170 islands scattered across the South Pacific near the International Date Line and just north of the tropic of Capricorn. Tonga remains a kingdom, its government a constitutional monarchy, and member of the British Commonwealth. The Head of State is King Taufa'ahau Tupou IV, son of the late Queen Salote. The capital is Nuku'alofa.

It is claimed that Tonga has been inhabited since 500BC and Tongans are descended from 'Lapita' people, the forerunners of today's Polynesians. The climate is cooler and less humid than most tropical areas. The average daily temperature is 24 degrees Celsius The hottest months are December/January. Seven days here will cost approximately $800 to $1,600 per person. There is a wide range of accommodation.

The Cook Islands
One of the best things about Rarotonga and the Cook Islands as a holiday destination is that it can be whatever you want to make it: sunshine, crystal clear lagoon waters, with swimming, sailing, windsurfing, scuba diving, tennis, golf, bowls, squash, canoeing and many more activities. Accommodation is varied with both budget and luxury hotels, the approximate cost for seven days being $1,300 to $2,600 per person.

THE GREAT OUTDOORS
New Zealand recreation is generally aimed at the great outdoors! The obvious beach activities include swimming, snorkelling and year round activities such as wind surfing and sailing.

Sport, fitness and leisure have played a key part in creating and shaping New Zealand's national image, both at home and abroad, and contribute much to the lifestyle New Zealanders enjoy. Everyone has the chance to take part in some form of sport or leisure activity and it is government policy to promote access to it for all New Zealanders.

An extensive and varied park system which includes national, forest and maritime parks, historic and scenic reserves, walkways and many local parks and reserves, showcases the environment and provides a full spectrum of recreational opportunity.

Top sports for people over the age of 15 years are swimming/ diving, cycling, snooker/pool, tennis and aerobics. In the recreational physical activity section walking comes out tops followed by running/jogging, cycling and fitness classes. In terms of favourite leisure activities reading is the most popular followed by watching television and videos, visiting friends, listening to music and gardening.

Marching is a New Zealand-born sport, originating in the early years of the 1930s Depression. The grades in marching cover four age groups, the senior grade for those 16 years and over, the junior grade for girls aged 12 to 16, the midget grade for seven to 12 year olds, and the introductory grade for six to 12 year olds.

There is a large following for big game fishing, lake and river fishing. Shooting and hunting is very popular, the principal game birds being duck, swan, pheasant, quail, geese and chukor. The season is, however, limited to six to eight weeks starting on the first weekend of May.

Skiing, mountaineering, tramping and walking offer an immense variety of venues to people in all age groups.

Golfing and bowls (indoor and outdoor) are also very popular, with a huge selection of clubs throughout New Zealand.

For the more daring, there is white water rafting, abseiling, mountain climbing, parachuting, gliding and bungy-jumping. You can find these and a lot more thrilling outdoor sports with up-to-date pricing on the Tourism New Zealand site *www.purenz.com*. Information can also be obtained from New Zealand Tourism Offices overseas.

DINING OUT

Over the past few years café style eating has become very popular. You will find tables to sit at outside cafés in most cities in New Zealand. Magazines and newspapers are available for you to read and an array of food and beverages from all-day breakfasts to vegan and vegetarian meals are on the menu.

Every style of restaurant and eating establishment is to be found now in most parts of New Zealand, with Thai, Italian, Spanish, Hungarian, Japanese, Chinese, New Zealand and European cuisines. You can expect to pay $20 to $30 for a fairly inexpensive meal, and for the high class establishments in top hotels and some of the more 'intimate' restaurants, somewhere in the region of $50 to $70 a head.

BYO – visitors will notice that many restaurants hold a 'byo' licence, that is, these establishments are permitted by law to allow clients to 'bring your own' liquor with them, to be consumed with their meal. There is usually a 'corkage' charge of $1–$3. Restaurants of this nature are distinct from those who are licensed to sell liquor on their premises.

A new feature of dining out which is becoming quite popular is the 'dessert' restaurants like 'Death by Chocolate' and 'Strawberry Faire'. Here you choose a dessert and finish up with coffee.

A Final Word

BECOMING A KIWI

Pubs

The New Zealand way of life is quite different from the British. Until recently there were no cosy pubs where you could wind down at the end of the day, or enjoy an entertaining evening out. A few smaller pubs have now started to appear but on the whole the pubs are large and noisy, with strange elbow-high tables scattered around the rooms where the men seem to enjoy standing and leaning while drinking their beer. Until roughly 25 years ago, drinking was referred to as 'the six o'clock swill'. That was because pubs closed at 6.00 p.m., and everyone had to drink their drink quickly and leave.

Restaurants

A new trend that seems to be becoming extremely popular is 'dining out'. In Wellington alone there are enough restaurants for you to dine out at a different one every day of the year! Wine bars are also very popular with the younger set, and in some you may find live music.

Cinema

It would seem, according to recent figures in the local press, that New Zealanders are the world's most avid cinema-goers. Cinema complexes which hold two, three or even four screens are springing up all over the main cities.

'Bring a plate'

It is very common to be invited to an evening gathering of friends and be asked to 'bring a plate'. This doesn't mean an empty plate! You are expected to concoct some delicacy and share it with everyone else who will be doing the same thing. When I first came to New Zealand I innocently took along an empty plate, thinking perhaps that the hostess was running short of crockery – I remember the strange looks I got!

Dress

Dress here is rather casual, so aim for the middle of the road look if you are unsure as to how you should dress for an event that doesn't indicate the requirements. Shirts and trousers for the men, both can be short in the summer. Until you are sure of the expectations, the ladies should dress simply, not over dressy. Don't wear the crown jewels until you have found your ground.

PLAYING THE GAME

Sport is the life, blood and soul of a great majority of New Zealanders, the national game being rugby. Weekends during the season are taken up with games being played all over the country, and television is completely taken over at weekends with replays, and then replays of the replays!

Parents of young children can be seen huddled against the cold supporting their young prodigy's efforts on the field. Very young kiwis can even be seen doing the 'haka' before their interclub matches begin. They all have aspirations to be another Jonah Lomu. Netball is very popular for girls, as is hockey. In the summer tennis clubs are popping at the seams with likely players, and there will invariably be a waiting list to join.

New Zealand is generously endowed with wonderful golf courses. The green fees vary, but at weekends you can expect to pay around $20 for 18 holes.

Water sports are high on the activity list with sailing being very popular. After winning the America's Cup in 1995, the continual talk has been of yachting. The harbours and lakes can be seen to be cluttered with a myriad of sailing boats. In fact most families enjoy time on the water during the summer, whether being propelled by wind or motor.

SOME TOPICAL ISSUES IN NEW ZEALAND

There are several topical issues concerning the New Zealand public, and you are likely to find them widely discussed. These are some of them.

Hardcore unemployment

People are becoming quite concerned at the growing number of redundancies, and the fact that so many people in the middle years are unable to find another job. The Government is now trying to encourage children to stay on at school, rather than leave and go 'on the dole': even after going to university and graduating, many young people are still unable to find work. There is also concern that there will be a core of people who will never be able to find employment in their lifetime again.

Health and education reforms

The Government has reorganised the health services, within the Ministry of Health, and people are worried when they see wards and hospitals closing down in the smaller areas. The Ministry of Health is leading the process of changes in the health sector and overviews the local and area Health Boards – they are working to make health services and hospitals become commercially viable organisations, rather than just a 'service'.

Schools have also been organised to run themselves, instead of the Education Department being responsible. School heads have been increasingly turned into administrators and schools are run by boards of trustees, elected from among the parents. The boards hire and fire, and because they have a strict budget to operate must hire to fit their budget; if they are short of money, they may feel obliged to hire less qualified teachers.

Crime

There is concern at the growing number of rapes, attacks of violence, murder and robbery. It is generally felt by the public that the punishment does not fit the crime. Offenders may be sentenced to eight to ten years, but this can be substantially reduced for good conduct. Also, white collar crime has increased, and seemingly 'stable' organisations have collapsed overnight when misappropriation of funds has been discovered. The prison population seems to be growing out of control.

Racism

Of concern to a lot of people is the Government's handling of the Treaty of Waitangi Appeals, and its 'hand-outs' to the Maori tribes. People in general feel that the other races in New Zealand are being disadvantaged because of this and instead of New Zealanders being 'one people' they are now split into 'them' and 'us'.

Many New Zealanders question the advisability of the Government's policy which allows large immigration of Asians. Some people are now shouting out against the seemingly 'over-run' situation. Asians are becoming prime targets for criminal elements.

A beautiful country

When Captain James Cook came ashore on the east coast in the late 1700s, he named the area the Bay of Plenty, and this it certainly is. Everything grows here aplenty. Grapefruit, orange and lemon trees are everywhere, dropping their fruit over lawns, road sides and fields.

Throughout New Zealand things grow in abundance. In the North Island you will see freesias growing wild at the roadside, arum lilies growing in fields, clematis growing amongst the trees in forest areas. In our garden in Tauranga in the Bay of Plenty, we grew outdoor tomatoes; the vines grew as abundantly as weeds, and black and green grapes were everywhere. There were plum trees, peach trees, guava trees, lemon and orange trees, to name but a few.

The commercialism so evident in most countries is still not alarmingly evident here. You will certainly not find the equivalent of Blackpool and the 'Golden Mile'. New Zealand has no really 'old' buildings, as it has only just been weaned in a historical sense. You will find several historic villages, where time seems to have stood still since the arrival of the early settlers; these are really a 'must' to view.

You will never grow bored with the scenery which changes continually as you travel. The South Island is very grand with mountains to rival Switzerland. The peace you will feel because of the low population density is very captivating and you will feel very well rested after a holiday here.

Nuclear testing

In June 1995 the French Government announced the resumption of nuclear underground testing at Mururoa Atoll. This is a Pacific Island approximately 1,200km west of New Zealand. The people of New Zealand and other countries around the Pacific are very displeased with the arrogance of the French wanting to pollute our 'back garden'. The new Greenpeace *Rainbow Warrior* continues to police the environment of the southern hemisphere.

Gambling is alive and well in New Zealand

Many people live in the obscure hope that they will win a large fortune and retire into the lap of luxury. It is now more than a dream. New Zealand has extended the hand of opportunity to many by opening a casino in the South Island in Christchurch. My husband and I visited the casino in May 1995, and were amazed at the sight of people sitting patiently feeding 20c coins into the jaws of voracious slot machines lined up on two floors. Across the road from the casino was a prosperous pawnbroker, with many large diamond rings in his window, and next door a business that hired out appropriate clothes to punters to gain entry into the casino. Obviously the idea that 'one could lose one's pants at the races' could apply to the casino too. Auckland opened its magnificent casino in 1996 and one is planned for the waterfront in Wellington.

Black Magic!

The success of the New Zealand team in the Americas Yachting Cup in January 2000 was widely celebrated. Tickertape parades brought all the main New Zealand cities to a complete standstill. With the challenge that returned to Auckland's shores again in 2002 the land close to the coast and around the viaduct area was promoted by entrepreneurial real estate agents.

HOT OFF THE PRESS

♦ The health system is once again being restructured. As in the United Kingdom patients are being denied vital operations due to quotas being imposed upon Health Authorities by government funding.

♦ The police are undermanned – computers are being put in offices rather than constables on the beat.

♦ Violent crime is on the increase and education standards are dropping.

♦ The Maori voice is being heard more, especially in Parliament with New Zealand now having the first Maori Deputy Prime Minister.

♦ The legal change of drinking regulations has occurred with the official lowering of the age limit to 18 years.

New plan to curb flood of migrants
The New Zealand Government is constantly looking for ways to slow the flood of new immigrants. This is reflected in the ever changing immigration requirements. It is very important to check with your nearest immigration department for the latest information.

POSTSCRIPT
Once you have discovered what a great place New Zealand is, you will need to give some serious thought to making the big move to live here, or whether you will just come for the holiday of a lifetime.

As far as my family and I are concerned, New Zealand has become our true home. My daughters have both graduated at university, and remember very little about England.

My husband and I are enjoying a type of semi-retirement, playing a little golf and writing books. We hope in the future to include lots of travel in our itinerary.

Don't be a 'nearly did'. Many people in England, upon hearing of our intentions to settle in New Zealand, said 'Oh, I nearly did that, but . . .' I decided there and then that I was never going to be a 'nearly did'. Life can be exciting if you give it a chance.

Good luck!

A Guide to Speaking New Zildish

One feature of New Zealand speech often commented on by visitors is the inordinate fondness for abbreviations which end in ie or y.

We put our cardies on when it's cold, our gummies when its muddy, our pinnies when cooking, our cossies when we go swimming, our nighties when going to bed.

Our buildings are usually erected by chippies, our boats are unloaded by wharfies, our mail delivered by posties. We buy food at the deli, send children to kindy and sometimes give a small donation to the Sallies. We fight for the best possie in front of the telly, to watch the footie. If it's an important match against the pommies we pull a sickie and take the day off work.

In summer we buy aerosols to spray the mozzies and blowies. We eat bickies and smoke ciggies. Some of us have been known to pull swifties and throw wobblies. Military types belong to the Terries. If the weather isn't iffy we have a barbie, and most of us have been to Aussie.

New Zildish translations

sickie	a day off work
togs & cossies	swimming costumes
barbie	barbecue
snarlers	sausages
Sallies	Salvation Army
possie	position
gummies	gum boots (wellingtons)
footie	football
chippies	builders
kindy	kindergarten
mozzies	mosquitoes
wobblies	tantrums
smoko	tea break time
chooks	chickens
this arvo	this afternoon
Pakeha	the Maori name for a European
she'll be right	everything will be fine
cobber	friend
mate	a quick name when you have forgotten!
your shout	your turn to buy drinks
chick	woman
Terries	Territorial Army
ciggies	cigarettes
Aussie	an Australian
Pom or Pommie	Englishman
the loo or dunny	the toilet
kick in the guts	give it all you have got
rough as guts	crude, unrefined, impolite
as full as a boot	drunk
surfie	surf board rider

nuddie	in the nude
wrinklies	old people
lollies	sweets, candy
dairy	the corner shop, sells a bit of everything, usually open seven days per week
to be sucked in	to be tricked into believing a lie

Useful Addresses

GENERAL INFORMATION ABOUT NEW ZEALAND

Christchurch Information Centre, corner of Worcester Boulevard and Oxford Terrace, Christchurch. Tel: 03 379 9629. Fax: 03 377 2424.

Hamilton Visitor Information Centre, Angelsea Street, Hamilton. Tel: 07 839 3580.

New Plymouth Public Relations & Marketing Office, Private Bag 2025, New Plymouth. Tel: 06 759 6086. Fax: 06 759 6073. Email: *info@newplymouth.govt.nz*.

North Shore Visitor Information Centre, 49 Hurstmere Road, Takapuna, Auckland. Tel: 09 486 8670.

Wellington Visitor Information Centre, 101 Wakefield Street, Wellington. Tel: 04 802 4860. Website: *www.wellingtonNZ.com*

Newspapers UK

Destination New Zealand, Outbound Publishing, 1 Commercial Road, Eastbourne, East Sussex BN21 3QX. Tel: (01323) 726040.

New Zealand News UK, 25 Royal Opera Arcade, London SW1Y 4UY. Tel: (020) 7930 6451.

New Zealand Press Association, 12 Norwich Street, London EC4. Tel: (020) 7353 5430.

New Zealand Outlook, Consyl Publishing Ltd. 3 Bruckhurst Road, Bexhill-on-Sea TN40 1QF. Tel: (01424) 223111. Fax: (01424) 224992. Monthly newspaper.

TRAVEL (UK)

New Zealand High Commission Tourism Office, 80 Haymarket, London SW1Y 4TQ. Tel: 0839 300 900. Fax: (020) 7839 8929.

New Zealand Travel Information Service, 225 Riverside

Gardens, London W6. Tel: (020) 8748 4455.

IMMIGRATION OFFICES

New Zealand Consulate General, Springsiedelgasse 28, A-1190 Wien, AUSTRIA. Tel: (1) 318 8505. Fax: (1) 377 660.

New Zealand Embassy, Boulevard du Regent 47-48, 1000 Brussels, BELGIUM. Tel: (2) 512 1040. Fax: (2) 513 4856. Email: *nzembbru@.compuserve.com.*

New Zealand High Commission, Suite 727, Metropolitan House, 99 Bank Street, Ottawa, Ontario K1P 6G3, CANADA. Tel: (613) 238 5991. Immigration: (613) 238 6097. Fax: (613) 238 5707. Email: *nzhcott@istar.com.*

New Zealand Consulate General, Suite 1200-888 Dunsmuir Street, PO Box 10-071, Pacific Centre, Vancouver, British Colombia V6C 3K4, CANADA. Tel: (604) 684 7388. Fax: (604) 684 7333.

New Zealand Embassy, 7 ter, Leonard de Vinci, 75116 Paris, FRANCE. Tel: (1) 4500 2411. Fax: (1) 4501 2639. Email: *nzembassv.paris@wanadoo.fr.*

New Zealand Immigration Service, Atrium Friedrichstrasse 60, 10117 Berlin, GERMANY. Tel: (30) 206 210. Fax: (30) 206 21114.

New Zealand Consulate General, Heimhuderstrasse 56, 20148 Hamburg, GERMANY. Tel: (40) 442 5550. Fax: (40) 425 5549.

New Zealand Consulate General, c/o Coopers & Lybrand, 24 Xenias Street, Athens 115 28, GREECE. Tel: (1) 771 0112. Fax: (1) 777 7390.

New Zealand Consulate General, 6501 General Plaza, 18 Harbour Road, Wanchai, HONG KONG, SAR China. Tel: 2525 5044. Immigration: 2877 4488. Fax: 2845 2915. Immigration: 2877 0586.

New Zealand Consulate General, 46 Upper Mount Street, Dublin 2, IRELAND. Tel: (01) 676 2464. Fax: (01) 676 2489.

New Zealand Embassy, Via Zara 28, Rome 00198, ITALY. Tel: (06) 441 7171. Fax: (06) 440 2984. Email: *nzemb.rom@flashnet.it.*

New Zealand Consulate, Villa Hampstead, Oliver Agius Street, Attard BZNO3 MALTA. Tel: (435) 025. Fax: (437) 200.

New Zealand Embassy, Embajada de Nueva Zelandia, Jose Luis Lagrange 103, 10th Floor, Colonia Los Morales,

Polanco, 11510, Mexico DF, MEXICO. Tel: (5) 281 5486. Fax: (5) 281 5212. Email: *kiwimexico@compuserve.com.mx*.

New Zealand Embassy, Carnegielaan 10, 2517 KH The Hague, THE NETHERLANDS. Tel: (70) 346 9324. Immigration (70) 365 8037. Fax: (70) 363 2983. Immigration (70) 364 0116. Email: *nzemb@bart.nl*.

New Zealand Consulate, Rua de S. Felix, 13-2, 1200 Lisboa, PORTUGAL. Tel: (1) 350 9690. Fax: (1) 572 004.

New Zealand Embassy, 3rd Floor, Plaza de la Lealtad 2, 28014 Madrid, SPAIN. Tel: (1) 523 0226. Fax: (1) 523 0171.

New Zealand Consulate General, 28A Chemin du Petit-Saconnex, CH-1209 Geneva (PO Box 334, CH-1211 Geneva 19), SWITZERLAND. Tel: (22) 734 9530. Fax: (22) 734 3062. Email: *newzeal@pop.unicc.org*.

New Zealand Immigration Service, New Zealand House, Haymarket, London SW1Y 4TQ, UNITED KINGDOM. Tel: 09069 100100. Fax: (020) 7973 0370.

New Zealand Embassy, 37 Observatory Circle NW, Washington DC 20008, UNITED STATES OF AMERCA. Tel: (202) 328 4800. Fax: (202) 667 5227. Email: *nz@nzemb.org*.

New Zealand Consulate General, Suite 1150, 12400 Wilshire Boulevard, Los Angeles, CA 90025, UNITED STATES OF AMERICA. Tel: (310) 207 1605. Fax: (310) 207 3605.

New Zealand High Commission, Eastgate Centre (8th Floor Greenbridge), corner of Robert Mugabe Road and Second Street (PO Box 5448), Harare, ZIMBABWE. Tel: (4) 759 221. Fax: (4) 759 228.

New Zealand Offices

New Zealand Immigration Service, Private Bag, Wellesley Street, Auckland, New Zealand. Tel: 09 914 4100. Fax: 09 914 4119.

New Zealand Immigration Service, 5th Floor Westpac Building, Victoria Street, Private Bag, Hamilton, New Zealand. Tel: 07 838 3566. Fax: 07 838 0059.

New Zealand Immigration Service, Level 7, Regional Council Centre, 142-146 Wakefield Street, PO Box 27-149, Wellington, New Zealand. Tel: 04 384 7929. Fax: 04 384 8243.

New Zealand Immigration Service, Carter House, 81 Lichfield Street, PO Box 22-111, Christchurch, New Zealand. Tel: 03

365 2520. Fax: 03 365 2530.
Website: *www.immigration.govt.nz*.

IMMIGRATION CONSULTANTS

Auckland

AIC Immigration Consultancy (AUCK) Ltd, Dilworth Building, Level 2, corner of Queen and Customs Streets. Tel: 09 302
2091. Fax: 09 302 2096. Email: *105312.672@compuserve.com*
Specialises in all aspects of immigration including business
immigration, points system, family, citizenship, investments,
property and employment.

Dorchester and Smythe Ltd, Level 11, Tower 2, The Shortland
Centre, 55–65 Shortland Street, Auckland. Tel: 09 479 8911.
Website: *www.dorchesterimmigration.co.nz*

Excellence Consultancy Group, 87 Albert Street, Auckland. Tel:
09 377 9338.

Fay Pryor Immigration Services, Level 3, MDC House, 142
Broadway, Newmarket. Tel: 09 529 2745.

Global Immigration Services (NZ) Ltd, 10 New North Road,
Eden Terrace, Auckland. Tel: 09 307 6988. Website:
www.globalimmigration.co.nz

Harder; Christopher, 40 Kingston Street, Auckland. Tel: 09 377
8440. Fax: 09 377 8454. Deals with all immigration related
problems including business and work permits, permanent
residency, applications and appeals.
Website: *http://home.xtra.co.nz/nots.christopher*

Herne Bay Law, 128 Jervois Road, Herne Bay. Tel: 09 378 0511.

International Immigration Consultants, PO Box 80079, Green
Bay, Auckland. Tel: 09 629 0602.

Kermani Consultants Ltd, PO Box 6565, Wellesley St, Auckland. Tel: 09 307 3123.

Legget IBIS International Limited, 401 Queen Street, Auckland.
Tel: 09 534 1961. Fax: 09 534 1965.
Email: *imigr8@leggetibis.com* Website: *www.leggitibis.com/*
Specialises in employment search and relocation at business,
professional and executive level, family reunification and all
NZ immigration and citizenship requirements.

Lothian Consultants Limited, 45a Bleakhouse Road, Howick,
Auckland. Tel: 09 535 6811.

Lucas France & Partners, 185 Great South, Manurewa, Auckland. Tel: 09 269 2844. Professional immigration lawyers providing complete legal services connected with permanent residence, business, general and family migration.

Malcolm Pacific International Ltd, Level 12, 49 Symonds Street, PO Box 6219, Wellesley Street, Auckland. Tel: 09 309 4187. Fax: 09 366 4730. Website: *www.malcolmpacific.co.nz* Free consultation and assessment and money-back guarantee.

Marshall Bird and Curtis, Campbell's Building, Level 4, 16 High St, Auckland. Tel: 09 377 5543. Fax: 09 377 5544. Website: *http://legaleagle.co.nz* Lawyers specialising in obtaining work permits and permanent residence in New Zealand.

New Horizons, PO Box 11-125, Ellerslie. Tel: 09 525 4052. Services include: immigration solutions, professional registration assistance and translations. Mandarin and European languages spoken.

New Zealand Association for Migration and Investment, 71 Devonport Road, PO Box 518, Tauranga. Tel: 07 578 1883.

New Zealand Immigration and Investment Services, 5/138 Queen Street, Auckland. Tel: 09 366 0378.

North Shore Immigration Service Ltd, 17 Corinthian Drive, Albany, Auckland. Tel: 09 415 3392. Fax: 09 415 5934. Website: *www.nsis.co.nz* Free assessment interview for applications of residence.

Prospects Immigration, PO Box 38-880, Howick. Tel: 09 577 5895. Fax: 09 577 5894. Website: *www.access-nz.co.nz/profile* Specialists in permanent residence and work permit applications and job search. Free assessment.

Tika Ram Immigration Consultants, 3rd Floor, S302A, Dilworth Building, 24 corner of Queen and Customs Streets. Tel: 09 379 0387. Fax: 09 358 1728.

Turner Hopkins, 400 Lake Road, Takapuna. Tel: 09 486 2169. Fax: 09 486 2160. For assistance with immigration problems including applications and appeals.

WASAN International Co Ltd, BNZ Tower, Floor 9, 125 Queen Street, Auckland. Tel: 09 308 9998.
Email: *immigration@bizonglobe.com* Immigration specialists dealing with permanent residency, appeals, work permits, student and visitor's permits and job search.

Worldwide Immigration Services Ltd, Level 12, 242 Queen
Street, Auckland. Tel: 09 358 0884.

Christchurch
Brockett; James, 77 Hereford Street, Christchurch. Tel: 03 366
1487. A firm of barristers and solicitors offering professional
advice.
Business Immigration (NZ) Limited, PO Box 2286, Christch-
urch. Tel: 03 341 3340. Members of the New Zealand
Association for migration and investment and specialists in
permanent residency.
Lane Neave Ronaldson, Price Waterhouse Centre, 119 Armagh
Street, Christchurch. Tel: 03 379 3720. Fax: 03 379 8370.
Specialising in all matters relating to residency applications
(points system, business investment, family category and
humanitarian). Website: *www.laneneave.co.nz*
New Zealand Immigration Ltd, PO Box 11-073, Christchurch.
Tel: 03 365 3306. Fax: 03 365 3460. Email: *forbes@net2.co.nz*
Investment and permanent residence applications.
Weston Ward and Lascelles, 211 Gloucester Street, Christch-
urch. Tel: 03 379 1740 or call free: 0800 529 937. Fax: 03 379
1789. A firm of barristers and solicitors providing advice on
application problems.

Wellington
Execucorp Migration Services, 49 Ridgeway, Wanganui. Tel: 06
347 2776. Advises on all immigration matters including
visas, work permits and New Zealand residency.
Malcolm Pacific, 276 Lambton Quay, Wellington. Tel: 04 473
9615. Fax: 04 499 6559. Offers professional service for
migrants and employers, free assessments. Performance
guarantee independently underwritten by professional in-
demnity insurance company.

EDUCATION

Ministry of Education Offices
(Website: *www.minedu.govt.nz*)
National Office, 45–47 Pipitea Street, PO Box 1666, Thorndon,

Wellington. Tel: 04 463 8000. Fax: 04 499 1327.

Regional Offices:

39–45 College Hill, Private Bag 47-911, Ponsonby, Auckland 1034. Tel: 09 374 5400. Fax: 09 374 5401.

Corner of Grey and Bridge Streets, Private Bag 3011, Hamilton. Tel: 07 838 3705. Fax: 07 838 3710.
Email: *sheila.richmond@minedugovt nz.*

Box 2522, Christchurch, New Zealand. Tel: 03 365 7386. Fax (operations): 03 34 1631. Fax (property): 03 364 1667.

PO Box 1225, Dunedin, New Zealand. Tel: 03 474 0152. Fax: 03 479 0250.

New Zealand Post Primary Teachers Association (PPTA), PO Box 2119, Wellington. Tel: 04 384 9964. Fax: 04 382 8763.

New Zealand University Students Association, 354 Lambton Quay, PO Box 10-191, Wellington. Tel: 04 498 2500. Fax: 04 473 2391.

Independent Schools Council, PO Box 5222, Wellington. Tel: 04 471 2022.

Polytechnics

Waikato Polytechnic, Tristram Street, Private Bag 3036, Hamilton. Tel: 07 834 888. Fax: 07 838 0707.

Taranaki Polytechnic, Main Bell Street, New Plymouth. Tel: 06 757 3100. Fax: 06 757 8261. Website: *www.taranaki.ac.nz.*

Wellington Institute of Technology, PO Box 39803, Petone, Wellington. Tel: 04 920 2400. Fax: 04 920 2401.

Christchurch Polytechnic, PO Box 22-095, Coventry Street, Christchurch. Tel: 03 379 8150. Fax: 03 366 6544.

Otago Polytechnic, Forth Street, Private Bag 1910, Dunedin. Tel: 03 477 3014. Fax: 03 477 6032.
Email: *info@tekotago.ac.nz.* Website: *www.tekotago.ac.nz.*

Southland Institute of Technology, Tay Street, Invercargill. Tel: 03 218 2599. Fax: 04 214 4977.
Email: *marketing@southpoly.ac.nz.*

Association of Polytechnics, 114 The Terrace, Wellington. Tel: 04 471 1162. Fax: 04 473 2350.

Schools

Kamo Christian College, 55 Great North Road, Whangerei. Tel: 09 435 2458. Fax: 09 435 0458. Email: *postmaster@kcc.school.nz*.

Hato Petera College (ages 13–18), 103 College Road, Northcote, Auckland. Tel/Fax: 09 480 7784.

Kirstin School (ages 5–18), 360 Albany Highway, Albany, PO Box 87, Auckland. Tel: 09 415 9566. Fax: 09 415 8495.

Diocesan School for Girls (ages 5–18), Margot Street, Epsom, Auckland. Tel: 09 520 0221. Fax: 09 520 6778.

Collegiate School (ages 5–18), Liverpool Street, Private Bag, Wanganui. Tel: 06 349 0210. Fax: 06 349 0280. Email: *wcs@collegiate.school.nz*.

The Correspondence School, 11 Portland Crescent, Private Bag, Wellington. Tel: 04 473 6841. Fax: 04 471 2406.

Colleges of Education

Auckland College of Education, Private Bag 92-601, Symonds Street, Auckland. Tel: 09 623 8899. Fax: 09 623 8898.

University of Waikato, Hill Crest Road, Hamilton. Tel: 07 856 2889.

Massey University College of Education, Private Bag 11-222, Palmerston North. Tel: 06 356 9099. Fax: 06 350 5799.

Wellington College of Education, Donald Street, PO Box 17-310, Karori, Wellington. Tel: 04 924 2000. Fax: 04 924 2149. Website: *www.wce.ac.nz*.

Christchurch College of Education, Dovetail Avenue, PO Box 31-065, Christchurch. Tel: 03 348 2059. Fax: 03 348 4311. Website: *www.cce.ac.nz*.

Dunedin College of Education, 145 Union Street East, Private Bag 1912, Dunedin. Tel: 03 477 2289. Fax: 03 477 6573. Website: *www.dce.ac.nz*.

A helpful directory

A *Directory of New Zealand Schools and Tertiary Institutions May 1999* is available at a cost of NZ$30.00 from Learning Media Ltd. PO Box 3293, Wellington, New Zealand. Tel: 04 472 5522. Fax: 04 472 64444. Website: *www.learningmedia.co.nz*

EMPLOYMENT AGENCIES

Auckland

Aacorn International Ltd, PO Box 105-355 Auckland Central. Tel: 09 309 7862. Fax: 09 309 9043.
Email: *aacorn@aacorn.co.nz* Website: *www.aacorn.co.nz* Specialising in computer recruitment.

APS Personnel, 611 Great South Road, Manukau. Tel: 09 263 4322 or call free 0800 654 322. Fax: 09 837 0824. Deals with temporary and permanent labour hire (tradesmen, engineering, etc.) office and secretarial staff, hotel and leisure staff and executive leasing.

A & S Consultants International Ltd, 15 Edsel St, PO Box 21-761, Henderson. Tel: 09 837 4220. Fax: 09 837 4290. Website: *www.asconsultants.co.nz/* Specialising in technical recruitment: engineers, draftsmen and architects. Permanent and temporary placements catered for.

Accountant Recruitment Limited, PO Box 7209, Wellesley Street, Auckland. Tel: 09 309 2623. Website: *accrec.co.nz/* Specialists in the placement of temporary accountants and financial executives.

Acorn Healthlink, Suite 1, Level 1, 72 Dominion Road, Mount Eden, Auckland. Tel: 09 623 8006. Fax: 09 630 9622. Website: *healthlinknz.co.nz*

Ad People, NZ Post Building, 51 Hurstmere Road, Takapuna. Tel: 09 486 1922. Specialising in permanent placements and temporary personnel for advertising agencies and associated industries.

Alectus Recruitment Consultants Ltd, Ports of Auckland Building, Quay Street, Auckland. Tel: 09 366 3866.
Email: *contactus@alectus.co.nz* Specialists in secretarial, reception, administration, promotional and accounts recruitment.

Allied Workforce, 41 Station Road, PO Box 12-832, Penrose. Tel: 09 526 8770. Website: *alliedworkforce.co.nz* Auckland-wide specialists in temporary personnel.

Alpha Personnel Recruitment Ltd, Level 3, 27 Gillies Avenue, PO Box 99-256, Newmarket. Tel: 09 524 2336. Specialising in office staff recruitment together with career counselling, software crosstraining, salary surveys, outplacement, staff assessment, training needs and résumé preparation.

Arrow Personnel Ltd, Ellerslie Business Centre, 101 Main Highway, Ellerslie. Tel: 09 525 3650. *Website: www.arrowprsonnel.co.nz/* Specialist suppliers of temporary and permanent staff.

Ascent Supported Employment, 114–16 Great South Rd, Newmarket, Auckland. Tel: 09 529 4153.

Auckland Medical Bureau, PO Box 37-753, Parnell. Tel: 09 377 5903. For nationwide GP and hospital locums.

Automotive & Technical Personnel Ltd, PO Box 17-343, Greenlane, Auckland. Tel: 09 636 7300.
Website: *www.autojobs.co.nz* Email: *cv@autojobs.co.nz*
Specialising in motor industry recruitment – sales, technical, parts, administration and management, automotive, heavy automotive and heavy equipment.

Banking Personnel Ltd, West Plaza Building, corner of Albert and Customs Street West, Auckland. Tel: 09 358 0888.

Bridge Personnel and Management Consultants Ltd, PO Box 89-043, Torbay, Auckland. Tel: 09 366 3741. Website: *www.ubd-online.co.nz/*

Centacom Staff Ltd, 31 Dean Street, Grey Lynn, Auckland. Tel: 09 360 2455. Fax: 09 360 1022.

Central Farm Employment, RD 1, Tukau. Tel: 09 232 8005.

Clayton Ford Ltd, Level 19, Westpac Trust Tower, 120 Albert Street, Auckland. Tel: 09 379 9924. Fax: 09 379 7785. Website: *www.claytonford.co.nz* Handles finance, banking and accountancy recruitment.

Credit Control Co Ltd, PO Box 28-196, Auckland. Permanent and temporary employment in office and accounting (Tel: 09 524 2003) sales and marketing (Tel: 09 520 4292) executive and management (Tel: 09 524 7766).
Website: *www.cccpersonnel.co.nz*

Drake International, 7th Floor, Tower Centre, corner of Queen and Customs Streets, Auckland. Tel: 09 379 5610. Specialises in general office, management, medical and industrial positions either temporary, permanent or contract. Also offers advice and assessment on career moves.

Enterprise Staff Consultants NZ Ltd, Third Level, The Ferry Building, 99 Quay Street, PO Box 1799, Auckland. Tel: 09 306 2160. Fax: 09 307 1285. Email: *office@enterprise.co.nz*

Flavell Personnel Consultants, Level 7, Harbour View Building, 152 Quay Street, Auckland. Tel: 09 300 9464. Fax: 09 307 0385. Website: *www.flavell.co.nz*

Gaulter Russell (NZ) Ltd, Level 3, 128 Broadway, Newmarket, PO Box 37-557, Parnell, Auckland. Tel: 09 529 2334. Fax: 09 529 2339.

Hendriks Human Resources, PO Box 105-244, Auckland. Tel: 09 302 3003 or call free 0800 220089. Fax: 09 375 3563. Email: *service@hendriks.co.nz*

Job Connections, 8 Kirkbride Road, PO Box 59070, Mangere, Manukau. Tel: 09 275 3557. Fax: 09 275 3531. Provides employment services for people with disabilities.

KC Temps Ltd, PO Box 331 256, 415 Lake Road, Takapuna. Tel: 09 486 4796. Fax: 09 486 5207.

Kelly Services, Level 9, Price Waterhouse Centre, 66 Wyndham Street, Auckland. Tel: 09 303 3122. Fax: 09 366 7097. Website: *www.kellyservices.co.nz/* Email: *auckland@kellyservices.co.nz* Provides training and employment opportunities for temporary and permanent office and industrial placements. No unsolicited CV's.

Lampen Group Limited, Level 16, Telstra Business Centre, 191 Queen Street, PO Box 2438, Auckland. Tel: 09 357 9800. Fax: 09 357 9800. Specialises in technical and office recruitment and provides consulting services, including psychological assessments and career counselling.

Law Staff (NZ) Ltd, 11th floor, Price Waterhouse Coopers, 66 Wyndham Street West, Auckland. Tel: 09 377 2248. Website: *www.law-staff.com* Email: *jobs@lawstaff.co.nz*

Legal and Corporate Staff Ltd, 11th Floor, Price Waterhouse Coopers, 66 Wyndham Street West, Auckland. Tel: 09 377 2248.

New Zealand Employment Service, Three Kings Plaza, 536 Mount Albert Road, PO Box 27-203, Auckland. Tel: 09 624 2042. Fax: 09 629 3229.

OPAL Consulting Group, Level 13, Westpac Tower, 120 Albert Street, PO Box 7067, Auckland. Tel: 09 379 0200. Fax: 09 377 4127. Website: *www.opal.co.nz* Email: *opal@opal.co.nz* OPAL is a full service recruitment consultancy.

Progressive Personnel Ltd, 3/272 Parnell Rd, Parnell, Auckland. Tel: 09 307 6413. Fax: 09 528 6945.

Quinn Staff Recruiters Ltd, Level 7, Landmark House, 187 Queen Street. Tel: 09 309 8821. Fax: 09 309 8364.
Email: *recruit@quinnstaff.co.nz*

Reed Recruitment Ltd, Level 4, 87–89 Anzac Avenue, Auckland. Tel: 09 915 8900 Fax: 09 915 8915.
Website: *www.reedrecruitment.co.nz*
Email: *respond@reedrecruitment.co.nz* Human resources specialists dealing with temporary, permanent and contract employment in accounting, administration, computing, engineering, executive, industrial, management, marketing, reception, sales, secretarial and technical posts.

Schofield Services, 535 Riddell Road, Glendowie. Tel: 09 575 7732. Specialists in accounting placements.
Email: *lps@schofieldservices.co.nz*

Select Appointments, Level 7, Bridgecorp House, 37 Kitchener Street. Tel: 09 307 2042. Fax: 09 307 2041.

Student Job Search, Auckland Institute of Technology, PO Box 5418 Wellesley Street, Auckland. Tel: 09 309 7800. For part time jobs all year and full time summer jobs – no agency fee.

Tempforce, Level 25, ASB Bank Centre, 135 Albert Street, Auckland. Tel: 09 379 2308 or call free 0508 836 736. Fax: 09 379 2307. Website: *www.tempforce.co.nz*

Travel Personnel Ltd, PO Box 28-463, Remeura, Auckland. Tel: 09 521 3060. Fax: 09 520 4237.

Triangle Recruitment Ltd, 235 Broadway, Newmarket. Tel: 09 520 5102. Email: *triangle@trianglerecruitment.co.nz*

Walbrook Appointments Ltd, 123 Manakau Road, Epsom. Tel: 09 623 1414. Fax: 09 623 1714.

Westaff, Head Office, Level 2, Emcon House, 115 Queen Street, PO Box 105028, Aukland. Tel: 09 307 2225 or call free 0800 436 756. Fax: 09 307 2231. Website: *www.westaff.co.nz*
Email: *headoffice@westaff.co.nz* *All levels of recruitment, permanent, temporary and contract.*

Christchurch

Advanced Personnel Services Ltd, Ist Floor, 829 Colombo Street, PO Box 21-348, Christchurch. Tel: 03 365 4322 or call free 0800 365 4322. Fax: 03 365 7356.
Website: *www.advancedpersonnel.co.nz*
Email: *enquiries@advancedpersonnel.co.nz* Handles vacan-

cies for office and secretarial staff, information and technology staff, building trades people, store people, labourers, drivers, receptionists, accountants, draughting, design engineers and engineering and hospitality staff.

Drake International Ltd, Level 4, Glasson Building, ANZ Chambers, 160 Cashel Street, Christchurch. Tel: 03 379 5940. Fax: 03 279 2091. Website: *www.drake.co.nz* Handles vacancies for general office and sales staff and industrial, secretarial, production, administration, accounting, distribution, process and stores staff. Also drivers and labourers for all trades.

Kelly Services (NZ) Ltd, Level 10, Price Waterhouse Centre, 119 Armagh Street, Christchurch. Tel: 03 379 2963. Handles vacancies for secretarial, hospitality and medical staff, data entry, WP operators and receptionists, spreadsheet operators, accounting, clerical, sales and marketing, legal, labourers, truck and van drivers, trades people, mobile plant operators, warehouse staff and process workers.

Lampen Group Ltd, 9th floor, NZI Building, 96 Hereford Street, PO Box 3790, Christchurch. Tel: 03 374 9222. Fax: 03 374 9223. Website: *www.lampen.co.nz* Permanent, contract and temporary staff in office based positions specialising in call centre and customer service.

Mature Employment Service, Community House, 141 Hereford St, PO Box 13-026, Christchurch. Tel: 03 377 2141. Fax: 03 377 2181. Email: *mature@snap.net.nz*

New Zealand Employment Service, 54 Cass Street, PO Box 57, Ashburton. Tel: 0800 559 009. Fax: 03 308 1560. Also 231 High Street, PO Box 22-495, Christchurch. Tel: 03 365 3133. Fax: 03 366 4283.

Workbridge Inc, corner of Durham and Armagh Streets, Christchurch. Tel: 03 377 2188.
Website: *www.workbridge.co.nz* Specialises in employment and training for people with disabilities.

Wellington

AIESEC New Zealand Inc, PO Box 11–126, Manners Street, Wellington. Tel: 04 499 6480. Website: *www.aiesec.org.nz*

Andersen Contracting, Level 11, Westpac Trust Centre, 125 The Terrace, Wellington. Tel: 04 471 1530. Fax: 04 471 1585.

Website: *www.swcontracting.com.au*

Centre Consulting Group, Level 2, Willbank House, 57 Willis St, PO Box 24 307, Wellington. Tel: 04 472 7092. Fax: 04 472 9002. Website: *www.centreconsulting.co.nz*

Challenger Consulting, 1st Floor, 45 Buick Street, Petone, Lower Hutt. Tel: 04 568 2982. Fax: 04 568 2984. Website: *www.challenger.co.nz*

Clayton Ford Limited, Level 6, Clayton Ford House, 132 The Terrace, Wellington. Tel: 04 473 6223. Fax: 04 471 2100. Web: *www.claytonford.co.nz*
Email: *wellington@claytonfordco.nz* Handles finance, banking and accountancy recruitment.

Cooney and Associates. Now known as Search Works Ltd, Level 4, 326 Lambton Quay, PO Box 10 438, The Terrace, Wellington. Tel: 04 913 3700. Fax: 04 471 4833. Website: *www.searchworks.co.nz*

Drake International, Exchange House, 5-7 Willeston Street, Wellington. Tel: 04 472 6972. Fax: 04 473 4930.

GBL Personnel Ltd, 256 Lambton Quay, PO Box 10-435, Wellington. Tel: 04 472 0140. Fax: 04 499 1619. Website: *www.gbl.co.nz* Email: *mailbox@gbl.co.nz* Handles temporary and permanent recruitment of secretarial and office support.

Hawkins Associates, Level 7, 26 Brandon Street, Wellington. Tel: 04 499 9199. Fax: 04 472 8620.
Website: *www.hawkins4accountants.co.nz* Handles vacancies in accounting and finance, information technology, human resources/payroll and administration/secretarial.

Hutt Valley Personnel, AA Centre, Level 2, 29 Waterloo Road, Lower Hutt. Tel: 04 569 5648. Fax: 04 566 4436.

Interchange Corporation Ltd, PO Box 9965, Marion Square, Wellington. Tel: 04 389 6482.

Kelleher Consulting Group, 8/138 The Terrace, Wellington. Tel: 04 473 9094. Handles both temporary and permanent recruitment.

Kelly Services (NZ) Ltd, Level 9, BDO House, 99–105 Custom House Quay, Wellington. Tel: 04 499 2825. Fax: 04 499 2821. Also at: Level 2, 119 Queen's Drive, Lower Hutt. Tel: 04 569 5200. Fax: 04 569 2899.

Lampen Group Limited, Level 2, 107 Custom House Quay,

Wellington. Tel: 04 472 4157. Fax: 04 471 0958. Website: *www.lampen.co.nz*

Match 2 Recruitment, ISP Centre, 14 Laings Road, Lower Hutt. Tel: 04 570 0199. Fax: 04 570 0122. Website: *www.match2.co.nz* Email: *cv@match2.co.nz* Handles vacancies in engineering, science, sales, management and manufacturing.

Mature Employment Support Hutt, 72 Queens Drive, Lower Hutt. Tel: 04 566 9778.

Mercury Consulting Group, Level 9, AMP Centre, 1 Grey Street, PO Box 10-605, Wellington. Tel: 04 499 2624. Website: *www.mercuryrecruit.co.nz* Specialists in recruiting IT and computer professionals and telecommunications and electronic engineers.

Mid City Personnel Ltd, Terrace Plaza, Level 105, The Terrace, Wellington. Tel: 04 472 5281.
Website: *www.midcitypersonnel.co.nz*

New Zealand Employment Service, Ballantrae House, 192 Willis Street, PO Box 9340, Wellington. Tel: 04 801 9900. Fax: 04 385 4797.

Opal Consulting Group. Now known as Stratum Consulting Group, Level 5, 8 Willis St, Wellington. Tel: 04 498 7500. Fax: 04 498 7519. Website: *www.stratumconsulting.co.nz*

Quin Workforce Ltd, PO Box 45-044, Wellington. Tel: 04 586 2761. Fax: 04 586 2762.
Website: *www.nzbuilders.com/quin_workforce.htm*
Building and trade.

Rob Law Consulting Group Ltd, 105 The Terrace, PO Box 10-080, Wellington. Tel: 04 499 8800. Website: *www.roblaw.co.nz* Specialising in technical personnel, both permanent and contract.

Sapphire Technologies, 2 Hunter Street, Wellington. Tel: 04 473 3333. Website: *www.sapphire.nz.com*

Select Appointments, Level 6, Clayton Ford House, 132 The Terrace, Wellington. Tel: 04 916 6740. Fax: 04 916 6754. Website: *www.selectappointments.co.nz*

Stanford Recruitment Consultants Ltd, Level 2, James Cook Arcade, 294–296 Lambton Quay, PO Box 1505. Tel: 04 472 0861. Fax: 04 499 4994.
Website: *www.womens-business.org.nz* Permanent and tem-

porary work in corporate market, all areas of support, accounting/finance, etc.

Stewart; K P and Associates, 15 The Masthead, Whitby. Tel: 04 234 8226.

Temp Centre, Level 2, Willbank house, 57 Willis St, Wellington. Tel: 04 473 6833.

Wellington Student Job Search, Student Union Building, Kelburn Parade, Kelburn, PO Box 9193, Wellington. Tel: 04 472 8105. Fax: 04 471 1181. A professional service specialising in the selection of students for employment during vacation periods and throughout the year. No referral fee.

Westaff, Level 24, Grand Plimmer Tower, 92–94 Boulcott St, Wellington. Tel: 04 473 4361. Fax: 04 499 0261. Email: *wellington@westaff.co.nz* All levels of recruitment, permanent, temporary and contract

EMPLOYMENT CONTRACT NEGOTIATORS

Auckland

Arbitration and Alternative Dispute Resolution Centre (NZ) Ltd, PO Box 9166, Newmarket. Tel: 09 638 9995 or call free 0800 ARBITERS.

Bowerman; Clinton N, 9/47 High Street, Auckland. Tel: 09 366 0131. Licensed investigator for all personal grievance disputes and contract negotiation.

Dean J Organ and Associates Limited, 20 Puriri Avenue, Greenlane, Auckland. Tel: 09 520 4948. Employment solutions consultancy dealing with advocacy, personal grievances, employment relations advice and arbitration.

Employment and Manufacturers Association (Northern) Inc, 159 Khyber Pass Road, Grafton, Auckland. Tel: 09 367 0909. Fax: 09 367 0902. Website: *www.ema.co.nz*
Email: *ema@ema.co.nz* Employment relations consultancy for employers.

Employment Disputes and Dismissal Compensation Services, 87 Albert St, PO Box 105-564, Auckland Tel: 09 917 3720. Deals with unfair dismissals, redundancies, wage arrears and representation.

Employment Relations and Advocacy Services Ltd, Level 7/17

Albert Street, Auckland. Tel: 09 377 6510. Fax: 09 358 5325. Deals with personal grievances and employment contracts.

Christchurch
Phil Butler & Associates, Cashel Chambers, 224 Cashel Street, Christchurch. Tel: 03 365 2150. Fax: 03 365 0259. Website: *www.employment-law.co.nz* Email: *phil.butler@xtra.co.nz* Specialising in employment contract design and negotiations, mediation, personal grievances, employment tribunal advocacy.

Cheyne; Philip, 3 Armagh Court, 78 Armagh Street, Christchurch. Tel: 03 379 5718. Specialist advocates in employment law matters.

Gough Irving Rotherham, 137 Hereford Street, Christchurch. Tel: 03 366 8751. Fax: 03 365 2388.
Email: *email@gir_law.co.nz* For help with wrongful dismissal and other employment contract problems.

Wellington
Bargaining Agents, 68 Queens Drive, Lower Hutt, PO Box 31-496. Tel: 04 566 8923. Specialising in labour relations and employment related matter, including safety, health and welfare.

Employers and Manufacturers Association (Central) Inc, 95-99 Molesworth Street, Thorndon, PO Box 1087. Tel: 04 473 7224. Fax: 04 473 4501. Website: *www.emacentral.co.nz*

Employment Contract Services Ltd, Wakefield House, 104 The Terrace, Wellington. Tel: 04 471 1720. Fax: 04 473 7495.

Jamieson Partners, 30-32 Mahina Road, Lower Hutt. Tel/Fax: 04 562 7231. Specialises in employment law and tribunal advocacy.

Keenan Consulting, 146a Karori Road, Karori. Tel/Fax: 04 476 7056. Specialists in developing employment contracts, performance agreements, remuneration systems and the related information systems.

FOR WOMEN
Rural Women, 5 Ward Street, Wellington. Tel: 04 528 7556.
Website: *www.ruralcomen.org*.

Email: *ruralwomen@clear.net.nz*.
Ministry of Women's Affairs, 48 Mulgrave Street, PO Box 10-
049, Wellington. Tel: 04 473 4112. Fax: 04 472 0961.
Website: *www.mwa.govt.nz*. Email: *mwa@mwa.govt.nz*.

MOTORING
Avis Car Rentals
Level 2, Building 4, Central Park 666, Great South Street,
Auckland. Tel: 09 526 2847. Fax: 09 526 2828.
Christchurch Airport, 76 Orchard Road, Christchurch. Tel: 03
358 9661. Fax: 03 379 4602.

Hertz Fleetlease
Corner of Tory and Buckle Streets, Wellington. Tel: 04 384
3809.
99 Grafton Road, Auckland. Tel: 09 375 6200.
46 Lichfield Street, Christchurch. Tel: 03 366 0549.

AA Automobile Association Inc. Website: *www.aa.co.nz*
342–352 Lambton Quay, Wellington. Tel: 04 470 9999.
99 Albert Street, Auckland. Tel: 09 377 4660. Fax: 09 309
4564.
210 Hereford Street, Christchurch. Tel: 03 379 1280.
410 Anglesea Street, Hamilton. Tel: 07 839 1397.
Motor Trade Association Inc. 79 Taranaki Street, PO Box
9244, Courtenay Place, Wellington. Tel: 04 385 8859. Fax: 04
385 9517. Website: *www.mta.co.nz*.
Email: *mta@motor-trade.co.nz*.

PROFESSIONAL AND TRADE ASSOCIATIONS

General
Booksellers New Zealand, Survey House, 21–29 Broderick
Road, Johnsonville, Wellington. Tel: 04 478 5511.
Bus and Coach Association (NZ) Ltd, Tourism and Travel
House, 79 Boulcott Street, PO Box 9336, Wellington. Tel: 04
499 7334.
Canterbury Employers Chamber of Commerce, 57 Kilmore
Street, Christchurch. Tel: 03 366 5096.

Chartered Institute of Transport, 298a Wairau Road, Glenfield. Tel: 09 444 4261.

Hospitality Association of New Zealand, Education House, 178–182 Willis Street, Wellington. Tel: 04 385 1369.

Independent Schools Council, PO Box 5222, Wellington. Tel: 04 471 2022.

New Zealand Chamber of Commerce UK, 393 The Strand, London WC2. Tel: 020 7379 0720. Fax: 020 7379 0721.

New Zealand Chambers of Commerce, Level 9, 109 Featherston Street, PO Box 11–043, Wellington. Tel: 04 914 6500. Fax: 04 471 1767. Website: *www.wgtn-chamber.co.nz* Email: *info@wgtn-chamber.co.nz*.

New Zealand Employers Association, Level 6, Microsoft House, 3–11 Hunter Street, PO Box 1925, Wellington. Tel: 04 496 6555. Fax: 04 496 6550. Email: *nzef@nzef.org.nz*

New Zealand Institute of Management Canterbury Division, 307 Madras Street, PO Box 13-044, Christchurch. Tel: 03 379 2302. Fax: 03 366 7069. Website: *www.nzim.co.* Email: *canty@nzim.co.nz*

New Zealand Painting Contractors Association (Inc), 63 Miramar Avenue, Miramar. Tel: 04 388 1516.

New Zealand Recreation Association, Education House, Level 5 (Westblock), 178–182 Willis Street, PO Box 11132, Manners St, Wellington. Tel: 04 915 5640.

New Zealand Road Transport Association, 41 Carlyle Street, Christchurch. Tel: 03 366 9854.

New Zealand Tourism Industry Association, 4th Floor, Paxus House, 79 Boulcott Street, Wellington. Tel: 04 499 0104. Fax: 04 499 0827. Email: *nztia@xtra.co.nz*

New Zealand University Students Association, 354 Lambton Quay, PO Box 10-191, Wellington. Tel: 04 498 2500. Fax: 04 473 2391.

Retail Merchants Association, PO Box 13-877, Christchurch. Tel: 03 366 1308.

Wellington Regional Chamber of Commerce, Gen-i Tower, Level 9, 109 Featherston Street, PO Box 1590, Wellington. Tel: 04 914 6500. Website: *www.wgtn-chamber.co.nz* Email: *info@wgtn-chamber.co.nz*

Medical

Dental Council of NZ, 108 The Terrace, PO Box 10-448, Wellington. Tel: 04 499 4820. Website: *www.dcnz.org.nz*

New Zealand Association of Occupational Therapists, PO Box 12-506, Thorndon. Tel: 04 473 6510.

New Zealand Association of Optometrists, 49 Boulcott Street, Wellington. Tel: 04 473 2322. Fax: 04 473 2328. Website: *www.nzaot.com*

New Zealand Medical Association, PO Box 156, Wellington. Tel: 04 472 4741. Fax: 04 471 0838.
Website: *www.nzma.org.nz*. Email: *nzma@nzma.org.nz*.

New Zealand Nurses Organisation, 57 Willis Street, Wellington. Tel: 04 385 0847. Fax: 04 382 9993.

New Zealand Veterinary Association, 69 Boulcott Street, Wellington. Tel: 04 471 0484. Fax: 04 471 0494.

Pharmaceutical Society of New Zealand, 124 Dixon Street, Wellington. Tel: 04 802 0030. Fax: 04 382 9297.
Website: *www.psnz.org.nz*

Pharmacy Guild of New Zealand Inc. National Headquarters, Pharmacy House, 124 Dixon Street, Wellington. Tel: 04 802 8200.

Researched Medicines Industry Association NZ Inc. Level 8 Castrol House, 36 Custom House Quay, PO Box 10-447, Wellington. Tel: 04 499 4277. Fax: 04 499 4276.

Farming

AGCARM Agricultural Chemical and Animal Remedies Manufacturers Association of New Zealand Inc, 142 Featherston Street, PO Box 5069, Wellington. Tel: 04 499 4225. Fax: 04 499 4223.

Deer Industry New Zealand, PO Box 10702, Wellington. Tel: 04 382 8626. Website: *www.dinz.org*

Federated Farmers of NZ Inc., Corner of Featherston and Johnston Streets, Wellington. Tel: 04 473 7269. Fax: 04 473 1081.

Nursery and Garden Industry Association of New Zealand Inc. PO Box 3443, Wellington. Tel: 04 918 3511.

New Zealand Berry Fruit Growers' Federation Inc, 12 Johnston Street, Wellington. Tel: 04 473 5387.

Vegetable and Potato Growers Federation (Inc), Huddart

Parker Building, Post Office Square, Wellington. Tel: 04 472
3795. Fax: 04 471 2861. Email: *information@vedfed.co.nz*

Legal
New Zealand Law Foundation, 26 Waring Taylor Street,
Wellington. Tel: 04 915 1288. Fax: 04 915 1285.
New Zealand Police Association Inc., PO Box 12-344, 57 Willis
Street, Wellington. Tel: 04 496 6800. Fax: 04 471 6819.
Website: *www.police.org.nz*

Technical
Aviation Industry Association of New Zealand Inc., Agricul-
ture House, 12 Johnston Street, Wellington. Tel: 04 472
2707.
Canterbury Manufacturers' Association Inc., corner of Cam-
bridge Terrace and Manchester Street, Christchurch. Tel: 03
353 2540. Website: *www.cma.org.nz*
Electrical Contractors Association of New Zealand Inc., 220
Thorndon Quay, Wellington. Tel: 04 494 1540. Fax: 04 385
4645.
Employers and Manufacturers Association (Central) Inc, 95-99
Molesworth Street, Wellington. Tel: 04 473 7224. Fax: 04 473
4501.
Institute of Environmental Science & Research, PO Box 12-444,
Wellington. Tel: 04 914 0700.
Institute of Geological & Nuclear Sciences Ltd (GNS), PO Box
30-368, Lower Hutt, Wellington. Tel: 04 570 1444. Fax: 04
570 4600. Website: *www.gns.cri.nz*.
Institute of Professional Engineers New Zealand, PO Box 12-
241, Thorndon, Wellington. Tel: 04 473 9444. Fax: 04 473
2324.
ITANZ (Information Technology Association of New Zealand
Inc), 9th Floor, 108 The Terrace, PO Box 1710, Wellington.
Tel: 04 472 2731. Fax: 04 499 3318.
Website: *www.itanz.org.nz*. Email: *info@itanz.org.nz*.
New Zealand Architects Co-op Society, 69 Rutherford Street,
Lower Hutt, Wellington. Tel: 04 566 4762.
New Zealand Chemical Industry Council, Agriculture House,
12 Johnston Street, Wellington. Tel: 04 499 4311. Fax: 04 472
7100.

New Zealand Computer Society, Level 5, Old Wool House, 139 Featherston Street, Wellington. Tel: 04 473 1043. Fax: 04 473 1025. Website: *www.nzcs.org.nz*

New Zealand Meat Industry Association (Inc), Wool House, 10 Brando Street, PO Box 345, Wellington. Tel: 04 473 6465.

New Zealand Minerals Industry Association, PO Box 5039, Wellington. Tel: 04 499 9871. Fax: 04 499 9873.
Website: *www.Minerals.co.nz* Email: *nzmia@xtra.co.nz*

New Zealand Retail Meat and Allied Trades Federation, Molesworth House, 95–99 Molesworth Street, Wellington. Tel: 0800 880099. Fax: 04 472 0807.
Website: *www.retailmeat.org.nz/*
Email: *enquiry@retailmeat.org.nz*

New Zealand Timber Preservation Council, 2 Maginnity Street, Wellington. Tel: 04 472 3733. Fax: 04 472 1071.

Petroleum Exploration Association of New Zealand, PO Box 5227, Wellington. Tel: 04 472 1933. Fax: 04 472 3968. Website: *www.peanz.org.nz*

Printing Industries NZ, PO Box 39-039, Lower Hutt. Tel: 04 569 2110.

Recording Industry Association of New Zealand, 11 York Street, PO Box 37–442, Auckland. Tel: 09 308 0510. Fax: 09 930 4977.

Retail Merchants Association, PO Box 13-877, Christchurch. Tel: 03 366 1308.

Wellington Master Plumbers Association, 108 Taranaki Street, PO Box 6606, Wellington. Tel: 04 384 4184. Fax: 04 384 2456.

Financial

Institute of Chartered Accountants, Cigna House, 40 Mercer Street, PO Box 11-342, Manners Street, Wellington. Tel: 04 474 7840. Fax: 04 473 6303. Website: *www.icanz.co.nz.*

Insurance Institute of New Zealand Inc., Guardian Assurance House, 111–115 Custom House Quay, Wellington. Tel: 04 499 4630. Fax: 04 499 4536.

New Zealand Bankers Association, Level 12 Grand Arcade Tower, 16 Willis Street, Wellington. Tel: 04 472 8838. Fax: 04 473 1698. Website: *www.nzba.org.nz*
Email: *accopland@nzba.org.az*

Further Reading

TRAVEL GUIDES

Beautiful New Zealand, Peter Morath (Hale, 1993).

Christchurch: A City and its People, Philip Temple (Pacific, 1987).

Collins Illustrated Guide to New Zealand, Elizabeth Booz (Collins, 1989).

Cycle Touring in Neu Zealand, J. B. Ringer (Mountaineer Books, USA, 1989).

Fragile Eden: A Ride Through New Zealand, Robin Hanbury-Tenison (Arrow, 1990).

Guide to Auckland, Brigid Pike (Hodder & Stoughton, 1987).

Homeplaces: Three Coasts of the South Island of New Zealand, Keri Hulme (Hodder & Stoughton, 1989).

Insider's Guide to New Zealand, Kirsten Ellis (Moorland, 1993).

Insight Guides: New Zealand (APA Publications, Hong Kong, 1992).

Introduction to New Zealand, Elizabeth Booz (The Guide Book Co, Hong Kong, 1991).

Mobile New Zealand Travel Guide, D. & J. Pope, two vols (North Island and South Island) (Heinemann Reed, 1992).

New Zealand in Your Pocket, Arnold Schuchter (Horizon, 1990).

New Zealand 1993 (Fodor Gold Guides, 1993).

New Zealand Travel Survival Kit, Tony Wheeler (Lonely Planet, 1991).

New Zealand, Gift of the Sea, Brian Brake (Hodder & Stoughton, 1990).

West Coast Pictorial, John Burford (Whitcoulls, 1987).

Wild New Zealand (Reader's Digest Australia, 1993).

FOOD AND WINE

Jane MacQuitty's Pocket Guide to Australian and New Zealand

Wines, Jane MacQuitty (Mitchell Beazley, 1990).
New Zealand, the Beautiful Cookbook, Tui Flower (Weldon Australia, 1992).
New Zealand Food and How To Cook It, David Burford (Bateman, New Zealand, 1992).

SPORT AND LEISURE

Between the Posts: A New Zealand Rugby Anthology, Ron Palenski (Hodder & Stoughton, 1989).
Fishing the Wild Places of New Zealand, Tony Orman (Bush Press. New Zealand, 1991).
Golf Courses of South Canterbury, Peter Russell (Whitcoulls, 1985).
Golf Courses of Wellington, Peter Russell (Whitcoulls, 1985).

NATURAL HISTORY

Dragonflies of New Zealand, Richard Rowe (Auckland University Press, 1987).
Ferns of New Zealand, Susan Firth (Hodder & Stoughton, 1986).
Field Guide to the Birds of New Zealand, R. Falla (Collins, 1979).
Handbook of New Zealand Mammals, Carolyn King (Oxford University Press, 1990).
Living New Zealand Forest, Robert Brockie (Bateman, New Zealand, 1992).

EDUCATION

Family, School and Community, Peter Ramsay (Allen & Unwin, 1984).
The New Zealand Education Directory (annual), available from Consyl Publishing, 3 Buckhurst Road, Bexhill-on-Sea, TN40 IQF.
Towards Successful Schooling: Conference Proceedings, Hugh Lauder & Cathy Wylie (Falmer, 1990).

BUSINESS & LAW

Business Review Monthly Newspaper, available from Consyl Publishing, 3 Buckhurst Road, Bexhill-on-Sea TN40 IQF.

Corporatization and Privatization: Lessons from New Zealand,
Ian Duncan & Alan Bollard (Oxford University Press, 1993).
Economic History of New Zealand, M. F. L. Prichard (Collins,
1970).
Fair Trading in New Zealand, B. Hill & M. Jones (Butterworth
NZ, 1989).
Family Law Policy in New Zealand, Frank Henaghan & W.
Atkin (Oxford University Press, 1993).
Introduction to Financial Markets in New Zealand, G.
Karacaoglu (Victoria University Press, 1988).
Introduction to the New Zealand Legal System, R. D.
Mulholland (Butterworth NZ, 1990).
The New Zealand Economy: A Personal View, Robert Muldoon
(Endeavour NZ, 1985).
Takeover New Zealand, W. B. Sutch (Reed, 1972).
Towards Prosperity, Roger Douglas (Bateman NZ, 1991).
*Turning it Around: Closure and Revitalization in New Zealand
Industry*, John Savage & Alan Bollard (Oxford University
Press, 1991).

HISTORY

Forever the Forest: A West Coast Story, Neville Peat (Hodder &
Stoughton, 1987).
Fifth Wind: New Zealand and the Legacy of a Turbulent Past,
Robert MacDonald (Bloomsbury, 1989).
Historic Places of New Zealand, Automobile Association/
Historic Places Trust (Hodder & Stoughton, 1981).
History of New Zealand, Keith Sinclair (Penguin, 1989).
Hokianga, Jack Lee (Hodder & Stoughton, 1987).
*Maori Magna Carta: New Zealand Law and the Treaty of
Waitangi*, Paul McHugh (Oxford University Press, 1992).
Ka Whawhai Tonu Matou: Struggle Without End, Ranginui
Walker (Penguin, 1990).
New Zealand: A Short History, Laurie Barber (Hutchinson,
1990).
Oxford Illustrated History of New Zealand, Keith Sinclair
(Oxford University Press, 1990).
The Past Today: Historic Places in New Zealand, John Wilson
(New Zealand Historic Places Trust/Pacific, 1987).
Oxford History of New Zealand, W. Oliver & B. Williams

(Oxford University Press, 1993).

GOVERNMENT AND POLITICS

Democracy and Power in New Zealand, Richard Mulgan (Oxford University Press, 1989).

The Ideal Society and its Enemies: The Foundations of Modern New Zealand Society, Miles Fairburn (Auckland University Press, 1989).

Justice, Ethics and New Zealand Society, Graham Oddies & R. Perrett (Oxford University Press, 1993).

Local and Regional Government in New Zealand, Claudia Scott (Allen & Unwin, 1979).

Maori: The Crisis and the Challenge, Alan Duff (HarperCollins 1993).

New Zealand in Crisis, D. Novits & B. Willmot (GP Publications, 1992).

New Zealand Foreign Affairs Handbook, Steve Hoadley (Oxford University Press, 1993).

Nuclear Free the New Zealand Way, David Lange (Penguin, 1990).

Politics in New Zealand: A Reader, Steven Pevine (Allen & Unwin, 1978).

Unbridled Power: An Interpretation of New Zealand's Constitution and Government, Geoffrey Palmer (Oxford University Press, 1987).

Women's Suffrage in New Zealand, Patricia Grimshaw (Auckland University Press, 1988).

LITERATURE, MUSIC AND ART

Anthology of Twentieth Century New Zealand Poetry, Vincent O'Sullivan (Oxford University Press, 1987).

Goodbye to Romance: Stories by New Zealand and Australian Women Writers 1930-88, E. Webby & L. Wevers (Unwin, 1990).

History of New Zealand Music, John Masefield Thompson (Oxford University Press, 1991).

Introduction to New Zealand Painting 1839-1980, Gordon Brown (Bateman, NZ, 1992).

Oxford History of New Zealand Literature in English, Terry Sturm (Oxford University Press, 1992).

Penguin Book of Contemporary New Zealand Poetry, Miriam Evans (Penguin, 1990).

Two Hundred Years of New Zealand Paintings, Gil Docking (Bateman, NZ, 1992).

Index